LIBERTY

The SAGE Program on Applied Developmental Science

Consulting Editor

Richard M. Lerner

The field of Applied Developmental Science has advanced the use of cutting-edge developmental systems models of human development, fostered strength-based approaches to understanding and promoting positive development across the life span, and served as a frame for collaborations among researchers and practitioners, including policymakers, seeking to enhance the life chances of diverse young people, their families, and communities. The **SAGE Program on Applied Developmental Science** both integrates and extends this scholarship by publishing innovative and cutting-edge contributions.

LIBERTY

Thriving and Civic Engagement
Among America's Youth

Richard M. Lerner
Tufts University

SAGE Publications
International Educational and Professional Publisher
Thousand Oaks

For information:

 Sage Publications, Inc.
2455 Teller Road
Thousand Oaks, California 91320
E-mail: order@sagepub.com

Sage Publications Ltd.
1 Oliver's Yard
55 City Road
London EC1Y 1SP
United Kingdom

Sage Publications India Pvt. Ltd.
B-42, Panchsheel Enclave
Post Box 4109
New Delhi 110 017 India

Printed in the United States of America

Library of Congress Cataloging-in-Publication data

Lerner, Richard M.
Liberty : Thriving and civic engagement among America's youth / Richard M. Lerner.
    p. cm.
Includes bibliographical references and indexes.
ISBN 0-7619-2984-3 (pbk.)
    1. Youth—United States. 2. Social participation—United States.
3. Civil society—United States. 4. Liberty. 5. Developmental psychology.
I. Title.
HQ799.7.L467 2004
305.235'0973—dc22

                                        2003019258

04   05   06   07   08   10 9 8 7 6 5 4 3 2 1

Acquiring Editor:	Jim Brace-Thompson
Editorial Assistant:	Karen Ehrmann
Production Editor:	Sanford Robinson
Typesetter:	C&M Digitals (P) Ltd.
Copy Editor:	Pam Suwinsky
Indexer:	Monica Smersh
Cover Designer:	Michelle Lee

Contents

Foreword

Ideas must work through the brains and arms of good and brave men,
or they are no better than dreams.

Ralph Waldo Emerson

R ich Lerner confesses—no, proclaims—that this wonderful and
important book arose out of the depths of profound despair. In his
self-disclosing Preface, Lerner recounts how, like so many of us, his world
and worldview were shaken to the core by the events of September 11,
2001. Despite a lifetime committed to disciplined research, it was Rich
Lerner the outraged, saddened, and numbed father who needed to write
this book and for whom it serves as a citizen's anthem as hopeful as it is
healing. Rescued in large measure by Al Gore's invitation to co-teach a
seminar, Lerner rebounds with an urgent call for us to embrace a powerful set of ideas about the essential connections among thriving youth, civil
society, and vibrant democracy. That despair bordering on clinical depression could be transformed into a work so ultimately optimistic is powerful and eloquent testimony that we, and this idea, are in the care of an
author who indeed is good and brave.

Rich Lerner dedicates this book to Al Gore as a measure of thanks for
providing "inspiration and courage." There are a few hundred people
across the country who know that that is no praise required by the dictates of courtesy, celebrity, or friendship. I count myself within that fortu-
nate circle of folks who have accompanied Al and Tipper Gore on their
quest to reclaim the high ground on family policy. And it has been a journey of reclamation. Quite frankly, during the past three decades liberals
and progressives have ceded considerable terrain to social conservatives
and libertarians. Confronted with the choice of embracing "workfare" or

spending enough to make welfare a means to provide income security as well as a pathway out of poverty, liberals and progressives walked away from work, ceding that issue and, with it the high ground, to more conservative voices. Instead of wrestling with the dilemma of a nation adamant about keeping church and state separate but unwilling to eradicate expressions of faith from all public forums, liberals and progressives drew a line in the sand and pretended it was a self-evident solution to the problem. The middle ground was left to the right.

Much the same occurred with families. Liberals and progressives were unequal to the task of describing a view of "family" that holds men and women in equal regard, respects a woman's right to choose whether to bear a child, refuses to discriminate on the basis of sexual orientation, and is unapologetic about the importance of committed relationships and healthy marriages. Seemingly unable to braid these into a coherent vision, liberals and progressives assumed the fetal position when invited to join the debate on family values. They could have held social conservatives accountable for the practical consequences of viewing the family as a gendered sole proprietorship. Instead, the left mocked *Ozzie and Harriet*, celebrated *Murphy Brown*, and appeared indifferent to the fact that the late Daniel Patrick Moynihan's dire prognosis had morphed into prophecy, as more and more children were born into already poor single-parent single-income households.

Al and Tipper Gore chose not to mock the American family but to embrace and even celebrate it. The annual conference they hosted grew out of their conviction that the family was the cornerstone of society. They saw in the family unit a collection of assets and strengths that made the whole greater than the sum of its parts. These same assets and strengths were being ignored and undervalued as we hurried to identify, label, and treat individual pathologies. And from this perspective, what was needed were occasions and opportunities to bring the family together—to reimagine what health care and child care and work would look like if we put whole families at the center.

What began life as a statewide confab hosted by the senior senator from Tennessee matured into a national event hosted by the vice president and Mrs. Gore, drawing in some years the president and first lady of the United States. But what is far more interesting is the story behind the story. And this is the story of the widening circle of scholars, policy wonks, practitioners, and ordinary folks who, like swallows to Capistrano, returned to Nashville year after year. The circle grew larger. It grew stronger. Relationships blossomed. A network evolved. And slowly, ever so slowly, the liberals and progressives regained their voices, rejoined the fray, and set out to reclaim and recapture lost terrain.

Family Re-Union 3 presented one such opportunity. Planned around the theme "Fathers and Families," the conference provided an opportunity for intense dialogue among the usual suspects and several dozen practitioners who were first-time attendees. By the end of the session, there was broad consensus on a point of view that endures as bedrock for what we now call "the responsible fatherhood movement." Central to that point of view was the notion that men be required, encouraged, and enabled to accept the responsibility to contribute to the social, emotional, and economic well being of their children, regardless of whether those fathers lived in the same home as the children.

In many respects, the practical judgment, real-world experience, and ethnic diversity of practitioners seemed to embolden formerly silent liberals and progressives to find their voices, break the silence, and speak publicly and unflinchingly about personal and parental responsibility. Concerns about political correctness yielded to powerful evidence that children needed both parents. And in that space political support could be found across traditional ideological divides for helping young fathers to hone the skills and earn the resources needed to fulfill their parental role—once they accepted responsibility by acknowledging paternity.

In the decade that has followed Family Re-Union 3, we find liberals and progressives and social conservatives sharing personal responsibility as a common point of departure for a relatively invective-free conversation about how best to encourage and support responsible fatherhood.

Lerner authored a similar breakthrough with Family Re-Union 11 in October 2002. By the end of the two-day conference, Lerner had accomplished the goal he and the planning committee had announced on day one—to explode the long-held myth that healthy adolescent development requires separation from family. And he did so, in the presence and with the enthusiastic consent of the major thought leaders and practitioners in the youth development field. This was no small feat.

Candor requires disclosure that the "Family and Youth" theme of Family Re-Union 11 reflected the reality that Rich Lerner's suggestions prevailed and mine did not. Lerner does not know that. Or he is simply too gracious to let on. Earlier that year, I urged attention to rural families. I still do. But once the planning started, like so many others I was captured completely by the field-altering potential of having so many of the luminaries in the youth development field in one place, at one time, addressing an issue so many of them seemed to have avoided for so long:

families. And also like many others, I did not grasp immediately how the planning, content, and execution of this Family Re-Union would become an experiential immersion in Lerner's "Big Three" features of effective youth programs: positive adult–youth relationships, skill building; and meaningful opportunities for youth participation and leadership.

Like everyone else in attendance, I was mesmerized by the authenticity, sophistication, and raw power of the youth presenters. As I listened to and learned from these young people, I was grateful to Lerner for his uncompromising faith in the generations to come. And I do mean *faith*. Lerner's fiftysome books and 300 articles establish him as one of the world's preeminent researchers on life-span development. He is a scientist. He thrives on facts, evidence, and proof. In this work, however, Lerner the scientist is unmasked as citizen. However much he values research, Lerner reveres liberty and justice even more.

In a recent meeting, Rich and I took turns arguing for a more muscular approach to family policy and social justice, one that would recoup lost ideological and political ground by connecting to the core values of the American people. To do so, we argued, would mean reminding Americans that even the most economically secure among us are just one, two, or three generations removed from working poor families. And to stay the course, we have to believe that Americans will respond to the fundamental fairness of an agenda that seeks to ensure that today's working poor can become beacons of hope and agents of change for their children and grandchildren. After one exchange, Rich passed me this handwritten note:

> Ralph—The point I was trying to make is that you can't have a democracy, you can't have social justice or fundamental fairness, when you partition or allocate "hopeful futures" on the basis of race, class, language. . . . When we enact such partitions, we produce the child and family problems we claim we want to prevent [and/or] diminish.

I plan to keep that note. It will serve as my bookmark when I return, as I know I will, to *Liberty: Thriving and Civic Engagement Among America's Youth*. Every now and then, we all need to be reminded that even profound despair will succumb to the talismanic and transformative forces we unleash when we strive to secure a "hopeful future" for every child.

—Ralph Smith

Preface

Perhaps like many Americans on September 11, 2001, I was first overcome with numbing shock. Then screaming outrage took over, as I was appalled and sickened by the evil and cruelty that had befallen America. I could not help but imagine the agonizing last moments of the passengers and crews aboard the four planes that crashed, the desperation of the people dying in the towers of the World Trade Center and in the Pentagon, the coursing stabs of pain that pierced the bodies and souls of family members who knew their loved ones were dead, the numbing dread of my fellow citizens who realized the gravity of what was occurring, and the incomprehending fear of young children who could not fully understand, but only feel terror.

By the evening of September 11, and for several weeks that followed, I am certain I was—if not clinically depressed—at the borderline of this condition. My entire professional career has been devoted to the study of children and adolescents, and for a decade and a half, to trying to figure out ways to promote, through the marriage of research and application, the positive development of young people. I wanted my life contribution to increase the probability, if only by a miniscule percentage, that every child and adolescent could look forward to a future marked by hope, by the opportunity to pursue his or her goals, and by the freedom to actualize his or her potentials. Now I felt that not only was there no certainty of a positive future for anyone in the world, but, what seemed more likely in the dark depths of that moment, that there would be no future at all. I despaired that my own three children, and all the tens of millions of children around the world, would have their futures completely robbed by a relatively few fanatics who, because of pathological hatred or delusional beliefs that sanctity could emerge through slaughtering innocents, would destroy civil society, if not the very planet itself. In these moments I felt my entire life had turned out to be meaningless. With no hope of a future, there was also no rational reason for me to continue to seek to enhance the probability of positive development for the world's youth. With no future, there would be no development at all.

A call from Al Gore, or actually from one of his staff members, brought me out of this despair.

After the 2000 national election, Mr. Gore decided that, among the several things he wanted to do, he wished to develop and teach a course on Family Centered Community Building at two universities in Tennessee: Fisk University, a historically black college in Nashville, and Middle Tennessee State University (MTSU), the alma mater of his father, Al Gore, Sr., in Murfesboro. The idea for the course grew out of a series of annual conferences that Al and Tipper Gore had been convening for about a decade in Nashville, meetings they labeled "Family Re-Union." The purpose of these annual meetings was to discuss among the diverse communities and sectors of American society the important issues facing contemporary families. For example, how can parents balance the challenges of rearing their own children while, at the same time, caring for their own, now aged parents? What must a family do to assure that a child in the first three years of life has the resources and stimulation needed for healthy physical and psychological development and for later school and career achievement? How do people balance or integrate the world of work and the world of family in ways that benefit all family members?

The Gores had acquired a great deal of information of scholarly and applied importance during the decade that they had convened these meetings, and, more important, these meetings had resulted in several important outcomes: the Family Re-Union Conferences resulted in policy changes and new legislation, for example, that enabled families with sick children to take leave from their jobs during times of medical emergency; they changed business practices in ways that created more family-friendly workplaces through, for example, more flexible working hours and better and enhanced support for high-quality child care; and they created new partnerships among parents, schools, faith leaders, employers, police, social service providers, and young people. These partnerships identified the strengths that existed in communities and integrated them to support families in their efforts to raise healthy, productive young people. These and the other outcomes of the Family Re-Union Conferences created a deep understanding in the Gores of the importance of community building in the United States, especially community building that strengthened the capacity of families to rear their children successfully.

At the beginning of 2001, Mr. Gore decided that he would like to organize a college course around these learnings, and I was asked to be one of the faculty members who would assist in organizing and teaching the course at Fisk and at MTSU. We taught in the spring of 2001 a one-semester version of the course, and then, over the summer of 2001, worked to enhance and expand the course into an academic year-long, two-semester course.

Mr. Gore launched the two-semester version of the course in the beginning of September 2001. And then came September 11.

The call from Mr. Gore's assistant came at the end of September. I was reminded that the portion of the syllabus that I taught with Mr. Gore (which was on youth and families) was scheduled for early October, that I should make my plane reservations to Nashville, and let Mr. Gore know if there were any new handouts, overheads, or other materials that I wanted to suggest for our joint lecture.

Up until the time of this call, I had thought that I might never fly on a plane again, especially out of Logan Airport in Boston. I was finding it difficult to imagine having enthusiasm for my work sufficient to travel to my classes at Tufts University to lecture about positive youth development, much less travel on a plane to Nashville to do this. During the conversation with Mr. Gore's assistant, I was in fact wondering if and how I could tell her I was too afraid, too paralyzed emotionally, to travel. However, I just indicated throughout the conversation that I understood the details of the task that was being described.

Then, as the business portion of the phone call was ending, Mr. Gore's assistant added something personal. She said that the vice president wanted me to know that he not only really appreciated my collaboration with him in this course up to now but that, particularly at this point in our nation's history, it was especially important that he and I talk about positive youth development. Although on this occasion we would be speaking only to the students at Fisk and at MTSU, it was crucial that they and other young people know that there is reason for them to hope. There are ways to build a positive future, even in the midst of a war of singular historical dimensions besetting the nation, and our country is in fact especially suited to build this future in such an era.

As I put down the phone receiver I felt completely changed. Given the unique historical situation I knew surrounded Mr. Gore as a consequence of the events involved in the 2000 presidential election, as well as the family stresses he had experienced that year (for example, the passing away of his mother-in-law, his youngest child going off to college, and having to cope with an "empty nest"), I found his commitment to moving forward with the message of family-centered community building for the youth of America both courageous and inspirational. I also thought that there was more reason to convey the message of hope for the future of the young people of the nation than simply that America was best positioned to deliver it. I thought that this was a message we *ought* to deliver, both to our own nation and throughout the world. The essence of America is its standing as the beacon across history and in the contemporary world for democracy and freedom of opportunity. America gives hope to all people. By living in and supporting the institutions of American civil society, parents and children will be afforded a just and free present and an opportunity to pursue an even better future.

I believe we have an obligation to deliver to others this vision of our nation. Voltaire said that "every man is guilty of all the good he didn't do," and in this sense I realized then that conveying and supporting this view of America was part of the moral duty of its people. It is a moral requisite for all citizens enjoying the fruits of American liberty to explain, embrace, and pass onto future generations an understanding of how the American system of "liberty and justice for all" promotes and protects the health and positive development of each individual. Ours is a nation of civil institutions and of governmental structures and functions that support every individual's liberty. It is not only a matter of civic responsibility to support such a nation; it is what one ought to do. While in such a society one is free to ignore this obligation, it is nevertheless the case that, normatively, civic duty and moral action are merged.

I recognized as well that a key reason existed for why America was best suited to carry the message of liberty forward at a time of a war on liberty *and* why it was the moral obligation of America to do this. As I explain later, this link between what America *is* doing—leading the war against the terrorist onslaught against democracy and liberty—and what America *ought* to do derives from a historically singular integration of human evolutionary change and the changes that comprise across people's lives exemplary, healthy, or optimal development—*thriving*, if you will. This link between the *is* and the *ought* of human behavior involves a recognition that for human life to exist optimally—for individuals to thrive—people and their social worlds must be in a relationship wherein each support the other. I saw the situation in this way:

- Exemplary positive youth development—thriving—involves a young person who—within the context of his or her individual set of physical and psychological characteristics and abilities—takes actions that serve his or her own well-being and, at the same time, the well-being of parent, peers, community, and society. A thriving young person is on a life path that eventuates in his or her becoming an ideal adult member of a civil society.

- Thriving is enabled by a civil society that supports the rights of the individual to develop his or her abilities as best he or she can and in ways valued by the thriving person.

- A civil society supporting individual freedom and justice can only exist when the people in that society act to support, protect, and extend the societal institutions affording such liberty for all of its citizens. And

- When individuals do so because of their belief that such actions constitute the "right thing to do"—that these action define the morally correct path—there is, then, a mutual, or reciprocal, relationship between individual thriving and civil society, which may be represented as "thriving individual ← → civil society."

- This relationship involves the development in a person's life of a sense of self (a self-definition or an "identity") wherein civic engagement and moral thought and action are synthesized.

- This integrated civic and moral identity has its roots in humans' evolutionary heritage and in the translation of this history into human development across the life span.

- In human life, integrated moral and civic may emerge prototypically in adolescence, when the person's self-definition is undergoing significant and singular changes.

- The thriving individual ← → civil society relationship is actualized in youth by the attainment of several key characteristics of positive development (competence, character, confidence, social connections, and compassion) that coalesce to create a young person who is developing successfully toward an "ideal" adulthood, one marked by contributions to self, others, and the institutions of civil society.

- To ensure that our liberty is sustained, we need to translate knowledge about the thriving individual ← → civil society relationship into (1) programs that are effective in engaging youth productively and positively with their communities (through promoting what I term the "Big Three" features of effective youth programs: positive adult ← → youth relationships; skill building; and the opportunity for youth participation and leadership); and (2) policies that assure that all individuals will have the opportunity to be civically engaged and to thrive. I suggest that the concept of "family-centered community building for youth" provides a frame for such policy development.

My ability to persuade myself about these ideas, of course, did not mean that I could persuade others. Given the significance that I believe these ideas hold for the maintenance and perpetuation of our nation's values and institutions, both because of—at this writing—the continuing danger of substantial terrorist assaults on America and other democracies around the globe, and because the bases of the American idea of liberty have important implications for both science and applications to American domestic and foreign policies and social policies, I felt an obligation to try to persuade others. As a consequence, I wrote this book.

However, the birth of the idea for writing *Liberty* arose earlier than October 2001. Over the years, several other of my books—written in 1976, 1984, 1986, 1992, 1995, and 2002—"prepared" me for the ideas I present here regarding the systematic relationship between individuals and their social worlds that define the course of both human evolution and human development across the life span. In addition, conversations with my colleagues and students during these years—about evolution and human development, about moral development and spirituality, about positive youth development and thriving, and about civic engagement, citizenship, and civil society—helped me articulate and sharpen the ideas I present in this volume.

In particular, I want to thank my colleagues in the Eliot-Pearson Department of Child Development at Tufts University. Their comments and encouragement were invaluable. I am especially grateful to my department chairs during the time I was writing this book—Professors Ann Easterbrooks, David Elkind, and Fred Rothbaum. Their collegiality and support are deeply appreciated. Two other colleagues, Professors George Scarlett and Don Wertlieb, were particularly generous in conveying their wisdom to me. Their reading and commenting on full drafts of the manuscript were especially kind and incredibly helpful.

My colleagues in the Tufts University College of Citizenship and Public Service provided stimulating comments about the ideas presented in this book. Professor Anthony Schlaff was especially helpful. He provided several thoughtful and detailed commentaries about my work.

My students in the Applied Developmental Science Institute (ADSI) were enormously helpful and were tireless in providing insightful critiques, innovative ideas for improvement, and unwavering support. I thank Amy Alberts, Pamela Anderson, Elyse Archila, Aida Balsano, Rumeli Banik, Elise Christiansen, Elizabeth Dowling, Lisa Fishlin, Steinunn Gestdottir, Sarah Hertzog, Helena Jelicic, Angelica Lundquist, Lang Ma, Sophie Naudeau, Isla Simpson, Christina Theokas, and Brian Wright. It is a privilege to work with such enormously talented young people. I am especially grateful to four of the people who were my graduate students during my writing of this book—Elizabeth Dowling, Pamela Anderson, Sarah Hertzog, and Daniel Warren. Providing me with insightful feedback, recommendations for improvement, and unflagging enthusiasm, they were more colleagues than students throughout this project.

I also greatly appreciate the stimulation by, and my discussions with, the superb undergraduate students who were members of the spring 2003 undergraduate seminar I taught in applied developmental science. Many of the ideas in this book were first presented to the students, and their feedback was invaluable in advancing my thinking and improving the presentation of my views. I thank the students in the class—Sarah Bovaird, Allison Cohen, Deborah Durant, Jessica Gioia, Merissa Goldberg, Laura Irizarry, Laurie Konigsberg, Roxanne Kritzer, Hilary Van Dusen, Lauren Weintraub, Erica Weitz, and Marva Williams—and the three students who were teaching assistants—Sarah Foss, Sarah Hertzog, and Taryn Morrissey—for their truly significant contributions to the present work.

I am also greatly indebted to all of my colleagues in ADSI for their stimulation, critiques, and support. In particular, I want to thank Deborah Bobek, the Managing Director of ADSI, for the soundness of her advice, her engaging intellectual style, and her insight into and creativity about the thriving process and its importance for liberty. I am enormously appreciative of all the support given to me by Nancy Pare, my assistant. I am deeply grateful for her sense of perspective, her good humor, and all the myriad ways she supported my work and kept me on task. Leslie Daly, the Project Director of the Institute's 4-H Study of Positive Youth Development, and Maria Mallon, the Project Assistant for the Study, were constant sources of enthusiastic support. I am grateful for their talented and tireless contributions to the 4-H Study, a project that affords my students and me the opportunity to observe thriving youth across the nation.

I am also enormously grateful to Professor Joan Bergstrom, Chair-Ex Officio of the Institute's International Leadership Committee (ILC), and Tufts University President-Emeritus, Dr. John DiBiaggio, Chair of the ILC, for all their encouragement of this project and for the import ideas about its scholarly direction that they provided. Susan Ernst, the Dean of the College of Arts and Sciences at Tufts University, has also been an unwavering supporter of my scholarship and, as well, an enormously important substantive colleague in regard to my treatment of the biological dimensions of positive youth development.

The two Managing Editors of the Editorial Office within the Institute with whom I worked over the course of writing this book—Jennifer Davison and Karyn Lu—and the Editorial Assistant—Katherine

Connery—were invaluable colleagues. Their tireless enthusiasm and their professionalism and precision made this project into a product. They are all incredibly able, affable, and dedicated, and I am grateful for the opportunity to have worked with such superb editors on this book. Eleanora E. T. Cacciola was an undergraduate research assistant in the Editorial Office, and she contributed in several ways to the production of the manuscript. I am grateful for her commitment and the excellence of her efforts.

My editor at Sage Publications, James Brace-Thompson, has been both an unfailingly supportive advocate for this book and, as well, an insightful colleague. His thorough reading of the manuscript resulted in dozens of important and often provocative comments that sharpened my thinking and improved the quality of my presentation. I am enormously grateful for his support, encouragement, guidance, and friendship. I am also very grateful to Pam Suwinsky for her suburb copy editing of the manuscript. Her excellent work improved the book enormously.

Numerous colleagues outside of Tufts made significant contributions to this work. I am grateful to the reviewers of the manuscript—Professors Celia B. Fisher, Gary Greenberg, Lawrence Schiamberg, and Carl S. Taylor. Their wisdom and erudition were invaluable assets to me throughout my writing, and their advice improved every facet of the book. My colleague, Professor Jacqueline V. Lerner, provided thoughtful and insightful commentary about every draft of the manuscript and, in another one of her roles, as my spouse, she provided unfailing support and encouragement.

Several other sets of colleagues provided incomparable intellectual stimulation and models of how scholarship may be translated into effective actions that serve young people. My colleagues in the field of positive youth development with whom I am collaborating in the study of youth thriving—Dr. Peter Benson, Professor William Damon, Dr. Elizabeth Dowling, Professor James Furrow, Rev. Cynthia King Guffey, Bob King, Dottie King, Professor Pamela Ebstyne King, Dr. Peter Scales, and Professor Linda Wagener—have shaped my thinking and been unwavering in their encouragement of my efforts. In addition, Professor Margaret Beale Spencer has been indefatigable in her provision of scholarly insight and collegial support.

My colleagues at the National 4-H Council—Donald Floyd, President, Kashyap Choksi, Vice President, Strategic Intitiatives, and Susan Halbert, Senior Vice President—have been enormously supportive of this project and have provided critically important knowledge about how effective and exemplary youth development programs have fundamental significance for improving the lives of youth. Robert Granger, President, and Karen Hein, Immediate Past President, of the William T. Grant Foundation embraced the ideas presented in this book early in their development and, as such, gave me enormous encouragement to develop the work further. They also taught me a great deal about integrating policies and programs in the service of promoting positive youth development. My colleagues at the International Youth Foundation—Rick Little, Founder and Immediate Past CEO, and William Reese, Chief Operating Officer of the Foundation—have served as exemplars of scholar-practitioners, and have provided me with numerous models of how systems change promoting positive youth development may be achieved. Two other scholar-practitioners, Wendy Wheeler, President of the Innovation Center for Community and Youth Development, and Hartley Hobson, Vice President of the Innovation Center, were enormously helpful in teaching me more about the diverse ways community programs can promote positive youth development. Their commitment to youth participation and civic engagement is an exemplar for all community-based organizations. Dorothy Stoneman, President of YouthBuild USA, has served as a role model of vision, commitment, and creativity in the development of effective youth programs. Her incomparable commitment to improving the lives of all young people through empowering them as leaders, and her own inspirational leadership, are invaluable assets for America's youth.

I am also very grateful to Arthur J. Schwartz, Vice President for Research and Programs in Human Sciences, at the John Templeton Foundation, for his mentorship and collegiality regarding the links between spiritual development among youth and their positive development. The stimulating discussions I had with him regarding spiritual and religious development, and the importance of Benjamin Franklin's conceptions of virtue, where essential sources of the ideas I present in this book.

In teaching the Family-Centered Community Building course with Mr. Gore, and in collaborating with him and Mrs. Gore in the Family Re-Union Conference series, I have had the unique and humbling experience to work with and learn from two truly historically great American citizens. I have grown intellectually and personally from my continuing educational experiences with Tipper and Al Gore, and I thank them for being such thoughtful and generous instructors. I also owe an enormous debt to the other colleagues involved in the Family-Centered Community Building Course and in Family Re-Union—Lisa Berg, Audrey Choi, Neal Halfon, Nancy Hoit, Debbie Miller, Shelia Peters, Andy Shookoff,

Ralph Smith, Lisa Spinali, Peggy Ulrich-Nims, and Rebecca Webb. Their collegiality, collaboration, and mentorship were invaluable in shaping many of the ideas I have presented in this book.

Numerous individuals and foundations supported my work and the work of the Applied Developmental Science Institute during the time I wrote this book. I want to thank the National 4-H Council, the William T. Grant Foundation, the Jacobs Foundation, the John Templeton Foundation, the Wohlgemuth Foundation, the 484 Phi Alpha Foundation, the Innovation Center for Community and Youth Development, the Philip Morris Youth Smoking Prevention Program, Search Institute, the International Youth Foundation, Lawrence Erlbaum Associates, Publishers, Sage Publications, John Wiley & Sons, Inc., Prentice-Hall, ABC-Clio Publishers, Greenword Press, Drs. Joan and Gary Bergstrom, Paul and Joyce Barsam, Dr. Joan Kirschenbaum Cohn, Ms. Elaine Kasparian and Dr. Robert Watson, Dr. John Lapidus and Mrs. Randi Lapidus, Jon Leven, and Dr. Dotte Weber for their generous support.

Finally, I am especially grateful to Ralph Smith for writing such a generous foreword to the book. Ralph Smith is a visionary and effective advocate for, and leader of, societal actions in support of fairness and social justice for American youth, and I am honored to have this esteemed colleague and valued friend contribute so importantly to this book.

Although my personal experiences surrounding September 11, 2001, were the immediate impetus to my writing this book, its timing in no way reflects the wishes or will of any person involved in these experiences. As already emphasized, and as will be clear at several points in the book, I have been impressed by the vision and ideas of former Vice President Gore regarding family-centered community building. I hope I give adequate voice to the compelling and important perspective he has advanced. On the other hand, it is important to stress that except where I specifically and directly cite Mr. Gore or, in fact, any person, I take responsibility for all the ideas presented in this book. Nothing I write should be construed in any way as an endorsement by any person of any issue of science I present or of any point of policy I suggest. Indeed, I anticipate that even my most supportive colleague or devoted student will find something in this book with which to disagree. Other people will find even more ideas to which they object or believe are downright wrong.

Last, and as is almost obligatory to say, the deficits of the arguments I forward are not of the making of any of the colleagues, students, and friends I have acknowledged. However, in almost all cases the assets in this book may be attributable to their influence. Indeed, arguably the most important asset of this book, its existence, is certainly attributable to another person. Accordingly, this book is dedicated to Al Gore for giving me the inspiration and the courage to continue to try to make a difference for the youth of America and the world.

R. M. L.

August 2003

1

Ideals and Human Development

How do we know whether American children and adolescents are doing well in life? What words do American parents, teachers, policymakers, and young people themselves use to describe a young person—a person in the first two decades or so of life—who is showing successful development?

All too often in the United States we discuss positive development in terms of the absence of negative or undesirable behaviors. Typically, such descriptions are predicated on the assumption that children are "broken" or are in danger of becoming broken (Benson, 2003a, 2003b), and thus we regard young people as "problems to be managed" (Roth, Brooks-Gunn, Murray, & Foster, 1998). As such, when we describe a successful young person we speak about a youth whose problems have been managed or are, at best, absent. We might say, then, that a youth who is manifesting behavior indicative of positive development is someone who is *not* taking drugs or using alcohol, is *not* engaging in unsafe sex, and is *not* participating in crime or violence.

Benson (2003a) explains that the focus on problems in Americans' discussions of youth and the use by Americans of a vocabulary that stresses the risks and dangers of young people occurs because we have:

> a culture dominated by deficit and risk thinking, by pathology and its symptoms. This shapes our research, our policy, our practice. It fuels the creation of elaborate and expensive service and program delivery infrastructures, creates a dependence on professional experts, encourages an ethos of fear, and by consequence, derogates, ignores and interferes with the natural and inherent capacity of communities to be community. (p. 25)

1

Benson (2003a) also points out that:

> Intertwined with this social phenomenon is the contemporary dominance of what is often called the deficit-reduction paradigm. In this paradigm, research and practice are steered to naming, counting, and reducing the incidence of environmental risks (e.g., family violence, poverty, family disintegration) and health-compromising behaviors (e.g., substance use, adolescent pregnancy, interpersonal violence, school dropout). This paradigm, it has been argued, dominates the strategies chosen to enhance child and adolescent health and has historically driven resource allocation in the favor of federal and foundation initiatives (Benson, 1997). The point here is not that deficit-reduction as a way of thinking and mobilizing action is misguided. But as a dominating paradigm, it may unintentionally enhance both the over-professionalization of care and civic disengagement. These processes may well be symbiotic. That is, civic disengagement and professionalized forms of addressing child and adolescent health may feed each other. (p. 24)

The deficit model that shapes our vocabulary about the behaviors prototypical of young people results, then, in an orientation in America to discuss positive youth development as the absence of negative behaviors. In this context, Pittman and Fleming (1991) note that:

> For years, Americans have accepted the notion that—with the exception of education—services for youth, particularly publicly funded services, exist to address youth problems. We have assumed that positive youth development occurs naturally in the absence of youth problems. Such thinking has created an assortment of youth services focused on "fixing" adolescents engaged in risky behaviors or preventing other youth from "getting into trouble." Preventing high risk behaviors, however, is not the same as preparation for the future. Indeed, an adolescent who attends school, obeys laws, and avoids drugs, is not necessarily equipped to meet the difficult demands of adulthood. Problem-free does not mean fully prepared. There must be an equal commitment to helping young people understand life's challenges and responsibilities and to developing the necessary skills to succeed as adults. What is needed is a massive conceptual shift—from thinking that youth problems are merely the principal barrier to youth development to thinking that youth development serves as the most effective strategy for the prevention of youth problems. (p. 3)

Unfortunately, as recently as 1999, and even in programs purportedly focused on positive youth development, a predominant emphasis in the youth development field continued to be a reliance on the deficit model of youth and, as such, on defining positive youth development as the absence of adolescent problem behaviors. For instance, Catalano et al. (1999) noted that "currently, problem behaviors are tracked more often than positive ones and, while an increasing number of positive youth development interventions are choosing to measure both, this is still far from being the standard in the field" (p. vi). They go on to note that:

> A major obstacle to tracking indicators of positive youth development con-
> structs is the absence of widely accepted measures for this purpose.
> Although such outcomes as academic achievement, engagement in the work-
> force, and financial self-sufficiency are commonly used, many aspects of pos-
> itive youth development go unassessed due to the underdeveloped state of
> the assessment tools. (pp. vi–vii)

The absence of an accepted vocabulary for the discussion of positive youth development is, then, a key obstacle to evaluating the effectiveness of programs or policies aimed at promoting such change. People do not measure what they cannot name, and they often do not name what they cannot measure (T. Gore, personal communication, December 13, 2002).

In short, characterizations of young people as problems to be managed or as primarily people in need of fixing reflect both a deficit approach to human development and a belief that there is some shortcoming of character or personality that leads youth to become involved in risky or negative behaviors. Given the presence of such a deficit, the appropriate and humane action to take toward young people is to prevent the inevitable actualization of the problems they will encounter. Indeed, policymakers and practitioners are pleased when their actions are associated with the reduction of such problem behaviors as teenage pregnancy and parenting, substance use and abuse, school failure and dropout, and delinquency and violence.

Everyone should of course be pleased when such behaviors diminish. However, it is dispiriting for a young person to learn that he is regarded by adults as someone who is likely to be a problem for others as well as for himself. It is discouraging for a young person to try to make a positive life when she is continually confronted by the suspicion of substance abuse, problematic sexuality, and a lack of commitment to supporting the laws of society. What sort of message are we sending our children when we speak of them as inevitably destined for trouble unless we take preventive steps? How do such messages affect the self-esteem of young people, and what is the impact of such messages on their spirit and motivation?

America does of course have some words for describing the positive behaviors of youth, for example, pertaining to academic achievement and activities relating to current or potentially successful entrepreneurship. Nevertheless, the vocabulary for depicting youth as "resources to be developed" (Roth et al., 1998) is not as rich or as nuanced as the one for depicting the problematic propensities of young people. While Americans are justifiably pleased when rates of drug abuse or teenage crime decrease, there are few positive national indicators to which Americans point to reflect desirable, healthy, and valued behaviors among its children and adolescents.

America as a nation must do a better job of talking about the positive attributes of our young people. We must talk to our youth about what they should and can become, not only about what they must not be. We must then act on our statements, and work with young people to promote their positive development. In the context of nurturing and healthy adult–youth relationships we need to offer young people the opportunities to learn and use the skills involved in participating actively in their communities and in making productive and positive contributions to themselves and their families and society.

A Theory of Positive Youth Development

This book proposes a theory of what it means to develop as an exemplary young person—a young person who is healthy and thriving. In this book, I define a *thriving* young person as an individual who—within the context of his or her physical and psychological characteristics and abilities— takes actions that serve his or her own well-being and, at the same time, the well-being of parents, peers, community, and society. A thriving young person is on a life path toward a hopeful future (Damon & Gregory, 2003; Damon, Menon, & Bronk, 2003), a path that eventuates in the young person becoming an ideal adult member of a civil society. In other words, thriving young people show exemplary positive development in the present and become generative adults who make positive contributions to self, others, and civil society.

The theory of positive youth development that I propose regards the development of these contributions to self and society as a matter of *relationships* between changes in the young person and the nature of his or her social world. I argue that thriving young people—youth who make these mutually beneficial contributions to self and to society—are people whose senses of self involve a combined moral and civic commitment to contributing to society in manners reflective of their individual strengths, talents, and interest. Accordingly, thriving youth are on life journeys that involve productive civic engagement and valued contributions to other people and to the institutions of their communities. As well, thriving young people are individuals who live in a society that values and supports the freedom to take the initiative to make such individual contributions. I describe such a mutually beneficial relationship between person and society as *liberty*.

Although my theory capitalizes on the emergence of a new, positive vision and vocabulary about youth (e.g., Damon & Gregory, 2003; Roth & Brooks-Gunn, 2003a, 2003b; Roth et al., 1998), one stressing their strengths and their potential for healthy growth (e.g., Benson, 2003a; Blum, 2003; Pittman, 1996), the theory is rooted in an idea that has a long history within America. This is the idea that there is a connection between moral and civic life.

In specifying that ensuring liberty involves developing an integration of moral and civic identity in youth, a development that enables young people to contribute effectively and productively to a society that promotes individual freedom, I am in a sense proposing an idea found in the writings of Benjamin Franklin. Franklin believed that probity (honesty) and integrity were moral qualities of youth that, when present, enabled them to successfully contribute to their communities. Indeed, Franklin proposed 13 virtues (temperance, silence, order, resolution, frugality, industry, sincerity, justice, moderation, cleanliness, tranquility, chastity, and humility) as a means to frame the lives of individuals pursuing life courses marked by healthy and successful contributions to self, others, and society.

Thus, the connections in my theory between youth moral and civic identity, individual freedom, and liberty have a long tradition in America, and as exemplified by the virtues specified by Franklin and by his advice to young people, this relationship offers a strong counterargument to critics of American culture who claim that the subscription to virtue, not freedom, is the ultimate indicator of a good society. For example, as explained by D'Souza (2003), Islamic fundamentalist critics of America argue that virtue is a higher principle than is freedom, and that, in stressing virtue, albeit in the absence of any freedom to choose to be virtuous or not, fundamentalist Islamic societies are closer to the good than are those societies that promote liberty. However, there are two problems with this argument.

First, as D'Souza (2003) explains, coercing virtuous behavior from people obviates the behavior from being reflective of virtue. He notes that the wearing of a veil is not indicative of modesty *if* the person has no choice other than to wear the garment. He argues that only when virtuous behaviors are freely chosen from among options that are not indicative of the good is virtuous behavior being shown: "Virtue has special luster because it is freely chosen" (p. A23). D'Souza indicates that in America such choices are made daily by millions of free American people, and in the vast majority of the cases the virtuous path is taken. Freedom and virtue are integrated in America (see too Wilson, 1993).

Recognition of the nature of the contemporary choices of American citizens leads to the identification of the second problem with the Islamic fundamentalist critique of America. As reflected in today's behaviors of Americans, and as epitomized by the ideas of Benjamin Franklin, the ideals set for Americans' behaviors have always reflected the linkage between doing what is morally correct and doing what is civically beneficial (cf. Wilson, 1993).

A key point of this book is that this association between moral and civic life does not occur by happenstance, and, most certainly, it is not "in our genes" (Lewontin, 2000). Rather, the merger of moral and civic life is *developed*. If we create through our social policies and community-based programs the resources or assets needed by communities, families, and young people themselves to foster such development, we can assure this link between moral and civic life among all American youth. The purpose of my theory is to explain how this development occurs and how it may be promoted.

The theory I propose is, then, a model of how a social system characterized by liberty involves thriving youth whose civic engagement supports civil society (that is, the values and institutions of society, independent of government, that assure democracy and freedom; O'Connell, 1999). As well, the theory explains how the probability of youth thriving is strengthened and furthered when young people live within a strong and vibrant democracy that celebrates the diversity of its citizenry. The theory points, then, to the ideals of the American system— to the idea of America, if you will—as an exemplar of a social system that involves liberty. This system has the greatest potential of simultaneously promoting positive youth development and civil society, and of assuring the intergenerational continuity of democracy and of social justice.

The Purposes of Scientific Theory

Scientific theories have two purposes. They integrate existing information and they lead to the generation of new information. Accordingly, across the chapters of this book, I present information derived from different areas of science that are integrated into the ideas of the proposed theory of positive youth development. In turn, I also discuss issues about positive youth development that need to be addressed by future research. An important part of such research is a discussion of the role of innovations in social policies and of community-based programs in promoting thriving among youth.

As a consequence, I discuss the implications of the theory for some very practical concerns—what communities, families, and young people themselves can do to enhance the probability both of positive youth development and of civil society; what citizens can do to further liberty. I suggest actions that people can take to translate the idealized depiction of young people portrayed in the theory into policies and programs that increase the probability of positive youth development among all young people.

I place, then, a large burden on my theory of youth development. In more than 30 years of teaching and research about human development, I have often found that not only students new to the field but also colleagues from disciplines other than human development are not familiar with the characteristics, uses, and limitations of a theory of human development. Accordingly, in order to undertake the burden I have set for my theory, it is important to explain the ways in which not only scientific theory in general but a theory of human development in particular may be useful both for advancing scholarly research about young people *and* for framing practical and applied issues intended to improve the lives of youth in their real-world settings.

On the Nature of Human Development Theory

What are theories of human development theories *of*? To people unfamiliar with the science of human development, the answer is often surprising.

Jean Piaget, in his major treatise on moral development, *The Moral Judgment of the Child* (1965), provides an illustration of the fact that theories of human development may often have a focus that is counterintuitive. Piaget (1965) began his book by noting that:

Readers will find in this book no direct analysis of child morality as it is practised in home and school life or in children's societies. It is the moral judgment that we propose to investigate, not moral behaviour or sentiments. (p. 7)

Piaget argued that the study of moral behavior, or even of emotions associated with moral behaviors, missed the point of a developmental analysis, which was to provide an idealized representation of the process of growth underlying, and giving meaning to, the changes that characterized life; in the case of the moral developments in which he was interested, this process involved the alterations in the structure of the child's mind that gave meaning to the young person's moral decisions and actions.

The same behavior could be underlain mentally by very different moral rationales. As a consequence, a developmental theory pertinent to the growth of morality during childhood needed to account for the changing structure of thought that resulted in moral meaning across life.

Development Always Involves Change, But Not All Changes Reflect Development

Piaget's (1965) differentiation between what was and was not to be the focus of his instance of developmental theory illustrates what may be a surprising but general fact about developmental theories. Developmental theories constitute idealized visions about the course of human life. A developmental theory focuses on what are, among all the vast characteristics of humans that might be studied or that could change across life, the particular instances of human functioning seen as relevant to the changes of interest in the theory. Thus, while the occurrence of development always means that some change has taken place, not all changes are indicative of development. For example, in Piaget's case, his selection was to focus on judgments about what is moral, and not on behaviors in situations wherein a moral action is taken.

In other words, theories of development are statements about those elements, among all the possible things that can and do change in a person's life, that are of importance or relevance for understanding the nature of systematic change across life. Developmental theories constitute a template depicting the nature of a specific set of systematic changes, a template that enables a developmental scientist to decide if any changes in behavior that he or she may observe actually reflect human development—that is, whether they reflect systematic and successive change in some life process, such as thinking, moral functioning, personality, or positive development. A developmental theory is, then, an a priori (pre-empirical) statement that allows one to know which empirical observations, among the virtually infinite number of observations that can be made, fit with or constitute developmental change.

Accordingly, Piaget (1965) did not first study behavioral changes and changes in thought and then decide which domain of change was important to consider when developing ideas pertinent to his theory. His interest in the changing structure of knowledge led him to conclude that information about changes in children's reasons about moral actions and not their moral actions per se were therefore of relevance:

> With this aim in view we questioned a large number of children in the Geneva and the Neuchâtel schools and held conversations with them, similar to those we had before on their conception of the world and of causality. (p. 7)

Thus, before he collected any data, before making any observations relevant to moral development, Piaget knew what he wanted to observe. This knowledge also shaped the method he selected to make his observations; that is, he decided that interviewing children was the best way to study their moral reasoning.

In essence, then, when embedded within a theory of human development, the concept of development is not primarily an empirical term. Rather, it is a concept that is used to discriminate between changes that are either part of the process of changes pertinent to the theory *or* constitute changes that are irrelevant to the process of development. Without an a priori specification of what constitutes developmentally pertinent change, the theorist cannot partition the huge flux of life into relevant and irrelevant categories.

As another example, consider what are termed *classic,* or *strong,* developmental theories (cf. Reese & Overton, 1970), for example, those of Freud (1949, 1954) or Piaget (1960; Inhelder & Piaget, 1958). Such theories propose that there exists a series of qualitatively different stages of development. It is held that only changes congruent with the structure and content of these stages constitute development. The usefulness of these theories is found (as I have noted is the case with all scientific theories) in whether they usefully integrate existing information and lead to the generation of new information. In the case of these developmental theories, their use lies in whether they depict the character of behavior at successive points in the life span (the *ontogeny*) of individuals and whether they enable successful understanding and prediction of what behaviors are or are not seen at particular times in life.

The classic psychoanalytic approach to psychiatry is predicated on adherence to Freud's specification that there are five psychosexual stages of development and that certain events must occur within a particular stage (or period within a stage) for development to occur normally; failure of certain things to occur at specific times (e.g., oral incorporative stimulation during the first period with the Oral Stage) will create lasting problems (e.g., adult obesity) for the developing person; in turn, one can understand (within the terms of this theory) adult psychiatric problems by fitting their character to earlier stages of development. One does not first observe an adult who eats excessively and then try to figure out if such behavior is or is not an instance of a behavioral pathology; one knows that this behavior does reflect such a problem (an "oral fixation") because one has an a priori theory within which one fits one's observations. This theory enables one to predict other problems associated with the person's past (e.g., frustration occurred during the first six months of life) and present (e.g., other problems associated with incorporation should exist, such as greed or self-absorption).

In all cases, then, developmental theories are tested for a goodness of fit between their a priori—and idealized—specification of the changing structure and content of mind or behavior and observations pertinent to these specifications. The theory presented in this book offers, as well, an idealized view of human development. However, what, specifically, is this theory a theory of?

An Introduction to a Theory of Thriving and Civic Engagement Among Youth

This book presents a new theory of what can go *right* in a young person's life. It is a theory of how positive development is forged through the individual's active contributions to society. It envisions that, when young people define themselves, morally and civically, as individuals committed to making valuable contributions to self, family, community, and society, they thrive—they enter onto life paths marked by positive behaviors (such as competence, confidence, and compassion) and by active participation in their communities (by civic engagement), and they develop toward a future characterized by the sorts of contributions to which they have become committed.

Accordingly, this is not a book about what goes wrong in the lives of youth. It is not a book that dwells upon the problems or the crises of youth or that regards children and adolescents as being broken and in need of fixing (Benson, 2003a, 2003b). Instead, this book stresses the strengths that are inherent in all young people and in their communities. While not denying that problems of youth development exist and that it is important to diminish or prevent these undesirable features of children and adolescents (R. M. Lerner, 1995; Perkins & Borden, 2003), the theory presented in this book emphasizes that young people constitute resources that can be developed in ways that serve both them and society in mutually beneficial ways (Roth et al., 1998).

The theory leads to the idea that the best way to prevent problems is to promote the potential strengths of all children (Pittman, Irby, & Ferber, 2001). It suggests that society would be wise not to focus its efforts on building programs to "fix broken children" or on avoiding the actualization of purported deficits or weaknesses (Benson, 2003b; Benson, Mannes, Pittman, & Ferber, 2004; Benson & Pittman, 2001). Instead, efforts should be directed toward enhancing the community resources, assets, or "nutrients" for healthy development that exist in all communities, and toward strengthening these assets for positive development in order to improve the lives of all young people (Benson, 2003a, 2003b).

Biology and Culture Are Interrelated in Human Evolution

Humans are both biological and social creatures (Tobach & Schneirla, 1968). Accordingly, the theory proposed in this book describes (in Chapter 2) the intertwined changes between biology and culture that characterize humans' evolutionary heritage and, as well, humans' contemporary functioning. Humans' evolutionary history involved the slow rate of development of immature human infants (Gould, 1977) and the need for interdependent group life to maximize survival on the African savannah (Johanson & Edey, 1981). These conditions resulted in the emergence of family and community institutions (Fisher, 1982a, 1982b) and the need for these and other institutions of social life to protect the individual and his or her singular characteristics.

For instance, in order to enhance the innovations needed for entry into and survival within the new or changing physical ecologies within which humans roamed and settled, individuality—diversity—had to be prized and supported. In turn, this connection between the individual and the social context resulted in socialization practices (by parents and by institutions outside the family) that inculcated in the developing person a sense of the importance of contributing—through the exercise of his or her individual talents, abilities, and interests—to the maintenance and perpetuation of the social context that supported him or her (Fisher, 1982a, 1982b; Lewontin & Levins, 1978).

Accordingly, across human evolution a mutually supportive, bidirectional, or reciprocal relation emerged to characterize individuals and their social worlds (Johanson & Edey, 1981). The interdependency between individual and context that was a defining feature of human evolution is also a key aspect of what must be reflected in human development across life in order for individuals to survive and prosper (e.g., Brandtstädter, 1998; Gottlieb, 1992, 1997; Heckhausen, 1999).

There is, in other words, a connection between human *phylogeny* (the evolution of the species) and human *ontogeny* (the development of a member of the species from conception to death): The structure of the relation between individual and context enabled human survival and biological hegemony over all other forms of life on this planet. This structure involves mutually beneficial relations between individual and context, and corresponds to the structure of the individual–context relations that enable individuals to develop across their lives in healthy, positive ways (Gould, 1977; Johanson & Edey, 1981). When the structure of the relations between individuals and their social worlds is instantiated in ideal ways—when these structures involve exchanges that are beneficial to both "partners" in the relation—then young people manifest exemplary personal development *(thriving)* and their communities flourish.

Universal Structures Exist Along With Cultural and Historical Variation

These ideal structures are seen to be "universal" in that they describe regularities in the relations between individuals and contexts that are always involved in successful, positive, healthy, or "adaptive" characteristics of both people and their settings. Nevertheless, it is of course the case that how these structures are realized (that is, how the "content" of these structures is formed) varies across place and time. Different societies at one point in time and the same society across history may create different social institutions (e.g., systems of government, faith institutions, or educational systems). The theory posits that in any society, at any point in history, *adaptive* (healthy, positive, or mutually beneficial) relations create the structure for ideal individual and societal functioning and change.

I term the mutual relations between growing young people and their changing social worlds *developmental regulations*. When these relations are in fact mutually beneficial, I label them *adaptive developmental regulations*.

There may be societal variation in the content of developmental regulations. For example, it is possible that one society may instantiate adaptive developmental regulations between individuals and contexts through the creation of democratic governmental systems and the affording to individuals of personal freedoms. However, another society may instantiate such individual–context relations through the creation of a theocracy or a monarchy.

"Liberty" Maximizes the Probability of Adaptive Developmental Regulations

The theory thus specifies that there is not an isomorphism between the structure and the content of healthy person–context relations. However, the theory does postulate that the probability of thriving individuals and flourishing societies is maximized when the idealized structure is matched with (1) a society that affords individuals the freedom to pursue their individual goals and aspirations, while, at the same time, (2) socializing individuals to support the institutions of the society that guarantee these opportunities to all individuals (that is, when there is socialization for democracy).

As I have already explained, I term such a relation between free and thriving individuals and a flourishing, democratic society *liberty*. Patterson (1991) also sees liberty as involving a mutually beneficial relation between individual and society and, as well, links liberty to the democratic ideals of Western, if not American, culture. He notes that:

> At its best, the valorization of personal liberty is the noblest achievement of Western civilization. That people are free to do as they please within limits set only by the personal freedom of others; that legally all persons are equal before the law; that philosophically the individual's separate existence is inviolable. . . . All add up to a value complex that not only is unparalleled in any other culture but, in its profundity and power, is superior to any other single complex of values conceived by mankind. (pp. 402–403)

Wilson (1993), too, underscores the link between liberty and a social order that maintains individual freedom and a commitment to a civil society that guarantees such freedom to others. He notes that "political liberty, which is one of the greatest gifts a people can acquire for themselves, is threatened when social order is threatened" (p. 234). Wilson explains that people:

> have made it clear that they want freedom and will die for it. But the freedom they want is not unconstrained choice; it is rather the opportunity to express themselves, enrich themselves, and govern themselves in a world that has already been organized and defined by a set of intuitively understood commitments. Ordinary people understand this very well, as when they insist that individual freedom is meaningful only in an orderly society. (p. 234)

I believe that in societies having the structure and content of a social order reflective of liberty young people will find optimally productive ways to matter simultaneously to themselves, their families, their communities, and to society. They will have attained a noble purpose for their lives (Damon et al., 2003). Such a purpose seeks to maximize the likelihood for positive, healthy development for self, for other individuals, and for the social institutions that guarantee such development for all people.

In essence, then, when imbued by noble purpose, young people are committed to contributing not only to their own better lives but also to making contributions that extend beyond themselves in time and place (Damon et al., 2003). As discussed later in this book, such personal investment in matters that extend beyond one's self in time and place—such transcendence—is the essence of spirituality (R. M. Lerner, Dowling, & Anderson, 2003).

Of course, one might argue that human evolution could not have resulted in individuals investing their resources in people and institutions that transcend them and their own existence (or their own reproductive opportunities). However, the uniquely human intermeshing of biology and culture that characterizes human evolution (Gould, 1977; Johanson & Edey, 1981) means that such transcendence is part of what it means to be human. Consistent with this viewpoint, Wilson (1993) argues that:

> If Darwin and his followers are right, and I think they are, the moral sense must have adaptive value; if it did not, natural selection would have worked against people who had such useless traits as sympathy, self-control, or a desire for fairness and in favor of those with the opposite tendencies (such as the capacity for ruthless predation, or a preference for immediate gratifications, or a disinclination to share). Biologists, beginning with Darwin, have long understood this. But contemporary biologists sometimes give too narrow an account of this evolutionary process, because they attempt to link selfish genes directly to unselfish behavior without explaining the intervening psychological mechanism. (p. 23)

Accordingly, the theory of positive youth development that I present postulates that, in ideal circumstances, young people's discovery of their individual goals and purposes in life involves the attainment of a sense of self—an "identity"—wherein moral and civic orientations become merged, where the understanding of self involves in part a transcendence of self, a spiritual commitment to "do what is right" and serve family, community, and society, as well as self (Damon et al., 2003; R. M Lerner, Anderson, Balsano, Dowling, & Bobek, 2003). Liberty exists, then, when thriving youth, impelled by a spiritual sense of integrated moral and civic commitment, contribute to their own lives and the lives of a democratic community in mutually beneficial ways.

The theory suggests that, under ideal circumstances, or at least at some general level, American youth (and perhaps youth from other democracies) are socialized to instantiate person–context relations in manners reflecting American ideals and values. In other words, in optimal circumstances youth are socialized to engage in adaptive developmental regulations that reflect the commitment to the integration of individual freedom and civil society that is described by Wilson (1993). In short, to promote positive development, youth should be socialized to strive to enact the "idea of America."

The "Idea of America"

The United States of America is more than a place. It is an idea, a vision of social justice, equity, democracy, and individual rights and responsibilities. Admittedly imperfect in its enactment, the vision is of free individuals living in peace in a just, democratic society. The idea of America, even more so than the nation itself, stands across history and throughout the contemporary world as the exemplar of liberty.

Liberty is the right of an individual to pursue a life path of his or her own choosing within a society that places on the person the responsibility, the duty, of contributing to the maintenance and perpetuation of a social order that ensures that all individuals have this same right. Indeed:

> Duty is taken for granted by democratic politics. . . . Many Americans are attracted by the idea of requiring of all of our young people some period of community or national service. Whatever the legislative fate of that notion, it is a powerful indicator of how strongly many people feel that duty is an impulse that ought to be encouraged. (Wilson, 1993, p. 249)

Liberty exists when a society ensures justice, equity, and democracy for all individuals and when individuals believe it is necessary, that it is their duty, to support this society and, as well, when they act on this belief. Wilson (1993) captures well this dynamic relation between individual freedom and commitment to a social order guaranteeing freedom to others when he notes that "testing limits is a way of asserting selfhood. Maintaining limits is a way of asserting community" (p. 9).

Liberty is not a gift by governments to people. As framed in the Declaration of Independence, it is an inalienable right of people who, living in a society wherein this right is present, see it as their moral necessity to contribute to—and to protect and further—a society that accords this right to all its members. To people embracing the idea of America, the promotion and protection of liberty becomes a defining characteristic of their senses of themselves, of their self-definitions or "identities." Ensuring liberty becomes both a moral imperative and a civic responsibility. *The key "hypothesis" within the theory of positive youth development that I propose is that thriving young people have an integrated moral and civic identity and that this self-definition is linked to their active contributions to self, family, community, and civil society.*

Indeed, the link between moral functioning and civic contribution is not just a matter of understanding positive development among young people. Consistent with the idea that healthy individual development also benefits communities, the link has been, and remains, also a key facet of national policy:

> There has always been a debate over the destiny of this nation between those who believed they were entitled to govern because of their station in life, and those who believed that the people were sovereign. That distinction remains as strong as ever today . . . [and pertains to] nothing less than the future of democratic capitalism. And it cannot be rejuvenated unless the people and the politicians focus on the question: What is good for the whole? (Gore, 2002, p. 13)

Gore's conception of a diverse America peopled by free citizens who act to support the constitutional principles that unify us as a nation recalls the vision of Abraham Lincoln for equity and freedom for all people within the union he led and preserved. In 1857, after the Dred Scott decision had been announced by the Supreme Court, and thus before he became president, Lincoln spoke in Springfield, Illinois, about the nature of the equality accorded to all people in our nation by the framers of the Constitution:

I think the authors of that notable instrument intended to include all men, but they did not intend to declare all men equal in all respects. They did not mean to say all were equal in color, size, intellect, moral developments, or social capacity. They defined with tolerable distinctness, in what respects they did consider all men created equal—equal in certain inalienable rights, among which are life, liberty, and the pursuit of happiness. This they said, and this meant. They did not mean to assert the obvious untruth, that we were then actually enjoying that equality, nor yet, that they were about to confer it immediately upon them. In fact they had no power to confer such a boon. They meant simply to declare the right, so that the enforcement of it might follow as fast as circumstances should permit. They meant to set up a standard maxim for free society, which could be familiar to all, and revered by all; constantly looked to, constantly labored for, and even though never perfectly attained, constantly approximated, and thereby constantly spreading and deepening its influence, and augmenting the happiness and value of life to all people of all colors everywhere. (Basler, 1969, p. 60)

The visions of American democracy of both Gore and of Lincoln are one wherein the interests of all individuals are served by free citizens supporting laws that guarantee their individual liberties and the continuing pursuit of the enhancement of social justice and of the guarantee of liberty and justice for all. Such a view of the relationship between individuals and government—a view that involves the vision of free people actively engaged in the maintenance, renewal, and extension of civil society—is, as Gore makes quite explicit, quite different from one that sees power and prerogative residing in the already-powerful by virtue of the argument that the possession of power or position is self-justifying. The belief that political power should belong to the politically powerful is a form of Social Darwinism, the idea that people possess political and social power because they (or their hereditary line) have evolved to take a superior role in society (Tobach, Gianutsos, Topoff, & Gross, 1974).

Although Social Darwinism is, today, mostly a subtext to the sorts of political debates noted by Gore, there are some areas of contemporary biological and behavioral or social science that, in effect, countenance a comparable view (R. M. Lerner, 1992). As discussed in this book, these areas of science—for example, areas termed "behavioral genetics" (Plomin, 2000; Rowe, 1994) or "human sociobiology" (Rushton, 1999, 2000)—are associated with the ideas that heredity—genes—provides a direct and immutable blueprint for behavioral development, and that differences in social standing and healthy or problematic behaviors reflect—or can be *reduced* to—variation in genetic inheritance.

As I explain in greater detail later in this book, these reductionistic, hereditarian conceptions have implications for the understanding of individual development and of civil society. These implications contrast dramatically with those associated with the theoretical view of the relations between individuals and society I forward. My rejection of biological reductionist ideas is predicated on the association of my theory of positive youth development with a superordinate theoretical framework for understanding all of human development, a conception termed *developmental systems theory*.

An Overview of Developmental Systems Theory

Developmental systems theory eschews the reduction of individual and social behavior to fixed genetic influences. and in fact contends that such a hereditarian conception is counterfactual (Gottlieb, 1997, 1998). Instead, developmental systems theory stresses the *relative plasticity* of human development. This concept means that there is always at least some potential for systematic change in behavior.

This potential exists as a consequence of mutually influential relationships between the developing person and his or her biology, psychological characteristics, family, community, culture, physical and designed ecology, and historical niche. The plasticity of development means that one may expect that means may be found to improve human life.

Plasticity, then, legitimizes an optimistic view of the potential for promoting positive changes in humans. The presence of plasticity is an asset in attempts to enhance the human condition, and, as such, plasticity directs interest to the strengths for positive development that are present within all people. It also directs both science and applications of science— for example, involving public policies and the programs of community-based organizations (CBOs)—to find ways to create optimal matches between individuals and their social worlds. Such fits may capitalize on the potential for positive change in people and for promoting such development.

The dubious political stances and, implicitly, the related scientific positions criticized by former Vice President Gore may be able to be turned into delimiting or, in fact, dehumanizing social policy formulations. In contrast, I argue that the social policy implications of developmental systems theory counter such negative formulations about human capacity, potential, and freedom. Developmental systems theory affords a means to pursue human development as it might ideally be (Benson, 2003a, 2003b; Bronfenbrenner, 1974); that is, developmental systems theory provides a framework for creating conditions whereby human development unfolds in a society marked by liberty. In such circumstances, thriving across the life span may be promoted.

The influence of developmental systems theory on the model of positive youth development that I forward involves specific means through which the idea of America may be actualized. These ideas converge in ways to promote mutually beneficial relations between individuals and their civil society. To begin to present the details of this theory, it is useful discuss the relation between civic engagement and moral behavior.

Merging Civic Duty and Moral Action in Youth Development

The idea of America suggests that contributions to civil society are both moral acts and civic duties. People embracing the idea of America believe that behaviors that support justice, freedom, equity, and democracy and that support a social order that ensures the availability of liberty to all are the right actions to take. Indeed, they believe they are duty bound to take them (Wilson, 1993). As well, people adhering to the idea of America believe it is wrong to act in ways that take from or deny people these rights. At the same time, people believing in the idea of America recognize that it is necessary to contribute to and, at times, fight to defend a society that ensures liberty. Without such contributions, the ability of society to afford liberty to themselves and others may be jeopardized. Both moral values and civic responsibility impel us, then, to support the institutions of our civil society. We do this because society acts to support our individual rights and ensures our liberty.

Civil society—"the nexus of families, groups, neighborhoods, and associations" (Wilson, 1993, p. 246)—is composed of the social mores, customs, values, and ideals of a people that ensure democracy. These social constructions, or social institutions, are not the components of government. In fact, government is only a means created "by the consent of the governed" to make systematic the availability of social justice and democratic opportunities to citizens. Civil society is, then, the "space" between individuals and government that assures that social justice and democracy are features of the social order and not a "gift" of government (O'Connell, 1999).

Certainly, after the attacks on America of September 11, 2001, the ideas surrounding the concept of liberty have a clear patriotic theme. The vision and values of America are under assault by an enemy that would destroy every facet of liberty and of modern American life. However, it is more than a call to patriotism to point to the fact that our moral and civic identities as American citizens combine to impel us to defend civil society as it is enshrined in the idea of America. Of course, it is not surprising that American youth are socialized to believe in and to act in support of this idea. However, what it not obvious—but what is clearly controversial—is that this coupling between adaptive developmental regulations and commitment to the idea of America provides for both youth and society the greatest likelihood of positive, indeed exemplary, individual development (thriving) and of the presence of institutions guaranteeing individual freedom and opportunity (e.g., as indexed by institutions, policies, and social programs reflecting social justice and equity; cf. Patterson, 1991; Wilson, 1993).

The Essence of the Theoretical Ideas
Linking Liberty, Thriving, and Civic Engagement

From all that I have said to this point, it may be clear that there are five sets of interrelated ideas found in the theory of positive youth development presented in this book:

1. There is a universal structure for adaptive developmental regulations between people and their contexts. This structure involves mutually beneficial relations between people and their social worlds, and may be represented as *individual* ← → *social context*.

2. These mutually beneficial, individual ← → social context relations have their historical roots in humans' integrated biological and cultural evolutionary heritage.

3. When instantiated in ideal ways, adaptive developmental regulations involve reciprocally supportive relations between thriving individuals and social institutions supporting the freedom of individuals.

4. Thriving youth have noble purposes; they have an integrated moral and civic sense of self that impels them to transcend their own interests and contribute to others and to society in ways that extend beyond them in time and place.

5. This idealized relation between individuals and society may be realized within diverse cultural systems. However, when universal structures of mutually beneficial person–context relations are coupled with behavioral and social characteristics consistent with the idea of America, then liberty is most likely to exist: Youth are maximally likely to thrive and, reciprocally, free society is most likely to flourish.

Potential Applications of the Theory to Science and Social Policy

How might this theory be useful in advancing understanding of human development in general or youth development in particular? In turn, how may the theory be used to promote social policy changes that would maximize the fit between the idealized developmental pathways depicted in the theory and the actual life courses of young people? Policies reflect what a people value, what they believe is right; policies tell people where resources will be invested and what actions will be taken in support of beliefs and values. What is the action agenda that may be derived legitimately from the positive youth development theory I present, of the ideas and research evidence linking moral and civic identity and thriving within a system promoting liberty?

In answer to these questions, I note that the present theory of positive youth development helps organize and extend data pertinent to:

1. The integration of biology and culture across human evolution (e.g., Fisher, 1982a, 1982b; Gould, 1977; Johanson & Edey, 1981; Lewontin & Levins, 1978)

2. The links between evolution and individual development (e.g., Gottlieb, 1992, 1997, 1998; Gottlieb, Wahlsten, & Lickliter, 1998; Tobach, 1981; Tobach & Greenberg, 1984; Tobach et al., 1974)

3. Covariation between positive youth development, thriving, and youth civic engagement (e.g., Benson, 2003a, 2003b; Damon et al., 2003; Dowling et al., 2003, in press; Scales et al., 2000; Sherrod, Flanagan, & Youniss, 2002b; Yates & Youniss, 1966; Youniss, Yates, & Su, 1997); and

4. Noble purpose and civic and moral identity (e.g., Benson, 1997, 2003b; Damon, 1997; Damon & Gregory, 2003; Damon et al., 2003; Furrow & Wagener, 2003).

In turn, the theory provides a set of testable ideas about the differential likelihood of youth thriving in social contexts that vary in regard to their support of liberty. Moreover, to the extent that developmental theories provide a useful frame for describing and explaining extant and to-be-generated data, they also offer a means to optimize human development. We may test our understanding of the processes involved in the systematic changes comprising human development by altering the relations between individual and contexts in ways that should, if our theory is useful, result in the enhancement of the likelihood of positive development (e.g., Baltes, 1973). In this sense, research that tests our understanding of the basic processes of human development—of adaptive developmental regulations—is also applied, intervention research (R. M. Lerner, 2002a).

As such, applying our knowledge of human development in order to enhance the quality of the life course enables developmental scientists to "test the limits" of the developmental system (Baltes, Lindenberger, & Staudinger, 1998). It affords scientists the opportunity to ascertain how much capacity for systematic change (for "plasticity") exists within the system of person–context relations, and it enables them to gauge how close a fit can be established between the ideal pathway across life specified in a developmental theory and the actualities of human functioning.

Accordingly, as already noted, a useful developmental theory is not just a means for integrating data about what *is* in human life. As suggested by Bronfenbrenner (1974), the idealization of the course of life represented in a useful developmental theory provides a means for the scientist to generate data about what *might be* in human life.

It may of course turn out to be the case that a system of developmental regulation marked by what I have termed *liberty* is not the setting most beneficial for, or most likely to result in, thriving and civic contributions among youth. But, if, as the data integrated by the theory presented in this book suggests, liberty does constitute a comparative advantage over other systems of developmental regulation for the growth of thriving youth, then the benefits of policy and social program interventions that promote liberty are clear. The rationale for the policies and programs I recommend to promote positive youth development is advanced across the chapters of this book.

The Plan of This Book

In the chapters that follow, the ideas about positive youth development, civic engagement, and liberty that I present are used to afford understanding of existing and potential relations between young people and their social worlds. I use developmental systems theory to explain the evidence from human evolution and human development that supports my view that, when the idea of America is actualized, moral development and civic engagement coincide in human life to support the relations between individual liberty and civil society. This discussion underscores the idea that thriving in human development, energized by a spiritual commitment to make contributions to others and to society that transcend the self in time and place, creates across people a society predicated on noble purposes (Damon et al., 2003). As well, these ideas are used to offer ideas about policies and programs that may be pursued to enhance the fit between what we see in the lives of young people and what we regard as ideal paths to positive and productive personhood.

Accordingly, I discuss in Chapter 2 biological bases of the mutuality of influence between individuals and their social world that build the links between healthy individual development and civil society. I argue that the sweep of evolution and, most centrally, the history of human evolution have resulted in a specific and optimal survival strategy, one involving the maintenance (or the regulation) of mutually supportive relationships between individuals and their social worlds. This strategy is essential for the maintenance and perpetuation of humans and, when enacted in ideal ways, allows individuals and their social institutions to thrive. The existence of this strategy of mutual support between individuals and their social worlds constitutes a contribution of human evolution (the history of changes for the species *homo sapiens*) to human development (the course of people's lives, from conception to death).

The translation of this evolutionary strategy into the development of humans across their life spans involves people becoming more willing and more able across the life span to contribute to the maintenance and perpetuation of a social context that supports the health and prosperity of individual development. I argue in Chapter 2 that a society that supports such individual development is a civil society, and that when there are mutually beneficial exchanges (healthy developmental regulations) between individuals and civil society, then optimal development—*thriving*—is occurring. As well, when there is both maintenance and perpetuation of the institutions of civil society that enable individuals to contribute in healthy ways to self and to their social worlds, there is a thriving individual ← → civil society relationship. A society within which liberty exists is, then, the epitome of a social order enabling relations between people and contexts to develop in a manner consistent with the evolutionary strategy requisite for the survival and the optimal functioning of the human species and of individuals within it.

I argue as well that integrated moral and civic identities may emerge prototypically in adolescence, when the person's self-definition is undergoing significant and singular changes. When the thriving individual ← → civil society relationship is actualized through the attainment of a synthesis between moral and civic identity, young people attain several key characteristics of positive development. I suggest, as have others (e.g., Eccles & Gootman, 2002; R. M. Lerner, Fisher, & Weinberg, 2000; Roth & Brooks-Gunn, 2003a, 2003b), that "Five Cs" may be used to represent the key features of positive youth development: competence, character, confidence, social connections, and compassion. Together, these five characteristics enable an adolescent to make an optimal, or idealized, transition to the adult world. When these five characteristics place the young person on a life path toward a hopeful future, the youth is manifesting exemplary positive development: He or she is thriving. Such youth will become generative adults, persons who make simultaneously productive contributions to themselves, to family and community, and to civic life. The individual will develop, then, a "Sixth C," that is, contribution.

The idea of America, then, is not only a concept having its roots in the political, economic, and cultural history of a people. The idea of America—the provision and protection of liberty—reflects also the most evolutionary advanced strategy for the survival and potential further enhancement of the human species and, as well, the pathway in individual life for healthy, optimal development, for thriving, and for development into adulthood as a generative, successful member of one's family, community, and society.

Accordingly, the combined moral and civic identities of Americans constitute not only the political and cultural socialization of a people. The idea of America, when translated into the development of individuals within a civil society, reflects the actualization of an evolutionarily shaped life course optimal for thriving and moral action in support of a social order marked by liberty.

In making this claim I fully recognize that I may be adopting a version of what moral philosophers term the *naturalistic fallacy* (Kohlberg, 1971), that is, the derivation of universal *(ought)* statements from the observation of a set of "is"es or, in other words, saying what people ought to do by observing what they in fact do. Nevertheless, despite the history of warnings in philosophy about making this purported error (Kohlberg, 1971), I argue that the phenomena of human evolution and human development create in adaptive people the moral necessity to contribute to civil society (cf. Wilson, 1993). I defend my subscription to this instance of the naturalistic fallacy later in this book. Here, it is useful to note that, in essence, I argue that what *is*—the development of mutually supportive relations between the diverse individuals comprising America and the institutions of civil society—reflects what *ought* to be.

A moral and civic commitment to maintaining and to perpetuating a civil society marked by liberty means that one thinks and behaves in ways that make contributions beyond those that accrue to the self. Productive contributions to civil society involve acting to enhance people and institutions that extend in time and place beyond one's self. Such actions exemplify transcendence—feelings about and commitments to things that are beyond one's own existence. Transcendence is the essence of a sense of spirituality (R. M. Lerner, Anderson et al., 2003). This sense is a potent emotional force energizing individuals to invest their selves in other people—even those people not yet born; in their communities and larger society; and in ideas and values of their culture, for example, a religious faith or the idea of America.

In short, then, in comparison to other writers who have discussed moral development, I do not place the American pursuit of a nation of liberty within the realm of a conventional orientation to moral thinking or behavior, one that regards the maintenance of social order and the institutions of society as a moral end in themselves (e.g., see Kohlberg, 1971, 1978). Rather, I view a moral commitment to actions in support of civil society as reflective of what Emmanuel Kant (1781/1966) discussed as a "prior to society" orientation, as a perspective about moral action that antedates any social constructions about morality generated by human society and constitutes principles foundational to the moral existence of human life. These principles have deontological status (they exist prior to the being of humans), and they serve as categories of morality that constitute universal imperatives for moral action. As such, they transcend any specific moral construction developed by a society, and give people a set of *oughts* that are necessary to follow and to use as standards against which to judge the moral correctness of the "is"es of any society. Subscription to these categorical imperatives allows individuals to transcend the empirical features of their being and to articulate with deontological nature. Concretely, this moral orientation means that civic engagement in support of civil society may be enacted as much when youth question and seek to improve (or just change) extant social systems, mores, and laws, as it may be when youth may support the maintenance of any current standards or laws (Sherrod, Flanagan, & Youniss, 2002b).

In my view, such a foundational moral understanding involves a spiritual sense that one must transcend the bounds of one's own life and support the liberty of other individuals and of civic institutions that extend beyond one's own life span and place and moment in history. Such transcendence reflects, for an individual, exemplary human development, or what I have called *thriving*. A society composed of thriving individuals represents a model worldwide for social justice, equity, peace, and democracy. It represents America.

My view of moral development also stands in contrast to other theoretical conceptions that attempt to integrate human evolution and human development, for instance, sociobiology (Wilson, 1975). Rather than reduce moral development to the possession of "selfish" genes (Dawkins, 1976) that transform seemingly moral acts (e.g., altruism) into behaviors that serve only the reproductive interests of an individual, I argue that spirituality and moral development derive from relations between diverse individuals and contexts that simultaneously serve the interest (the survival and hence perpetuation) of both. As I have explained, this theoretical approach derives from contemporary, cutting-edge models of human development linked to developmental systems theories (R. M. Lerner, 1998, 2002a).

In sum, the approach to moral and civic identity I forward in this book has implications not only for distinguishing among scientific theories. The approach also has import for social action and public policy. The key to ensuring the positive development of youth—development marked by the emergence of an integrated moral and civic identity that results in contributions to self, family, community, and ultimately civil society—rests on developing policies that strengthen in diverse communities the capacities of families to raise healthy, thriving children. I describe in Chapter 7 a set of policy principles and policy recommendations that supports such family-centered community building for youth (Gore, 2003; Gore & Gore, 2002).

The journey from the idea of America to the creation of caring communities for young people began millions of years ago, at the dawn of human evolution on the African savannah. We begin, then, with an account of human evolutionary history.

2

Evolution and the
Emergence of Liberty

The facts of evolution indicate that the history of human survival involved individuals working together with groups that protected them as individuals in exchange for their supporting the group in its ability to serve its other individual members. Maintaining these individual–group, or person–context, relations across life in ways that are mutually beneficial to the health and perpetuation of both parts of the relationship (both the individual and the group or institution) is termed *developmental regulation.* An understanding of the details of the emergence in human evolution of developmental regulation—this bidirectional or reciprocal relationship between a person and his or her social world—points to the importance of concepts such as civic engagement, moral identity, transcendence of self, and spirituality in attaining an appreciation of the scientific foundations of the idea of America.

Evolution: Theory and Fact

Discussing the "facts" of evolution may strike some people as a contradiction in terms. Is not evolution a theory, as in "the theory of evolution"? If it is a theory, then how can it be factual? And what about creationism, the "theory" that is supposed to rival the theory of evolution? Creationist theory is based on what its proponents believe is an accurate interpretation of the Bible. It holds that man did not evolve but was created, fully formed, by God in his own image. Is this not as sound a scientific formulation as any other theory about the origins of humans, such as the theory of evolution?

At their core, all these questions and, more important, the idea of creationism are based on a misunderstanding of the meaning of the term *theory*. As I noted in Chapter 1, in science, a theory is a statement or set of statements that integrates existing facts and that leads to the generation of new facts. Theory is not equivalent to speculation. It can be judged by the logical coherence of its statements, by how efficiently and successfully it accounts for existing facts, and by how well its formulations lead to ideas *(hypotheses)* that are supported by the observation of new scientific *(empirical)* data.

An analogy will help explain the relation between theory and facts. Many people may recall that in 1994, O. J. Simpson stood trial for the murder of his ex-wife Nicole Brown Simpson and her friend Ron Goldman. The murder of these two people was not a point of dispute between Mr. Simpson's defense attorneys and the prosecuting attorneys. The murders were facts. Both of these people had been brutally killed. However, what was open to debate was who committed the murders and when and how the murders were carried out.

There were several other facts surrounding the murders that both sides of the case accepted—for example, where the bodies were found, what type of weapon was used to commit the murders, Mr. Simpson's whereabouts earlier on the day of the murder and a few hours after the murders, and so on. These facts were put together quite differently by the defense and by the prosecution. Each side had its own and quite distinct theory of the crime. The prosecution assembled the facts within the context of a theory that interpreted the information to mean that Mr. Simpson was guilty of the murders. The defense put the same facts together, but in the context of a theory that led to the interpretation that Mr. Simpson was innocent. The jury decided which of the two theories seemed more logical and put the facts together better. As well, the jury decided which theory led to another fact—the guilt or innocence of the defendant.

O. J. Simpson was found not guilty by the jury. Thus, in this instance the theory of the crime forwarded by the defense lawyers proved to be the better theory. However, this does not mean that the facts of the crime used by the prosecution were incorrect. The murders did occur, and this fact and others surrounding the case were accepted within both theories. Indeed, the facts of the case and the prosecution's theory of the crime were in essence accepted as the better theory in a subsequent, civil trial of Mr. Simpson.

Accordingly, when one speaks of the theory of evolution, one is discussing a theory of how to put together the facts about the successive changes the human species and its hominid (bipedal) ancestors have undergone over the course of eons of human history. There may be several different theories of evolution—and in fact there are. Darwin's (1859) theory of evolution stresses what is termed *gradualism*. Gradualism holds that a slow but continuous change of one species to another occurred through a process involving the concepts of natural selection and survival of the fittest. Gould and Eldridge (1977) have a theory of evolution that stresses what they term *punctuated equilibria*, that is, that long periods of no species change were followed by abrupt species changes brought about by rapid ecological alterations; for example, the dinosaurs died out in what, in evolutionary time scales, was a relatively short period of time, and after the occurrence of a catastrophic event, for example, after a meteor or asteroid (it has been hypothesized) collided with the Earth. However, both theories accept the same facts of evolution—the appearance of one species occurring after another has died out, the increase in complexity of a given species line, and so on. They just put these facts together in a different way.

Therefore, it is not a contradiction of terms to speak of the facts of evolution. Moreover, it is nonsensical to equate the unbridled speculations of creationism with either any scientific theory of evolution or, even more absurdly, with the facts of evolution. There is no factual basis for creationism. The fossil record shows that different species existed across millions of years, and some came into existence, flourished, and then died out millions of years before other species ever appeared.

To claim, then, that all species, including humans, were created within, using contemporary temporal reckoning, a calendar week is a preposterous assertion devoid of any scientific validity. To equate creationism with a scientific theory of any sort or to assert that its statements are in some way equivalent to empirical facts about evolution is either stupidity, ignorance, or a political or social agenda attempting to masquerade as theologically informed science.

The vacuity of creationism does not mean, however, that science and a belief in God or religious faith and science cannot coexist. Following science is not the only step one may take to attain knowledge. Science rests on *empiricism*, on the commitment to observation of events as the basis for gaining knowledge. However, not all knowledge requires empirical verification through scientific methods. Belief and faith by definition do not require such proof. We may know God simply because of the depth and certainty of our beliefs in him.

Moreover, science and faith are not necessarily incompatible, and the scholarship produced in or sponsored by the John Templeton Foundation provides several compelling demonstrations of this point (e.g., Templeton, 1995; Templeton & Herrmann, 1994). Much of this work has been framed by:

> a new concept of theology . . . which is called Theology through Science. This denotes the way in which natural scientists are meditating about the Creator on the ground of their observations of the astronomic and subatomic domains, but also on the ground of investigations into living organisms and their evolution, and such invisible realities as the human mind. (Templeton, 1995, p. 35)

Indeed, the explorations that are predicated on the Templeton Foundation Theology Through Science approach lead "in each case to a greater mystery with ever deeper and more profound implications about what is real" (Templeton, 1994, p. 8).

Thus, although the creationist attempt to link science and religion is a failure, it is not therefore the case that a belief in God and a commitment to science cannot be integrated. Indeed, as explained by J. M. Templeton (1994), scientists from a broad array of disciplines find ways to do this on a daily basis. I believe that a focus on some of the facts of evolution may enable this integration to be made by people interested in the links between human development and civil society.

I have suggested that a key fact of human evolution is that we as a species survive and, as I argue, thrive when we support a society that affords liberty to all its people. If God did indeed create humans in his own image, then what better system for human behavior could have come into existence than one that supports each person's freedom by having other free, morally and civically oriented people support it? If each of us is an image of God, then a system that supports each image by having every other image support it is a perfect way to honor and respect the semblance of God in all of us. We need not demand of God that he had to establish within one week this regulation—this "rule" that humans thrive when their individual identities are directed to serving a society that supports the identities of all individuals. The regulation of our development—the way we grow to be healthy and thriving people, as we develop a sense of self that contributes to a civil society marked by liberty and justice for all, and do so within a society that supports our individual development—may be both a God-given strategy for human survival and growth and an empirical outcome of millions of years of human evolution.

I leave for other venues a discussion of whether the facts of human evolution and of the importance of the growth across the life span of individual ← → context relations, or adaptive (health maintaining and promoting) developmental regulations, coincide with a theological analysis of the hand of God in these exchanges. In this book I focus on the facts of evolution and of human development, and I offer a scientifically verifiable theory to integrate these facts. I begin to address this task by discussing the inherent association between our biological and our social characteristics.

Human Evolution and the Biology–Society Link

As I have already emphasized, human life is both biological and social (Featherman & Lerner, 1985; Tobach & Schneirla, 1968). In fact, no form of life as we know it comes into existence independent of other life. No animal lives in total isolation from others of its species across its entire life span (Tobach, 1981; Tobach & Schneirla, 1968).

In regard to human development, early humans or proto-humans (the hominid species that were the close ancestors of humans) were relatively defenseless, having neither sharp teeth nor claws. Coupled with the dangers of living in the open African savannah, where much of early human evolution occurred, group living was essential for survival (Masters, 1978; Washburn, 1961). Therefore, human beings were more likely to survive if they acted in concert with the group than if they acted in isolation. Human characteristics that support social relations (e.g., attachment, empathy, a sense of civil duty, and a belief that moral correctness involves serving the society that serves you) may have helped human survival over the course of its evolution (Hoffman, 1978; Hogan, Johnson, & Emler, 1978; R. M. Lerner, Brentano, Dowling, & Anderson, 2002; R. M. Lerner, Dowling, & Anderson, 2003; Sahlins, 1978).

Thus, biological survival requires meeting the demands of the environment or attaining a goodness of fit with the context (Chess & Thomas, 1984, 1999; J. V. Lerner & R. M. Lerner, 1983; Thomas & Chess, 1977). Because this environment is populated by other members of one's species, adjustment to (or fit with) these other organisms is a requirement for survival (Tobach & Schneirla, 1968).

Given this biological contribution to or, better, fusion with the social ecology of human development, it is not surprising to learn that several scholars believe that human evolution (phylogeny) has promoted the link between biological and social functioning across the human life span (ontogeny; Featherman & Lerner, 1985; Gould, 1977). In other words, the integration across people's life spans of human biological and social functioning has been shaped by the evolutionary history of humans.

The scholarship of Stephen J. Gould (1977) provided singular contributions to the understanding of this linkage between *ontogeny* (the development of individuals from their conceptions to deaths or, simply, the course of human development) and *phylogeny* (the history, the evolution, of a species to which an individual belongs). A discussion of Gould's ideas about ontogeny and phylogeny allows us to understand the relevance of human evolution to the dynamic individual ← → context relations that propel a person's development across the life span.

Evolutionary Bases of Reciprocal Person–Social Context Relations

As evident from the title of his book, *Ontogeny and Phylogeny* (1977), Gould had an abiding interest in detailing the relation between ontogeny and phylogeny. He contended that "some relationship exists cannot be denied. Evolutionary changes must be expressed in ontogeny, and phyletic information must therefore reside in the development of individuals" (Gould, 1977, p. 2). However, this point in itself is obvious and unenlightening for Gould. What makes the study of the relation between ontogeny and phylogeny interesting and important is that there are *"changes in developmental timing* that produce *parallels* between the stages of ontogeny and phylogeny" (p. 2).

However, discussing the relation between ontogeny and phylogeny may raise the hackles of many scientists. This may be especially true for those trained in human development, where there is a long history of controversy regarding the "recapitulationist" ideas of the nineteenth-century embryologist, Ernst Haeckel (e.g., 1868), especially as they were adopted by G. Stanley Hall (1904), the founder of the scientific study of human development and the person who, in his 1904 book on adolescence, introduced the deficit model of youth into the scientific literature. In somewhat simplified form, Haeckel's theory was one of *recapitulation,* by which he meant that the mechanism of evolution was a change in the timing of developmental events such that there occurred a universal acceleration of development that pushed ancestral forms of bodily structures into the juvenile stages of descendants. For example, Haeckel (1868) interpreted the gill slits of human embryos as characteristics of ancestral adult fishes that had been compressed into the early stages of human ontogeny through a universal mechanism of acceleration of developmental rates in evolving lines.

It is unfortunate for the scientific study of links between ontogeny and phylogeny that people have come to equate Haeckel's recapitulation idea with all potential types and directions of evolutionary change in the timing of developmental events. This is because there is an alternative to the changes in timing specified by recapitulation, and it provides an evolutionary basis for viewing person–social context relations in a reciprocal manner, as individual ← → context relations.

To Gould (1977), this alternative is the key to human evolution and, centrally, to human *plasticity*, that is, to the capacity in humans for systematic change in their morphological structure (e.g., involving the growth of connections among nerve cells in the cerebral cortex) or behavioral function (e.g., learning new skills across life). To understand this alternative we need to introduce three interrelated terms: *heterochrony*, *neoteny*, and *paedomorphosis*. All terms relate to the concept of timing of development.

Timing and Human Evolution

According to Gould (1977), evolution occurs when ontogeny is altered in one of two ways. First, evolution occurs when new characteristics are introduced, at any stage of development. If the new characteristics (e.g., these "mutations") enhance survival and reproduction, they will be retained in future offspring; the new characteristics may then be sustained and have varying influences on later developmental stages.

The second way in which evolution occurs is when characteristics that are already present undergo changes in developmental timing. These changes involve the timing that, in the course of human life, particular characteristics appear within a species. For example, dentation (the emergence of teeth) may occur later in a descendant species (say at one year of age) than it did in another, ancestral species (where, say, it occurred at one month of age or perhaps even in utero). This second means by which evolutionary (phyletic) change occurs is termed *heterochrony*. Specifically, heterochrony is changes in the relative time of appearance and rate of development of characteristics already present in ancestors.

In human evolution, a specific type of heterochrony has been predominant. The type of heterochrony that has characterized human evolution is *neoteny*, which is a slowing down, a retardation, of development of selected somatic organs and parts. For instance, continuing with the example of times in life when dentation occurs, neoteny would exist if an ancestral species cut their baby teeth at, say, an average of three months of age and, in turn, if humans on the average cut their baby teeth at, say, ten months of age.

Heterochronic changes are regulatory effects; that is, they constitute "a change in rate for features already present" (Gould, 1977, p. 8). Gould (1977) maintains that neoteny has been a—and probably *the*—major determinant of human evolution. Neoteny is a key basis of the evolution of humans as plastic organisms.

For example, as explained in greater detail following, delayed growth has been found to be important in the evolution of complex and flexible social behavior and, interrelatedly, it has led to an increase in cerebralization by prolonging into later human life the rapid brain-growth characteristics of higher vertebrate fetuses. As such, this general evolutionary retardation of human development has resulted in adaptive features of ancestral juveniles being retained. That is, a key characteristic of human evolution is *paedomorphosis*, or phylogenetic change involving retention of ancestral juvenile characters by the adult. In other words:

> Our paedomorphic features are a set of adaptations coordinated by their common efficient cause of retarded development. We are not neotenous only because we possess an impressive set of paedomorphic characters; we are neotenous because these characters develop within a matrix of retarded development that coordinates their common appearance in human adults. . . . [and these] temporal delays themselves are the most significant feature of human heterochrony. (Gould, 1977, pp. 397, 399)

But what are some of the paedomorphic-neotenous characteristics? How do they provide an evolutionary basis of human plasticity and of reciprocal person–social context relations? Gould (1977) himself answers these questions, and in so doing indicates that humans' evolving plasticity both enabled and resulted from their embeddedness in a social and cultural context. He notes:

> Human evolution has *emphasized* one feature of . . . common primate heritage—delayed development, particularly as expressed in late instruction and extended childhood. This retardation has reacted synergistically with other hallmarks of hominization—with intelligence (by enlarging the brain through prolongation of fetal growth tendencies and by providing a longer period of childhood learning) and with socialization (by cementing family

units through increased parental care of slowly developing offspring). It is hard to imagine how the distinctive suite of human characters could have emerged outside the context of delayed development. (p. 400)

He also adds that:

In asserting the importance of delayed development . . . I assume that major human adaptations acted synergistically throughout their gradual development. . . . *The interacting system of delayed development–upright posture–large brain is such a complex:* delayed development has produced a large brain by prolonging fetal growth rates and has supplied a set of cranial proportions adapted to upright posture. Upright posture freed the hand for tool use and set selection pressures for an expanded brain. A large brain may, itself, entail a longer life span. (p. 399, italics added)

Thus, in linking neoteny with reciprocal relations between brain development and sociocultural functioning, Gould (1977) makes an argument of extreme importance for scientific analyses of human development. Species differences in the time course (heterochrony) of the ontogeny of brain organization are important for levels of plasticity finally attained across life. Parent–child relations promote the child's development toward a final level of functioning characterized by plasticity. In other portions of the evolutionary biology literature, and in the anthropology literature as well, there is support for the link suggested by Gould (1977) between plastic brain development and human social and cultural functioning.

Bidirectional Organism–Context Relations in Evolution

Several ideas in anthropology suggest that humans have been selected for social dependency. As noted already, the course and context of evolution was such that it was more adaptive for individuals to act in concert with the group than in isolation. For example, Masters (1978) notes that early hominids were hunters. These ancestors evolved from herbivorous primates under the pressure of climatic changes that caused the African forest to be replaced with savannah. Our large brains, he speculates (Masters, 1978, p. 98), may be the (naturally selected) *result* of cooperation among early hominids and hence, in an evolutionary sense, a social organ. Indeed, he believes that with such evolution the "central problem" in anthropological analysis—that of the origin of society—may be solved. Washburn (1961) appears to agree, pointing out as I did earlier that the relative defenselessness of early humans (lack of fighting teeth, nails, or horns), coupled with the dangers of living on the open African savannah, made group living and cooperation *essential for survival* (Hogan, Johnson, & Emler, 1978; Washburn, 1961).

There is some dispute in anthropological theory as to whether material culture or specific features of social relations—such as intensified parenting, monogamous pair bonding, nuclear family formation, and thus specialized sexual-reproductive behavior—were superordinate in these brain ← → behavior evolutionary relations. For example, some paleoanthropologists believe that there are five characteristics that separate human beings from other hominids: large neocortex, bipedality, reduced anterior dentation with molar dominance, material culture, and unique sexual and reproductive behavior (e.g., of all primates, only the human female's sexual behavior is not confined to the middle of her monthly menstrual cycle; Fisher 1982a). Some paleoanthropologists believe that early human evolution was a direct consequence of brain expansion and material culture. However, Lovejoy (1981), among others (e.g., Johanson & Edey, 1981), believes that:

> Both advanced material culture and the Pleistocene acceleration in brain development are sequelae to an already established hominid character system, which included intensified parenting and social relationships, monogamous pair bonding, specialized sexual-reproductive behavior, and bipedality. (Lovejoy, 1981, p. 348)

Other debates also exist. For instance, there are disputes about the roles that continual sexual receptivity and loss of estrus played in the evolution of human pair bonding (e.g., Fisher, 1982b; Harley, 1982; Isaac, 1982; Swartz, 1982; Washburn, 1982).

Such debate, however, exists in the midst of the general consensus indicated earlier: that the social functioning of hominids (be it interpreted as dyadic, familial, or cultural) was reciprocally related to the evolution of the human brain, that is, that individual brain ← → social relations characterized human evolution. Many evolutionary biologists appear to reach a similar conclusion.

For example, summarizing a review of literature pertaining to the character of the environment to which organisms adapt, Lewontin and Levins (1978) stressed that reciprocal, organism ← → environment processes are involved in human evolution. Such individual ← → context relations lead to a view that human functioning is one source of its own evolutionary development, and provides a biological basis for a key argument in this book, that promoting the young person's active (civic) engagement with his or her community context is a core component of exemplary youth development, of thriving. In this regard, Lewontin and Levins (1978) state that:

> The activity of the organism sets the stage for its own evolution. . . . The labor process by which the human ancestors modified natural objects to make them suitable for human use was itself the unique feature of the way of life that directed selection on the hand, larynx, and brain in a positive feedback that transformed the species, its environment, and its mode of interaction with nature. (p. 78)

Moreover, not only did Lovejoy (1981), as well as Fisher (1982a), give a graphic account of the history of the role of hominid social behavior in human evolution, but—in specific support of Gould's (1977) views—they show how the complex social and physical facets of this evolution led to human neoteny. Interestingly, while Fisher and (especially) Lovejoy tend to view the ecological pressures that led to the evolution of social behaviors as eventuating in bipedalism and then rapid brain development, they nevertheless both see these links in more of a circular than a linear framework, that is, there is a view of the individual and of the context that is consistent with the notion of individual ← → context relations involved in the present theory of positive youth development.

For instance, Lovejoy (1981) believes that it is not just that ecological changes led to social relationships, which in turn led to bipedalism and in turn to brain evolution. Instead, social relationships that led to brain evolution were themselves altered when larger-brained and more plastic organisms were involved in them; in turn, new social patterns may have extended humans' adaptational pressures and their opportunities for behavior and for survival into other arenas of functioning (involving the construction of tools or of weapons that then facilitated exploration, hunting, or new activities, for instance, agriculture, in different geographical regions). Such changes may have fostered further changes in the brain, in social embeddedness, and so forth. Indeed, Johanson and Edey (1981) describe Lovejoy's (1981) position as one that requires the examination of:

> the mechanism of a complex feedback loop in which several elements interact for mutual reinforcement. . . . If parental care is a good thing, it will be selected for by the likelihood that the better mothers will be more apt to bring up children, and thus intensify any genetic tendency that exists in the population toward being better mothers. But increased parental care requires

other things along with it. It requires a greater IQ on the part of the mother; she cannot increase parental care if she is not intellectually up to it. That means brain development—not only for the mother, but for the infant daughter too, for someday she will become a mother.

In the case of primate evolution, the feedback is not just a simple A–B stimulus forward and backward between two poles. It is multipoled and circular, with many features to it instead of only two—all of them mutually reinforcing. For example, if an infant is to have a large brain, it must be given time to learn to use that brain before it has to face the world on its own. That means a long childhood. The best way to learn during childhood is to play. That means playmates, which, in turn, means a group social system that provides them. But if one is to function in such a group, one must learn acceptable social behavior. One can learn that properly only if one is intelligent. Therefore social behavior ends up being linked with IQ (a loop back), with extended childhood (another loop), and finally with the energy investment and the parental care system that provide a brain capable of that IQ; the entire feedback loop is complete.

All parts of the feedback system are cross-connected. For example, if one is living in a group, the time spent finding food, being aware of predators, and finding a mate can all be reduced by the very fact that one is in a group. As a consequence, more time can be spent on parental care (one loop), on play (another), and on social activity (another), all of which enhance intelligence (another) and result ultimately in fewer offspring (still another). The complete loop shows all poles connected to all others. (pp. 325–326)

An illustration of this "complete loop," or system of reciprocal influence, is presented in Figure 2.1. This figure illustrates that the foundations of humans' plasticity evolved in a complex system of bidirectional relationships among social, ontogenetic, and neuronal variables.

From Phylogeny to Ontogeny

Our analysis of the links between Gould's (1977) ideas pertinent to the role of neotenous heterochrony in the evolution of human plasticity has drawn us into a discussion of the role of reciprocal relations between organisms and their contexts in human evolution and development, that is, to the role of individual ← → context relations as involved in both phylogeny and ontogeny. In the context of such links between phylogenetic and ontogentic change, it may be seen that neoteny provides adaptive

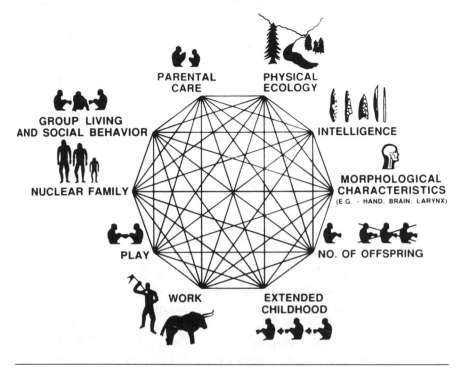

Figure 2.1   Components of the system of reciprocal influences that Lovejoy
(1981; Johanson & Edey, 1981) believes was involved in the
evolution of human neoteny and social embeddedness.

advantages for members of both older and younger generations.
Considering children first, the neoteny of the human results in the newborn child being perhaps the most dependent organism found among
placental mammalian infants (Gould, 1977). Moreover, their neoteny
means that this dependency is extraordinarily prolonged, and this requires intense parental care of the child for several years.

The plasticity of childhood processes, which persists among humans
for more than a decade, thus entails a history of necessarily close contact
with adults and places an "adaptive premium . . . on learning (as opposed
to innate response) . . . unmatched among organisms" (Gould, 1977,
p. 401). Gould agrees with de Beer (1959) that for the human:

> Delay in development enabled him to develop a larger and more complex
> brain, and the prolongation of childhood under conditions of parental care

and instruction consequent upon memory-stored and speech-communicated experience, allowed him to benefit from *a more efficient apprenticeship for his conditions of life* [italics added]. (de Beer, 1959, p. 930)

In other words, the neoteny of humans, their prolonged childhood dependency on others, and their embeddedness in a social context composed of members of the older generation who both protect them and afford them the opportunity to actualize their potential plasticity allow members of a new birth cohort to adapt to the conditions and pressures particular to their historical epoch.

Of course, such development in a new cohort has evolutionary significance for members of the older cohort as well. Gould (1977) points out that neoteny and the protracted period of dependent childhood may have led to the evolution of features of adult human behavior (e.g., parental behavior). The presence of young and dependent children requires adults to be organized in their adult–adult and adult–child interactions in order to support and guide the children effectively. Furthermore, since the period of childhood dependency is so long, it is likely that human history tended to involve the appearance of later-born children before earlier-born ones achieved full independence (Gould, 1977). Gould (1977) sees such an occurrence as facilitating the emergence of pair bonding, and further sees "in delayed development a primary impetus for the origin of the human family" (p. 403).

The Role of the Family in Positive Youth Development

In human evolution, then, the family was the social institution that maximized the successful rearing of the new generation. Families best assured that children would be nurtured in ways that facilitated their development as individuals with the skills requisite for survival; such social inculcation required as well that the child contributed to the social context (where his or her skills were needed for social maintenance and perpetuation). Families, then, are an evolutionary innovation that constituted the bridge between individual development and the support of the social world (that fed back to support the individual).

As such, current public policy interest in family-centered community building (Gore, 2003; Gore & Gore, 2002) reflects the importance and foundational value of investing social resources in improving communities' abilities to strengthen families' work to rear children who support civil society. Such an integrative vision for policy has a firm basis in human evolutionary heritage.

Conclusions

Several lines of evidence—from human evolutionary biology, sociology, and anthropology—converge to suggest that individuals and the other significant people in their lives (for instance, and perhaps most important for human development, children and their parents) interact in mutually beneficial and influential ways. In so doing, they promote their own and each other's mutual development. The evolutionary bases of individual ← → context relations are expressed in human development as the regulation of the exchanges that individuals have with their social worlds.

There is, then, a "translation" from evolution to human development of the individual ← → context relations that were integral for the survival and perpetuation of humans into relationships between individuals and their social world. Understanding and enhancing the development across the life span of these relationships are the keys to building (through social policies and community-based programs) communities and families that promote youth moral and civic identities (1) that are fueled by a sense of spirituality (transcendence); and (2) that create a commitment to a social organization marked by social justice, equity, and contributions to civil society. Accordingly, in Chapter 3, I discuss how these vital individual ← → context relations develop in childhood and adolescence.

3

Social Relationships
and Human Development

Converging with the nature of humans' evolutionary heritage, the forefront of contemporary developmental theory and research is associated with ideas that stress that bidirectional *relations* between individuals and contexts—which we represent as individual ← → context—provide the bases of human behavior and developmental change (e.g., Ford & Lerner, 1992; Gottlieb, 1997; R. M. Lerner, 2002a; Overton, 1998; Sameroff, 1983; Thelen & Smith, 1998; Wapner & Demick, 1998, are examples of developmental systems theories). The multiple levels of the context integrated with the person within developmental systems theories include biology, family, peer groups, communities, society, the physical and designed environment, culture, and history.

The emphasis in these developmental systems theories is on accounting for how the integrated developmental system functions. Within such theories, changes across the life span are seen as propelled by the dynamic relations between individuals and the multiple levels of the ecology of human development, all changing interdependently across time (history; R. M. Lerner, 2002a).

The embeddedness of human development in history (a relation that is termed *temporality*) means that there always exists the potential for change in individual ← → context relations. As I have noted, there are two important concepts associated with this optimistic view of the potential to enhance human life: developmental regulation and plasticity. Developmental systems ideas about developmental regulation derive from the concept of relative plasticity, which in turn, and as discussed in Chapter 2, is a facet of human functioning that emerged as central for human development over the course of neotenous human evolution.

Discussion of the implications of relative plasticity and developmental regulation results in an understanding, first, of the bidirectional, individual ← → context relations that create in individual development a sense of the transcendent significance of contributing integratively to self and society. Second, these concepts frame understanding of the importance for healthy human development of a socially just, democratic, civil society. Third, these ideas enable understanding of why the specific features of the individual ← → context relations that constitute the thriving process necessarily involve moral development, civic engagement, and spiritual development among youth.

The individual ← → context relations that propel development across the life span are, when reflective of adaptive (healthy) developmental regulations, marked by a balance between the positive effects of the individual on the context (for example, on his or her family, classroom, or community) and the supportive, nurturing, and growth-promoting influences of the social world on the individual. As explained in Chapter 2, the roots of adaptive developmental regulations are found during the earliest phases of infant life and involve the reciprocal relationships between infants and their parents.

Familial Foundations of Developmental Regulation in Infancy

There is an adage that says the child is father to the man. This saying means simply that individuals' characteristics when they are children relate to the characteristics they display during adulthood. However, there is another way of interpreting this saying: How we behave and think as adults—and especially as parents—are very much influenced by our experiences with our children. Our children rear us as much as we do them.

The very fact that we are parents makes us different adults than we would be if we were childless. But, more important, the specific and often special characteristics of a particular child influence us in very unique ways. How we behave toward our children depends on how they have influenced us to behave. Such child influences are termed *child effects* (R. M. Lerner, Rothbaum, Boulos, & Castellino, 2002).

Both across human evolution and in contemporary culture, parents are the major source of influence on their child's development. This is certainly the case from infancy through childhood and, arguably, even during the adolescent years (R. M. Lerner, 2002b). However, children influence the parents who are influencing them. Analogous to what Lewontin and Levins (1978) described as the productive role of individual action in the course of human evolution, children, across ontogeny, are then shaping a key source of their own life-span development. In this sense, children are producers of their own development (R. M. Lerner, 1982), and the presence of such child effects constitutes the basis of a *bidirectional* relationship between parents and children. Children influence the parents who are, at the same time, influencing them.

Of course, this bidirectional relationship continues when the child is an adolescent and an adult. And corresponding relationships exist between the individual and siblings, friends, teachers, and, indeed, all other significant people in the individual's life. To illustrate this core relationship, it is useful to continue our emphasis on "child" effects in regard to parents, recognizing of course that we can readily generate other examples that include adolescents, adults, the aged, or the parents with whom the child interacts.

How Does a Child Influence His or Her Parents?

Child effects emerge largely as a consequence of a child's individual distinctiveness. All children, with the exception of genetically identical (monozygotic) twins, have a unique genotype, that is, a unique genetic inheritance. Similarly, no two children, *including monozygotic twins,* experience precisely the same environment.

All human characteristics, be they behavioral or physical, arise from an interrelation of genes and environment (Anastasi, 1958; R. M. Lerner, 2002a). Given the uniqueness of each child's genetic inheritance and environment, the distinctiveness of each child is assured (Feldman & Lewontin, 1975; Hirsch, 1997, in 2004). In other words, every child is unique and therefore individually different from every other child. This individuality constitutes the first of the four key components of child effects. Following child individuality, the succeeding three components of child effects are (2) the stimulus characteristics of child individuality; (3) parental reactions to child stimulation; and (4) parental feedback to the child.

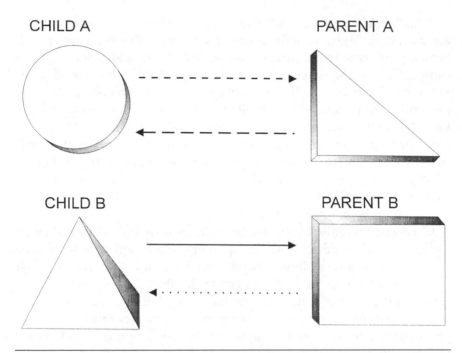

| **Figure 3.1** | Parents' behaviors toward their children are related both to their own and to their children's characteristics of individuality. |

Child Individuality

Child individuality is represented diagrammatically in Figure 3.1 in respect to Child A (represented as a circle) and to Child B (represented as a triangle). This individuality may be illustrated by drawing on the study of temperament (Chess & Thomas, 1999; Rothbart & Bates, 1998).

Temperament is a characteristic of children's behavior that describes how they act. For instance, all children eat and sleep. Temperament is the *style* of eating or sleeping shown by the child; if the child eats the same amount at every meal or gets hungry at the same time, then this child has, in regard to eating, a regular, or rhythmic, temperament. A child who gets hungry at different times of the day, or who may eat a lot or a little without any seeming predictability would, in regard to eating, have an arrhythmic temperament. Similarly, all children sleep. However, some children may sleep irregularly, that is, for seemingly unpredictable (at least to their parents) lengths of time, with periods of sleep interspersed with wakeful periods of crying and fussing. Imagine that Child A is an arrhythmic eater and sleeper, and that another child, Child B, sleeps and eats in a more regularly patterned way, or when awake shows more smiling and "cooing" than crying and fussing.

The Stimulus Characteristics of Child Individuality

The importance of these individual differences arises when we consider the second component of child effects. As a consequence of their individuality, children present different stimulation to parents. Child A and Child B present different stimuli to their parents as a consequence of their respective eating, sleep/wake patterns, and emotional characteristics; the experience of a parent of a pleasant, regularly sleeping child, who is predictable in regard to eating habits as well, is quite different from the experience of a parent who has a moody, irregularly sleeping and eating child. The different stimulation provided by Child A and Child B is also represented in Figure 3.1, by the short-dashed and solid-lined arrows going from Child A to Parent A and from Child B to Parent B, respectively.

Parental Reactions to Child Stimulation

Parents who are stimulated differentially may be expected to react differently. The different ways in which parents react to, or *process* (e.g., think and feel about), the stimulation provided by their children constitutes the third component of child effects. Child A might evoke feelings of frustration and exasperation and thoughts of concern in the parents (Brazelton, Koslowski, & Main, 1974; R. M. Lerner, 2002a; R. M. Lerner, Rothbaum, et al., 2002; Lewis & Rosenblum, 1974). And first-time parents especially might wonder if they will have the personal and marital resources to handle such a child (Chess & Thomas, 1999). We might expect, however, that the thoughts and feelings evoked in parents by Child B might be markedly different. Certainly, the parents of Child B would be better rested than Child A's parents. When their child was awake, they would have a child with a more regularly positive mood, and this too would present less stress on them as parents and as spouses.

Figure 3.1 also illustrates the presence of different types of reactions by the parents of Child A and Child B. The individual reaction of Parent A is represented as a right triangle, whereas the individuality of Parent B is represented as a rectangle.

The individuality of these parental reactions underscores the idea that parents are as individually distinct as are their children. Not all parents of an irregularly eating and sleeping, moody child will react with concern or frustration. Similarly, some parents will be stressed by even the most regular, predictable, and positive of children. Such parental individuality makes child effects more complicated to study. However, at the same time, parental individuality underscores the uniqueness of each child's context. This individuality leads to the fourth component of child effects.

Parental Feedback to the Child

As a consequence of the different stimulation received from their children, and in relation to their own characteristics of individuality, parents will provide differential feedback to their children. The differential feedback children receive from their parents, as a consequence of the stimulation they have presented to the parents, is the final component of child effects.

Such differential feedback may take the form of different behavior shown to children by parents or of different emotional climates created in the home (Brazelton et al., 1974; Chess & Thomas, 1999). For instance, the parents of Child A might take steps to alter the child's eating and sleep/wake patterns. In regard to sleeping, they might try to cut short naps during the day in order that the child will be more tired in the evening. In addition, when they are appraising the success of their attempts to put the child on a schedule, a general sense of tenseness might pervade the household. The parents might wonder, "Will we have another sleepless night? Will we be too tired to be fully effective at work?"

Figure 3.1 also illustrates the presence of differential feedback by the parents of Child A and Child B (see the long dashed and dotted arrows going from Parent A to Child A and from Parent B to Child B, respectively). This feedback becomes an important part of the child's experience. Moreover, this feedback is distinct in that it is based on the effect of the child's individuality on the parent. Thus, the feedback serves to further promote the child's individuality. This feedback creates a circular relation between parent and child.

Circular Functions and Bidirectional Socialization

The four components of child effects constitute a *circular function* (Schneirla, 1957) in individual development, one very similar to the feedback loops involved in the evolution of parent ← → child relations that were illustrated in Figure 2.1. Children stimulate differential reactions in their parents, and these reactions provide the basis of feedback to the child, that is, return stimulation that influences the children's further individual development.

The bidirectional child–parent relationships involved in these circular functions underscore the point that children (and adolescents and adults) are producers of their own development and that people's relations to their contexts involve bidirectional exchanges (R. M. Lerner, 1982; R. M. Lerner & Busch-Rossnagel, 1981; R. M. Lerner, Theokas, & Jelicic, in press; R. M. Lerner & Walls, 1999), that is, that individual ← → context relations epitomize the development of children. The parent shapes the child, but part of what determines the way in which parents do this is the children themselves.

Children shape their parents—as adults, as spouses, and of course as parents per se—and in so doing children help organize feedback to themselves, feedback that contributes further to their individuality and thus starts the circular function all over again (returns the child effects process to its first component). Characteristics of physical, behavioral, cognitive, and emotional individuality allow the child to contribute to this circular function.

However, this idea of circular functions needs to be extended. In and of itself the notion is mute regarding the specific characteristics of the feedback (e.g., its positive or negative valence) children will receive as a consequence of their individuality. In other words, to account for the specific character of child–context relations, the circular functions model needs to be supplemented. This is the contribution of the goodness of fit model.

The Goodness of Fit Model

Just as children each bring their characteristics of individuality to a particular social setting, there are demands placed on the children by the social and physical components of the setting. First, these demands may take the form of attitudes, values, or stereotypes that are held by others in the context regarding the child's attributes (their physical or behavioral characteristics). For example, some parents may have unfavorable attitudes about an infant waking at unpredictable times. Other parents, perhaps those with more flexible schedules, may have neutral attitudes about such a temperamental pattern.

Demands may also take the form of attributes (usually behavioral) of others in the context with whom the children must coordinate, or fit, their attributes (also usually behavioral) for adaptive interactions to exist. For example, a parent who must sleep uninterruptedly at night in order to feel effective at work the next day and an infant with irregular sleep patterns would not have behaviors that fit well with each other.

Third, demands may take the form of physical characteristics of a setting (e.g., the presence or absence of access ramps for the motorically disabled) that require the child to possess certain attributes (again, usually behavioral abilities) for the most efficient interaction within the setting to occur.

The child's individuality in differentially meeting these demands provides a basis for the feedback he or she gets from the socializing environment. For example, considering the demand "domain" of attitudes, values, or stereotypes, teachers and parents may have individual and distinct expectations about the behaviors desired of their students and children, respectively. Teachers may want students who show little distractibility, but parents might desire their children to be moderately distractible, for example, when they require their children to move from watching television to go to the dinner table or to bed. Children whose behavioral individuality was either generally distractible or generally not distractible would thus differentially meet the demands of these two contexts. Problems of adjustment to school or to home might thus develop as a consequence of a child's lack of match (or goodness of fit) in either or both settings.

Thomas and Chess (1977; Chess & Thomas, 1999) and J. V. Lerner and R. M. Lerner (1983, 1989) believe that if a child's characteristics of individuality provide a good fit (or match) with the demands of a particular setting, adaptive outcomes will accrue in that setting. Those children whose characteristics match most of the settings within which they act should receive supportive or positive feedback from the contexts and should show evidence of the most adaptive behavioral development. In turn, of course, poorly fit or mismatched children—those whose characteristics are incongruent with one or most settings—should show alternative developmental outcomes. Such characteristics of individuality involve what the children do, *why* the children show a given behavior, or how the children do whatever they do. This last characteristic of individuality raises again the example of the temperamental pattern associated with the child's behavior (Chess & Thomas, 1999), and I may underscore the importance of circular functions in the development of young people by again discussing individual differences in children's temperament (see too Rothbart & Bates, 1998).

Goodness of Fit and Infant and Child Temperament

Attributes of temperament that afford "difficulty" for caregiving—that is, that do not match with, or fit, the caregiver's demands—may be associated with distinct types of parental and family relations. "Difficult" children (e.g., children who, because they are moody and arrhythmic, do not fit with the preferences or expectations of caregivers) are arguably found more often in situations that cause them "trouble" (e.g., having problems involving social relationships) than is the case with children who have "easy" temperaments (e.g., rhythmic children who have positive moods and who fit more with caregiver preferences or expectations; Rothbart & Bates, 1998; Lee & Bates, 1985).

Understandably, mothers of difficult children often use intrusive, controlling techniques to keep them out of trouble. Nevertheless, these children resist their mothers' attempts at control and have relationships with them that are marked by conflict. People—even mothers—might be expected to try to avoid interactions with others—even their own children—if all that resulted was conflict. For example, scholars have been aware for more than two decades that mothers of infants are less likely to offer assistance to children with negative moods than to infants having positive moods, and that mothers of infants who are unable to adjust their behavior to changes in schedules or routines are less attentive to their infants, and interacted less with them, than is the case with mothers of infants high in adaptability (e.g., Campbell, 1979; Chess & Thomas, 1999; Dunn & Kendrick, 1980).

Furthermore, when babies' temperamental difficulty leads them to be insufficiently responsive to their mothers' caregiving attempts (for example, when they do not respond to their mothers' attempts to soothe or quiet them), classic research has demonstrated that mothers to a great extent stop trying to "mother" (Brazelton et al., 1974). In other words, the infant–caregiver relationship is severely strained and, as well, mothers of these infants suffer adverse emotional reactions (Chess & Thomas, 1999).

More recent data confirm these findings and indicate that a child's temperamental difficulty can influence parents' emotions (Rothbart & Bates, 1998). Activity level is one component of temperament that can be especially difficult for parents when it exists at truly excessive levels, that is, as *hyperactivity* (Chess & Thomas, 1999). Mothers of hyperactive children show high levels of stress and feel socially isolated, depressed, and self-blaming (Mash, 1984; Mash & Johnston, 1983). Such problematic child behavior not only can present difficulties in management but, in addition, has been found to produce marital conflict in parents (O'Leary & Emery, 1994) and mood disturbances, especially depression (Griest, Forehand, Wells, & McMahon, 1980; Patterson, 1980).

Of course, the negative emotions evoked in parents by their child's difficulty can be directed toward the infant. In this regard, mothers of difficult infants were more likely than were mothers of easy infants to have critical feelings toward their child; this is especially true if the child's difficulty was characterized by arrhythmicity (Chess & Thomas, 1999; Graham, Rutter, & George, 1973).

Temperamental difficulty (e.g., high intensity of response, irregularity in biological functions, negative mood, low adaptability, and withdrawal) also has been associated with less responsive caregiving or less stimulating contact from mothers (Chess & Thomas, 1999; Crockenberg, 1986; Crockenberg & Acredolo, 1983; Dunn & Kendrick, 1980; Linn & Horowitz, 1983; Rothbart & Bates, 1998). For instance, studies of maternal behavior and infant temperament have found that mothers are less engaged with their babies if the babies are difficult or irritable (Chess & Thomas, 1999; Crockenberg & Acredolo, 1983; Linn & Horowitz, 1983).

Among older children, those eighth graders' temperaments that best matched the demands for behavioral style in the classroom maintained by each student's classroom teacher and peer group had more favorable teacher ratings of adjustment and ability, had better grades, more positive peer relationships, fewer negative peer relationships, and more positive self-esteem than did students whose temperaments were less well matched with either teacher or peer demands (J. V. Lerner, 1983). In turn, for several temperament dimensions, and most notably for reactivity, fourth-grade students whose self-rated temperament best fit teacher demands not only had better teacher ratings of ability and adjustment, but also scored better on two standardized achievement tests (the Stanford Achievement Test for Reading and the Comprehensive Test of Basic Skills) than did less well-fit children (J. V. Lerner, R. M. Lerner, & Zabski, 1985).

Given the consistency of all these studies—showing that different person–context relations exist when individuals are temperamentally fit with contextual demands versus when individuals' temperaments are not fit with demands—we may conclude that individuals' styles of behavior exert an important influence on the significant others in their lives

(R. M. Lerner, Rothbaum et al., 2002; Rothbart & Bates, 1998). Indeed, there is also evidence that temperament influences the entire family. For instance, among children who had physical disabilities, the presence of family distress was much more likely if the disabled child had a difficult temperament (Korn, Chess, & Fernandez, 1978). About two-thirds of all such families found to be in distress had a child with a difficult temperament.

In sum, characteristics of child individuality, be they physical or behavioral, can influence the parent–child relationship, the spousal relationship, and the entire family. However, this is only one part of the "story" of bidirectional person–context relations. The breadth of the developmental system needs to be considered to understand developmental regulation, plasticity, and the nature of the bidirectional relations people have with their social worlds.

The child's context also influences bidirectional relations. Obviously, the parent is a key component of this context. However, it is important to view child–parent bidirectional relationships in respect to the broader social context of the child's development and, as such, to consider the other social settings and contextual influences (e.g., those derived from cultural and historical changes) that may influence children and parents, either separately or together.

Contributions of the Social Context to Bidirectional Person–Context Relations

To understand how the social context contributes to bidirectional person–context relations, we should emphasize that a child is *not* best thought of as merely similar to all other children, or as simply different from others in respect to only one, or even just a few, characteristics. Instead, individual differences exist in respect to numerous characteristics. Figure 3.2 illustrates the components that reflect some of representative dimensions of individuality within child and parent. For instance, children differ from each other in regard to their cognitive (thinking, intellectual) abilities, their personalities, their temperaments, and their health. The segment labeled "Others" is used to indicate that there are numerous other characteristics of individuality that might be mentioned. "Developmental Level" is used to indicate that all of the child's characteristics of individuality change over time.

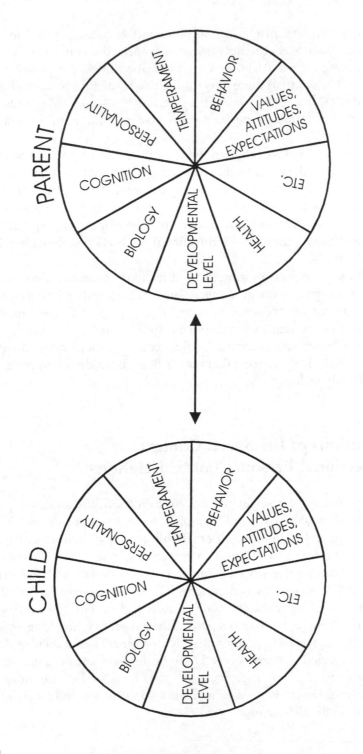

Figure 3.2 Multiple dimensions are involved in the bidirectional relations between a child and a parent.

We have illustrated how at least some of these changes occur through the bidirectional relationships children have with their parents in regard to temperament. However, what we have not illustrated yet is that parents too are made up of multiple dimensions of individuality that, as with children, develop across time (e.g., see Baltes, 1987, 1997; Baltes, Lindenberger, & Staudinger, 1998). The multiple dimensions of the parent are also presented in Figure 3.2, along with arrows to indicate the bidirectional relationships that exist between the child and the parent, that is, the parent ← → child relationship.

Another point not yet illustrated is that the parent ← → child relationship does not exist in isolation. Both the child and the parent have other social roles. These roles lead both children and parents into social relationships with other groups of people, that is, with other social "networks." Parents are also spouses, adult children of their own parents, workers, and neighbors. Children also may be siblings and friends of other children; and as they progress in childhood and adolescence, they become students and often part-time employees. The sorts of relationships in these other social networks in which children and parents engage when outside of their roles of child or parent can be expected to influence the parent ← → child relationship (Bronfenbrenner, 1977, 1979, 2001, in press; Bronfenbrenner & Morris, 1998).

Children's poor performance at school may influence their behavior in the home, and, especially, may alter the quality of the parent–child relationship. In turn, a problematic home situation—as is experienced by children in families wherein parental abuse or neglect of the child occurs—will affect the child's relationships with peers, with teachers, and with other family members (Baca Zinn & Eitzen, 1993; R. M. Lerner, Rothbaum et al., 2002).

For parents, strain in the spousal relationship can occur if the adults spend too much energy in their parental caregiving role (J. V. Lerner, 1994). For instance, a child's unpredictable sleep pattern and negative mood when awake can severely tax parents' energy. Energy and time needed for parents to be good spouses to each other may be unavailable. In addition, the fatigue caused by the demands of parental roles can be expected to influence parents' performance in the workplace (J. V. Lerner, 1994). It is difficult for people who have been up all night caring for a crying infant to be at their best at work the next morning. In turn, of course, problems at work can be brought home. Parents whose energies are significantly depleted outside the home may not have the stamina during the evening to be attentive, patient parents to their children or attentive, emotionally supportive spouses for their mates.

Thus, as illustrated by some of the temperament research reviewed earlier, and by research pertinent to child–parent interaction in regard to cognitive development (Bornstein, 1985, 1989), bidirectional relationships exist between the child and the parent (Bornstein, 1995, 2002; Bornstein & Tamis-LeMonda, 1990; R. M. Lerner & J. V. Lerner, 1987, 1989). These relationships are in turn reciprocally related to other social networks within which the parent–child dyad exists and to the broader societal and cultural context (Bornstein, 2002; Bornstein et al., 1992).

The Larger Ecology of Parent–Child Relationships

The model of bidirectional relations between children and their complex world that we have presented implies that young people and their context cannot be separated. Both are fused across all of life, and thus across history. One way to begin to understand what is involved in this relation, even for one person, is to consider Figure 3.3 (see R. M. Lerner, 1984, 2002a). Here we continue to use the representations introduced in Figure 3.2 to represent an individual child and parent. As before, the mutual influence between child and parent, their fusion with each other, is represented in the figure by the bidirectional arrows between them.

It is important to indicate at this point that we may speak of connections between parent and child that pertain to either *social relations* or *physical relations* (for instance, involving health or physiology). In regard to social relationships, for example, the parent demands attention from the child who does not show it; this lights the parent's "short fuse" of tolerance; the parent scolds the child, who then cries; this creates remorse in the parent and elicits soothing behaviors; the child is calmed, snuggles up to the parent, and now both parties in the relationship show positive emotions and are happy (e.g., see Tubman & Lerner, 1994).

In turn, we may illustrate dynamic interactions that involve not only the exchange of external social behaviors but also biological or physiological processes. For example, parental religious practices, rearing practices, or financial status may influence the child's diet and nutritional status, health, and medical care. In turn, the contraction of an infectious disease by either parent or child can lead to the other member of the relationship contracting the disease. Moreover, the health and physical status of the child influences the parents' own feelings of well-being and their hopes and aspirations regarding the child (Finkelstein, 1993).

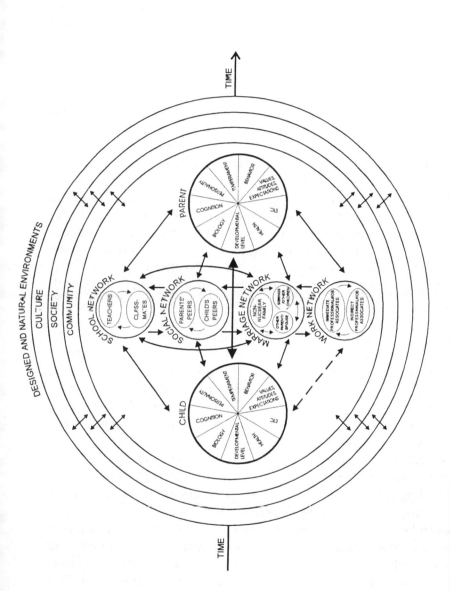

Figure 3.3 The developmental systems view of human development: Parent–child relations and interpersonal and institutional networks are imbedded in and influenced by community, societal, cultural, and designed and natural environments, all changing across time, and thus across history.

Thus, the children's physiological status and development are not disconnected from their behavioral and social context (in this example, the functioning of parents) and development (e.g., see Finkelstein, 1993; Ford & Lerner, 1992; Howard, 1978). The inner and outer worlds of the child are fused and dynamically interactive. In addition, of course, the same may be said of the parent and, in fact, of the parent–child relationship. Each of these foci—child, parent, or relationship—is part of a larger, enmeshed *system* of fused relations among the multiple levels that compose the ecology of human life (Bronfenbrenner, 1979, 2001, in press).

For instance, illustrated in Figure 3.3 is the idea that both parent and child are embedded in a broader social network, and each person has reciprocal reactions with this network. This set of relationships occurs because both the child and the parent play many more than just one role in life. As emphasized, the child may also be a sibling, a peer, and a student; the parent may also be a spouse, a worker, and an adult child. All of these networks of relationships are embedded within a particular community, society, and culture. And, finally, all of these relationships are continually changing across time and history. Simply, all portions of the system of individual $\leftarrow \rightarrow$ context or biology $\leftarrow \rightarrow$ environment relations comprising the ecology of human development (as conceptualized with developmental systems theories) change across time. Such change is an integral, indeed inescapable, feature of human life.

Thus, Figure 3.3 illustrates that within and among each of the networks depicted, one may conceive of bidirectional relationships existing among the people populating the network. A child effect may function, in a sense, like a small pebble thrown into a quiet lake. It can prompt a large ripple. In turn, of course, the reverse can occur. Events in settings far beyond the child–parent relationship can influence it. For instance, the resources in a community for child day care during the parent's working hours, the laws (e.g., regarding tax exemptions for money spent on child care) or social programs available in a society supporting day care, and the cultural values regarding families who place their infants in day care all exert an impact on the quality of the parent–child relationship.

The child $\leftarrow \rightarrow$ parent relationship, and the social networks in which it is located, are embedded in still larger community, societal, cultural, and historical levels of organization. These relations are illustrated also in Figure 3.3. As noted, time—history—cuts through all the systems. This feature of the figure is introduced to remind us that, as with the people populating these social systems, change is always occurring at all levels of the context of human development. Diversity within time is created as changes occur across time (across history). Diversity introduces important variation into all the levels of organization involved in the system depicted in Figure 3.3.

In other words, people develop: the family changes from one with infants and young children to one with teenagers to an "empty nest." In the last case, the children have left the home of their parents to live elsewhere and, very likely, to start their own families. Similarly, communities, societies, and cultures change too (Elder, 1974, 1998; Elder, Modell, & Parke, 1993; Garbarino, 1992; Hernandez, 1993). In addition, each of these multiple "levels" is embedded in the natural and human-designed physical ecology, a physical world that also changes. Changes at one or more of these levels produce changes in the other levels as well, given their bidirectional connections. In short, since all changes are embedded in history (Baltes, 1987, 1997; Baltes et al., 1998; Elder, 1974, 1998; Elder et al., 1993), which means that time therefore "cuts through" all levels of organization, the nature of parent–child relationships, of family life and development, and of societal and cultural influences on the child-parent-family system, are influenced by both "normative" changes (e.g., children graduate from school, marry, and have their own children) and "nonnormative" historical changes (e.g., wars, economic depressions, natural disasters; Baltes, 1987, 1997; Baltes et al., 1998).

In short, the essence of human development—of individual ← → context relations across the life span—involves (1) individual differences (diversity); (2) changes in both children and contexts; and, as a consequence (3) increases in individual differences. The multiple levels of change involved in individual ← → context relations may involve individuals at any point in their lives—whether they are infants or young children, on the one hand, or adults (and acting in roles such as parents, spouses, or teachers), on the other.

The possibility that bidirectional relations exist across the life span among all levels shown in Figure 3.3 represents a formidable state of complexity. However, behavioral and social science theory and research has accepted that it must address this complexity, both to understand human development and to apply the science of development in the service of enhancing the lives of diverse children and families (Bornstein, 2002; R. M. Lerner, 2002a; R. M. Lerner, Jacobs, & Wertlieb, 2003).

Conclusions

Applications of developmental science—be they programs for children and parents or public policies aimed at enhancing their lives—will insufficiently fit with the needs of the specific people intended to be served by these interventions, if these activities are insufficiently informed by knowledge about the specific characteristics of individuality of children and parents and of the dynamics of their relations—with each other and with the broader ecology of human development (see Figure 3.3). Accordingly, knowledge of the ways in which individual children influence their parents may be useful for parents in their attempts to provide their children with a healthy home setting that promotes their positive development.

The potential for such knowledge to be applied in ways that can, in fact, promote positive development among youth derives from the bidirectional relations that exist across the multiple levels of organization within the developmental system, relations that provide the basis for plasticity in human development. In other words, the temporality (historical embeddedness) of the developmental system means that all levels within it have the potential for systematic change. As in human evolution, plasticity is a key feature of adaptive—healthy, positive, and productive—human functioning, of adaptive individual ← → context relations.

I believe that the plasticity of human development is integral for the syntheses between individuals and contexts that eventuate in integrated moral and civic functioning, positive youth development and, in exemplary cases, thriving. These are the features of developmental regulation, of adaptive individual ← → context relations, that are requisite for liberty to exist. More generally, these are the features of changes across the life span that are emphasized within developmental systems theories of human development.

4

Developmental Theory as a Frame for Understanding Liberty

S cholars of human development and, more generally, students of human nature have put forward ideas about the defining features of public policy and social programs that are useful for promoting optimal human development and, as a consequence, for building an ideal human society (e.g., R. M. Lerner, 2002a, Lorenz, 1966; Proctor, 1988; Skinner, 1971). At their core, these ideas involve one or another theoretical account about the nature of human nature (Eisenberg, 1972), about the key features of human functioning on which we should focus if humanity is to be "perfected."

Across the history of scholarship that has an interest in the nature of human nature, the theoretical models of human nature have been associated traditionally with ideas that stress the primacy of influences on human development existing at one level of organization within the developmental system. These forays into using theories about human development to put forward a vision for policies and programs that purport to enhance if not perfect human life have resulted, most often, in the formulation of what may be termed *sociogenic, psychogenic,* or *biogenic* theories.

As explained later in the chapter, these approaches "split" or separate variables from one level of organization (biological, psychological, or sociological) from variables of other levels; they view the preferred level as "real" or primary and other levels as, at best, secondary or derivative or, at worst, a pseudo phenomenon (Overton, 1998, 2003). In either case, split conceptions reduce variables at non-preferred levels to ones at the preferred or "real" level (e.g., Plomin, Corley, DeFries, & Faulkner, 1990; Rowe, 1994; Rushton, 1999, 2000). Over the course of the history of developmental science, one type of split has involved separating nature (e.g., biology, genes) from nurture (e.g., experiences in the environment external to the person; see Gottlieb, 1997, 2004; Hirsch, 1997, 2004; R. M. Lerner, 2002a; Thelen & Smith, 1998).

More contemporary theoretical models—and certainly the perspective that frames my arguments in this book—stress that human development derives from integrative, or fused, relations among variables associated with the multiple levels of organization existing within the ecology of human development. I have explained that this developmental systems perspective emphasizes that relations among levels is crucial in the development of people, and that syntheses of variables across levels comprise the holistic reality of the human development process (e.g., Gottlieb, 1997, 1998; Magnusson, 1999a, 1999b; Thelen & Smith, 1998; Wapner & Demick, 1998).

In prior chapters I introduced ideas associated with developmental systems theories of human development and noted their use for understanding the relations between human evolution and human development. In this chapter I use the relational ideas of developmental systems theory to present a framework for policies and programs that are aimed at enhancing liberty. In the next chapters I use the framework developed here to discuss and illustrate how developmental systems theory frames specific features of my theory of positive youth development. In turn, I indicate how my theory of positive youth development facilitates understanding of the programs and policies that foster youth thriving and civic engagement and that promote the adaptive individual ← → context relations that are integral to liberty.

To employ developmental systems theory for these purposes requires a specification of its distinctive features as a framework for theory and application in human development. Accordingly, it is useful to contrast developmental systems models with split conceptions of human development.

Variation in Theories of Human Development

Several types of theories of development have provided frames for conceptualizing human development. One instance (one "family"; Reese & Overton, 1970) of such theories stresses *sociogenesis*, the idea that societal institutions create categories or sets of behaviors (roles) that individuals are channeled into enacting (e.g., Homans, 1961). Hartup (1978) termed these theories *Social Mold* models.

Essentially, these sociogenic theories stress social inculcation (nurture) and interpret all individual actions as not only societally embedded but as completely societally framed (Dannefer, 1984; Meyer, 1988). Society is, then, the "Puppet Master" that directs individual behavior and change. There is no agency (primary control) present in individuals, and, as such, psychogenesis is pseudo phenomenal. As B. F. Skinner (1971) asserted in his book, *Beyond Freedom and Dignity*, "a person does not act upon the world, the world acts upon him" (p. 211).

Psychogenic theories have traditionally stood in contrast to sociogenic models. In psychogenic views, macro-level variables are regarded as essentially pseudo phenomenal. They are conceived as linear combinations of individual–psychological variables (Featherman & Lerner, 1985). For instance, the family is not seen as a level of organization within the ecology of human development that is *qualitatively* distinct from the individual psychological functioning of the people who comprise the family. "Family" variables are merely quantitative additions of (and thus reducible to) individual level variables (e.g., an individual's attitudes, personality characteristics, temperamental attributes, intellectual abilities, and so on) associated with the people comprising the family. To understand spousal conflict or a mother's or a father's relationship with a child, all one must do (from this perspective) is additively combine knowledge of the psychological and behavioral characteristics (e.g., regarding personality or temperament) of each person in the relationship. Similar reductions—to individual-psychological elements—may be made in regard to social variables more macro than the family.

Biogenic theories are also reductionistic. As noted above in regard to sociogenic and psychogenic models, *biogenic* conceptions also "split" nature from its relation to nurture (Overton, 1998) and (obviously) emphasize the "reality" of nature and the pseudo phenomenal status of nurture. As discussed in Chapter 1, examples are hereditarian views such as human sociobiology (e.g., Rushton, 1999, 2000) and behavior genetics (Plomin, 2000; Plomin et al., 1990; Rowe, 1994). Social Darwinist conceptions of society and of government and public policy are also examples of such biogenic models of human behavior and development (Tobach et al., 1974). For instance, as discussed in more detail later in this chapter, Rowe (1994) believes that all socialization can be reduced to the actions of genes on behaviors. Biogenic models such as those proposed by Rowe (and Plomin et al., 1990, or Rushton, 1999, 2000) reduce the complexity of all levels of organization involved in human development (e.g., individual-psychological and societal levels) to *mechanistically acting* genetic determinants.

Developmental systems models are integrative conceptions. In contrast to split and reductionistic perspectives, such models take a relational, synthetic approach to understanding the multiple levels of organization involved in human development (R. M. Lerner, 2002a; Schneirla, 1957; Thelen & Smith, 1998). Theories derived from a developmental systems perspective focus on the integration (relation, fusion) of actions of one variable from one level of organization (e.g., the individual) and actions of variables from the other levels of organization comprising the ecology of human development (e.g., see Brandtstädter, 1998, 1999; Bronfenbrenner, 2001; R. M. Lerner, 2002a, 2002c), that is, developmental systems theories stress individual ← → context relations.

As illustrated in both Chapters 2 and 3, in my respective discussions of biological/evolutionary change (e.g., Gould, 1977; Lewontin & Levins, 1978; see too Lewontin, 2000) and of human ontogeny (e.g., Chess & Thomas, 1999; R. M. Lerner, Rothbaum et al., 2002), from a developmental systems perspective, human beings are active contributors to their own development (R. M. Lerner, 1982; R. M. Lerner & Busch-Rossnagel, 1981; R. M. Lerner, Theokas, & Jelicic, in press; R. M. Lerner & Walls, 1999). Humans are neither passive recipients of genes that compel their actions nor passive recipients of stimuli that impel their behavior. Humans are active, acting, goal oriented, effective shapers of the complex ecology of human development that influences their development. In addition, humans are relatively plastic organisms (R. M. Lerner, 1984) who thus can alter their structure or function to enable adaptation and, in ideal circumstances, well-being (R. M. Lerner, Bornstein, & Smith, 2003). From this perspective, infants, children, and adolescents as much shape the behavior of their siblings, parents, peers, and teachers as these social groups influence the young person (recall the discussion in Chapter 3 of child effects).

In other words, because children both influence and are influenced by their social world, the physical and the social ecology of human life are also active contributors to human development. Accordingly, the basic process of development is relational; it involves the integration or fusion of the person and the context, or of the individual and the ecology of human development (Bronfenbrenner, 2001; R. M. Lerner, 1991; Overton, 1998, 2003). It involves individual ← → context relations.

Developmental Systems as an "Alternative" to Hereditarian, Biogenic Models

The developmental process envisioned in the dynamic, relational, developmental systems perspective stands in marked contrast to the conceptualization of the developmental process found in split sociogenic, psychogenic, or biogenic positions. For example, developmental systems models such as developmental contextualism (R. M. Lerner, 2002a, 2000c; R. M. Lerner, Rothbaum et al., 2002) and the bioecological perspective (Bronfenbrenner, 2001, in press; Bronfenbrenner & Morris, 1998) have been forwarded to provide alternatives to the biogenic, hereditarian view of parenting in behavior genetics (e.g., Rowe, 1994).

As explained by Gottlieb (1992, 1997), in a developmental systems view of systemic change, of the developmental process, the key "conception is one of a totally interrelated, fully coactional system in which the activity of genes themselves can be affected through the cytoplasm of the cell by events originating at any other level in the system, including the external environment" (Gottlieb, 1992, pp. 144–145). As such, Gottlieb (1992, 1997) and other developmental systems theorists (e.g., Ford & Lerner, 1992; Magnusson, 1999a, 1999b; Sameroff, 1983; Thelen & Smith, 1998; Wapner & Demick, 1998) emphasize that neither genes nor the context by themselves cause development. The fusion among levels within the integrated developmental system means that relations among variables—not splits between nature and nurture—constitute the core of the developmental process.

Accordingly, although hereditarians argue that biological contributions exist in a one-to-one relation with genetic influences (e.g., Rushton, 1999), this equivalence is not seen as veridical with reality from the perspective of developmental systems theory or in light of the evidence about genetic action present in contemporary biological science (e.g., Garcia Coll, Bearer, & Lerner, 2004; Venter et al., 2001). For instance, although some hereditarians see constitutional variables (e.g., relating to brain volume, head size, size of reproductive organs, and stature) as all based on heredity (Rushton, 1999), within developmental systems:

> "Constitutional" is not equivalent to "genetic," and purposely so. Constitutional includes the expressed functions of genes—which, in themselves require some environmental input—but constitutional includes the operations of the central nervous system and all the biological and environmental experiences that impact organismic functioning and that make constitutional variables part of the dynamic change across the life span as they affect the development of and the decline of behavior. (Horowitz, 2000, p. 8)

In short, in contemporary, cutting-edge developmental science, developmental scientists have ceased engaging in the pursuit of theoretically anachronistic and counterfactual conceptions of gene function, or in the search for a way to reduce human development to the independent (split) action of genes (Rowe, 1994; Rushton, 1999, 2000). Indeed, significant advances in the science of human development are occurring through embedding the study of genes within the multiple, integrated levels of organization comprising the dynamic developmental system of person–context relations (Garcia Coll et al., 2004; Gottlieb, 1997, 1998; Thelen & Smith, 1998). To illustrate this contribution, it is useful to contrast a developmental systems theoretical approach to developmental science with the one found in, arguably, the key current instance of the hereditarian approach to developmental science, that is, behavioral genetics.

The Non-Challenge of Behavioral Genetics

Citing contemporary research using behavioral genetic analyses of purportedly contextual influences (e.g., Behrman & Rosenzweig, in press), Duncan and Magnuson (2003) suggest that this approach to developmental science constitutes a challenge to interpretations of person–context relations associated with theories other than biogenic ones. However, the fatal conceptual and methodological flaws of behavioral genetics research mean that any supposed challenge of this field to alternative theories, especially relational, developmental systems ones, is in fact a non-challenge.

According to Plomin (2000):

> Behavioural genetics is the genetic study of behaviour, which includes quantitative genetics (twin and adoption studies) as well as molecular genetics (DNA studies) of human and animal behaviour broadly defined to include responses of the organism from responses measured in the brain such as functional neuroimaging to self-report questionnaires. (p. 30)

The goal of behavior genetic analysis is to separate (partition) the variation in a distribution of scores (e.g., for a personality trait, temperamental characteristic, or intelligence) into the proportion due to genes and the proportion due to the environment. Although behavior geneticists admit that genes and environments may be correlated or may interact, they most typically seek to compute a score—termed a *heritability coefficient*—that (in its most frequently used form) denotes the independent contribution of genetic variance to the overall variance in the distribution of scores for a given individual characteristic. For such heritability scores to be meaningful estimates of the differences among people due to differences between them in the genes they possess, there must be genetic contributions that are independent of (not correlated or interactive with) the context within which genes exist. However, genes do not work in the way that behavior geneticists imagine.

Fatal Flaws in the Behavior Genetics Model of Gene Function

Neither cell biologists (McEwen, 1997, 1998, 1999; Meaney et al., 1988) nor molecular geneticists (e.g., Elman et al. 1998; Ho, 1984; Müller-Hill, 1988; Venter et al., 2001) place credence in the model of genetic function involved in behavioral genetics. In fact, Venter and his colleagues (2001), the group that successfully mapped the sequence of the human genome, emphasize that there are two conceptual errors that should not be made in the face of the advances they and others are making in understanding the structure and functional consequences of the human genome. They stress that:

> There are two fallacies to be avoided: determinism, the idea that all characteristics of the person are "hard-wired" by the genome; and reductionism, the view that with complete knowledge of the human genome sequence, it is only a matter of time before our understanding of gene functions and interactions will provide a complete causal description of human variability. (Venter et al., 2001, p. 1348)

These are precisely the fallacies embodied in behavior genetics. Accordingly, contemporary, cutting-edge thought in molecular genetics thus rejects the idea that genes are structures that act *on* supragenetic levels and, instead, adopts a position consistent with a dynamic, developmental systems view (Gottlieb, 1992, 1997, 1998; R. M. Lerner, 2002a; Lewis, 1997; Magnusson, 1999a, 1999b; Thelen & Smith, 1998). For instance, Braun (2004) notes that:

> The controversy over the origin of human traits, whether disease traits or behavioral traits, has been framed historically as one of the relative contribution of "nature versus nurture" or "genes versus environment," and scientists have invested considerable efforts in developing precise quantitative

measures to assess each component separately. Given such a dualistic framework, it is not surprising that explanations for variability oftentimes have taken the form of crude genetic or environmental determinism. (p. 140)

However, she goes on to explain that:

There is abundant evidence that DNA cannot be assembled without proteins and that gene expression is regulated by micro and macro environmental influences. No credible biologist would defend the idea that the genome is fully "encapsulated," as the complexity of intracellular and extracellular networks controlling cellular function is well established. For example, it has long been known that intricate positive and negative feedback networks regulate hormone function. (Braun, 2004, p. 141)

In essence, then, we have in the field of behavior genetics (e.g., Plomin, 1986, 2000; Rende, 2004; Rowe, 1994) the use of a model of genetic structure and function that is specifically rejected by those scientists who study the action of genes directly. There are conceptual, methodological, and empirical reasons for this rejection.

Methodological and Interpretational Problems in Heritability Computations

I have noted that the traditional way in which behavior genetics researchers attempt to reach their goal of understanding how variation between people in their genes is associated with variation in their behavior and development is through the computation of heritability estimates (e.g., Plomin, 2000; Rende, 2004). As Jerry Hirsch (1997) has explained, however, *heritability* does not mean *inheritance*. To give an example of how misleading heritability interpretations can be in regard to understanding the role of environmental influences, let us consider first an imaginary example.

Suppose a society had a law pertaining to eligibility for government office. The law was simply that men could be elected to such positions and women could not. Consider what one would need to know in order to divide completely correctly a group of randomly chosen people from this society into one of two groups. Group 1 would consist of those who had greater than a zero percent chance of being elected to a leadership post and Group 2 would consist of those who had no chance. All that one would need to know to make this division with complete accuracy was whether a person possessed an XX pair of chromosomes or an XY pair. In the first case, the person would be a female (since possession of the XX chromosome pair leads to female development). In the second, the person would be a male. One could thus correctly place all possessors of the XY pair into the "greater than zero chance" group and all possessors of the XX pair into the "no chance" group.

In this example, then, *all* the differences between people with respect to the characteristic in question—eligibility for office—can be summarized by genetic differences between them, that is, possession of either the XX or the XY chromosome pair. In this case the heritability of "being eligible" would be 1.0. In other words, in this society eligibility is 100 percent heritable. But, by any stretch of the imagination, does this mean that the eligibility characteristic is inherited, or that the differences between men and women with respect to this characteristic are genetic in nature? Is there a gene for "eligibility," one that men possess and women do not?

Of course, the answer to these questions is no. Although heritability in this case is perfect, it is the social ("environmental") variables—laws regarding what men and women can and cannot do—that determine whether or not someone has a chance of being elected. Indeed, if the law in question were changed, and women were now allowed to hold office, then the heritability of the eligibility characteristic would—probably rather quickly—fall to much less than 1.0.

Hebb (1970) offers another useful example of the problems associated with the measurement and interpretation of heritability, one drawing on a "modest proposal" put forth by Mark Twain:

> Mark Twain once proposed that boys should be raised in barrels to the age of 12 and fed through the bung-hole. Suppose we have 100 boys reared this way, with a practically identical environment. Jensen agrees that environment has *some* importance (20% worth?), so we must expect that the boys on emerging from the barrels will have a mean IQ well below 100. However, the variance attributable to the environment is practically zero, so on the "analysis of variance" argument, the environment is not a factor in the low level of IQ, which is nonsense. (p. 578)

In Hebb's example, environment had no *differential* effect on the boys' IQs; presumably in all boys it has the same (severely limiting) effect. In having this same effect, environment could contribute nothing to differences between the boys. No differences—or variation—existed in the environment, and so the environment could not be said to have contributed anything to differences between people. Yet, it is also obvious that environment had a major influence on the boys' IQ scores. Even with IQ heritability equal to +1.0, the intelligence of each of the boys would have been different had he developed in an environment other than a barrel.

A third example is based on the research of Partanen, Brunn, and Markkanen (1966). These researchers analyzed data from 172 monozygotic (MZ) and 557 dizygotic (DZ) male twin pairs. MZ twins are siblings from the same fertilized ovum that splits after conception; thus, MZs are genetically identical. DZ twins are siblings from two different fertilized eggs and thus have no greater genetic resemblance than do siblings born from different pregnancies.

All participants in the Partanen et al. (1966) study were alcohol users. The aim of the study was to estimate the degree to which alcohol abuse is genetically determined. When measured by frequency of alcohol consumption, alcohol abuse seems to have at least a modest genetic component (e.g., a heritability estimate of 0.40). However, if one uses the amount of alcohol consumed on each occasion, the heritability estimate drops considerably (to 0.27). A third measure of alcohol abuse, the number of citations and other social conflicts resulting from drinking, yields a heritability estimate of 0.02. Thus, judgments concerning heritability can depend largely on the definition and operationalization of the behavior under study.

The Inadequacy of Behavior Genetics as a Frame for Studying Human Development

Despite this criticism by their colleagues in the field of psychology, and the lack of credence given to behavior genetics by molecular geneticists (see Garcia Coll et al., 2004), eminent population geneticists (e.g., Feldman & Lewontin, 1975), and evolutionary biologists (e.g., Gould, 1981, 1996), there are some developmental scientists who continue to act *as if* behavioral genetics provides evidence for the inheritance of behaviors and links among (1) the role of the "environment" in human development (Harris, 1998; Plomin, 1986, 2000; Plomin & Daniels, 1987; Rowe, 1994), for example, socioeconomic status, or SES; (2) parenting (e.g., Harris, 1998; Scarr, 1992); and (3) child development outcomes such as intelligence (Jensen, 1969, 1998), morality (Wilson, 1975), temperament (Buss & Plomin, 1984), and even television watching (Plomin et al., 1990)! The work of these colleagues is ill founded.

To understand the problems with the use of behavior genetics as a frame for studying or explaining parent behaviors and of the effects of parenting on child and adolescent development, Collins et al. (2000) note that:

Large-scale societal factors, such as ethnicity or poverty, can influence group means in parenting behavior—and in the effects of parenting behaviors—in ways that are not revealed by studies of within group variability. In addition, highly heritable traits also can be highly malleable. Like traditional correlational research on parenting, therefore, commonly used behavior-genetic methods have provided an incomplete analysis of differences among individuals. (p. 220)

Accordingly, Collins et al. (2000) conclude that:

Whereas researchers using behavior-genetic paradigms imply determinism by heredity and correspondingly little parental influence (e.g., Rowe, 1994), contemporary evidence confirms that the expression of heritable traits depends, often strongly, on experience, including specific parental behaviors, as well as predispositions and age-related factors in the child. (p. 228)

Moreover, there are reasons to be skeptical about whether the various methodologies associated with behavior genetics can generate useful data pertinent to SES, parenting, and child development. For example, Collins et al. (2000) noted that:

One criticism is that the assumptions, methods, and truncated samples used in behavior-genetic studies maximize the effects of heredity and features of the environment that are different for different children and minimize the effects of shared family environments. . . . A second criticism is that estimates of the relative contributions of environment and heredity vary greatly depending on the source of data. . . . Heritability estimates vary considerably depending on the measures used to assess similarity between children or between parents and children. . . . The sizable variability in estimates of genetic and environmental contributions depending on the paradigms and measures used means that no firm conclusions can be drawn about the relative strength of these influences on development. (pp. 220–221)

Similarly, Horowitz (2000) noted that:

One sees increasing skepticism about what is to be learned from assigning variance percentages to genes. . . . The skepticism is informed by approaches that see genes, the central nervous system and other biological functions and variables as contributors to reciprocal, dynamic processes which can only be fully understood in relation to sociocultural environmental contexts. It is a perspective that is influenced by the impressive recent methodological and substantive advances in the neurosciences. (p. 3)

The cutting-edge study of the neurosciences within the developmental systems perspective noted by Horowitz (2000) is exemplified by the work of Suomi (1997, 2000; Bennett et al., 2002), who has sought to identify how genes and context fuse within the developmental system. Because of the close genetic similarity of rhesus monkeys to humans, he has studied these organisms as a means to provide a model for the investigation of this system.

In one recent instance of this long-term research program, Suomi (2000; Bennett et al., 2002) has found that young rhesus monkeys show individual differences in their emotional reactivity (or *temperament*). Some young monkeys are highly reactive. For example, they become quite excited and agitated when they experience environmental stress, such as separation from their mothers. Other monkeys show low reactivity in such situations. For instance, they behave calmly in the face of such separation. Suomi (2000; Bennett et al., 2002) discovered that these individual differences in behavior are associated with different genetic inheritances related to the functioning of serotonin, a brain chemical involved in neurotransmission and linked to individual differences in such conditions as anxiety, depression, and impulsive violence.

Accordingly, in order to study the interrelation of serotonergic system genes and environmental influences on behavioral development, Suomi (2000; Bennett et al., 2002) has placed high- or low-reactivity rhesus young with foster rhesus monkeys who were also either how or low in emotional reactivity. When young monkeys with the genetic inheritance marking high reactivity were reared for the first six months of life with a low-reactivity mother, they developed normally and, for instance, despite their genes, they did not show high reactivity even when removed from their foster mothers and placed in a group of peers and unknown adults. In fact, these monkeys showed a high level of social skill (e.g., they took leadership positions in their group). However, when young monkeys with this same genetic marker for high reactivity were raised by high-reactivity foster mothers, they did not fare well under stressful conditions and proved socially inept when placed in a new social group.

Moreover, Suomi (2000; Bennett et al., 2002) found that the interaction between the serotonin transporter genotype and early experience not only influences rhesus monkey behavior but, as well, brain chemistry regarding the use of serotonin. Despite having a high-reactivity genotype, the monkeys whose early life experiences were with the low-reactivity foster mothers had brain chemistry that corresponded to monkeys with a low reactivity genotype. Accordingly, Suomi (2000) concluded that:

> The recent findings that specific polymorphisms in the serotonin transporter gene are associated with different behavioral and biological outcomes for rhesus monkeys as a function of their early social rearing histories suggest that more complex gene-environment interactions actually are responsible for the phenomenon. It is hard to imagine that the situation would be any less complex for humans. (p. 31)

Finally, in addition to the fatal conceptual and methodological flaws associated with the study of heritability through behavior genetics (e.g., Braun, 2004; Garcia Coll, Bearer, & Lerner, 2004; Gottlieb, 1997, 2004; Hirsch, 1970, 1997, 2004; R. M. Lerner, 2002a), Velden (2003) identifies two critical empirical shortcomings of this area of work that are associated with (1) the population specificity of heritability estimates; and (2) the relation of these estimates to the issue of whether the characteristic for which heritability is being estimated is malleable, or plastic. Velden (2003) demonstrates that as a consequence of the vast, multidimensional differences that exist in the ecologies of populations, there would need to be a heritability estimate computed for every imaginable population-in-context situation. In addition, he demonstrated that a heritability estimate affords no useful prediction whatsoever about the plasticity of a characteristic. Given these empirical problems, Velden (2003) recommends that the field of heritability research should be abandoned given the absence of any theoretical or practical use for this work.

In sum, there are several serious and insurmountable scientific problems with *any* approach to human development that splits the actions of genes from the actions of the context, and behavior genetics is just one of several egregiously flawed instantiations of such perspectives. Sociobiology (as, for instance, represented by Rushton, 1999, 2000; see R. M. Lerner, 2002a, for a review and critique) is another, and, in an earlier era, instinct theory, as represented in the work of Konrad Lorenz (1940a, 1940b, 1943a, 1943b, 1965, 1966; also see R. M. Lerner, 2002a, for a review and critique), was yet another.

Nevertheless, such split, genetic reductionist conceptions continue to influence public discourse and, as well, to find their ways into public policy discussions about youth. Indeed, these conceptions of splits between genes and context enable deficit models of youth to be retained in policy discussions since, if one can speak of genes as separate from context, and as such as if one can therefore ignore the dynamic developmental system that affords plasticity in human development, then one can explain "bad kids" as having the deficit of "bad genes."

Braun (2004) points to the potential policy mischief that can be caused by such split conceptions. Commenting on the views of Rende (2004) regarding behavior genetics, Braun notes that:

> It is open to question, however, whether artificial distinctions between genes and environment, even for analytical purposes, will "promote our understanding" as Rende hopes, or close off knowledge that would lead to deeper understanding. Certainly, such a distinction creates conceptual barriers to challenging the dominant genetic paradigm. Even more fundamentally, the distinction takes on a life of its own, and when transformed into data, published in scientific journals, and popularized in the media acquires the authority of objective, neutral, and value-free knowledge.
>
> Nor does Rende's proposal to substitute the notion of "susceptibility" genes for that of dominant genes move us closer to understanding the ways in which genes and environment are mutually constitutive. For inherent to the idea of "susceptibility"—for both scientists and the public—is the idea of genes as causes. This point is clearly illustrated in a recent article in the *New York Times*, entitled "Schizophrenia May Be Tied to 2 Genes, Research Finds." In this article, the *New York Times* reporter Nicholas Wade (2002) notes that schizophrenia is a complex disorder with a complex etiology. However, Wade goes on to state that researchers "have found clues that point to a specific gene as a possible cause of schizophrenia." The hope is that, despite the frustrating history of schizophrenia research marked by reports of the isolation of genes associated with schizophrenia, this discovery "will illuminate the fundamental mechanisms of the disease and might lead to new treatments." Only in the last three sentence paragraph is the role of the environment even mentioned. This cannot be dismissed as "misunderstanding" by the media. Wade is an experienced and scientifically sophisticated reporter. Moreover, the editor of the *American Journal of Human Genetics* where the two papers were published also expressed the hope that "we might finally be getting close to some genes that predispose people to this important disease." To talk about genes for predisposition in the absence of the context within which those genes operate is to create a powerful rhetorical argument for the genes as primary causes and environment as having "residual" effects—and rhetorical arguments produce "knowledge." (2004, pp. 142–143)

Rhetorical arguments also produce policies and programs. It is crucial, then, that we evaluate how split conceptions versus ideas based on developmental systems theory have different policy and program implications for understanding and for potentially enhancing youth development.

Policy Implications of Split Versus Developmental Systems' Conceptions of Human Development

As suggested by Leventhal and Brooks-Gunn (2003), extensions of flawed ideas to the arena of public policy and social programs can be dangerous to human welfare, social justice, and civil society. While *any* model of human development, including those associated with developmental systems theories, can be misused, I believe that split conceptions of human development, whether they are biogenic, psychogenic, or sociogenic, are substantially more likely to have negative impacts on policies and programs pertinent to human development.

Policy Implications of Split Conceptions

Consider, for example, a society that developed policies derived from a split, sociogenic perspective. Such a society may well deny the value of all genetic inquiry and would believe in virtually limitless developmental plasticity.

For example, in order to capitalize on (beliefs in) the infinite malleability of children's behavioral development, efforts to enhance school achievement might involve policies that standardize the school curriculum for all students, mandate a common performance test for all students, and evaluate all schools by the application of an identical standard. In turn, individual parents taking actions predicated on these strict environmentalist ideas might place their newborn on the waiting list for entry into an "elite" preschool, in order to enhance the child's later life achievements, or they might participate in programs that expose fetuses or newborns to classical music in an attempt to improve later cognitive functioning (i.e., they might pursue the purported but fallacious *Mozart Effect*; Bruer, 1999). In fact, despite the lack of scientific evidence for such an effect, in the late 1990s attempts were made in Georgia and Missouri to create legislation for funding for the purchase and distribution of classical music audiotapes and CDs to newborns in these states (Bruer, 1999, p. 62).

By contrast, a society with policies derived from a split, biogenic perspective could well support policies that invest in genetic counseling programs or in incentives for some people to reproduce more and for others to reproduce less. In addition, miscegenation laws might be enacted to assure that the genes that (purportedly) provided the basis of desirable individual differences would not be "diluted" by those genes associated with undesirable individual differences and deficits of human character (e.g., see Lorenz, 1940a, 1940b, 1943a, 1943b).

Thus, a split, biogenic belief that fixed genes, given at conception, exclusively or primarily control a child's development has the potential to lead parents, youth-serving professionals, or policymakers to believe that there is little that can be done through childrearing to diminish undesired behaviors or to promote positive ones; such views may lead people to look with favor on reproductive control policies and programs. Pessimism about the role of environmental influences on behavior and development in the face of genes received from parents may be intensified when some scientists claim to have demonstrated that parent socialization strategies are, at best, largely irrelevant or merely epiphenomenal and reducible to genetics actions (e.g., as in Rowe, 1994).

Policy Implications of Developmental Systems' Conceptions

A society based on relational, dynamic, developmental systems beliefs would more likely support policies that invest in parent education programs that emphasize the importance of assessing a child's individuality and enhancing the goodness of fit with the specific characteristics of his or her context (e.g., Chess & Thomas, 1999; Thomas & Chess, 1977). In addition, such a society might provide resources (e.g., grants, scholarships, tax incentives) to lead all parents to place their children in high-quality child care and educational programs that foster such fits while, at the same time, recognizing the significance of and providing support for basic biological research pertinent to both organismic individuality and to the presence of and limits on relative plasticity across the life span (Baltes et al., 1998; R. M. Lerner, 2002a).

For example, programs derived from this policy perspective would support leave from employment, school, or military service for parents of all socioeconomic levels during times of work or family transition or crisis. More generally, programs derived from such a policy perspective would enable all parents to provide their children with the key resources needed for well-being and positive youth development (e.g., R. M. Lerner et al., 2002a), for example, a healthy start in life, an education linked to marketable skills, the presence of an adult in the child's life committed completely to his or her positive development, a safe living environment, the opportunity to become an active and engaged citizen in a civil society, and freedom from prejudice and discrimination (R. M. Lerner, Fisher, & Weinberg, 2000). In short, policies derived from developmental systems theory would suggest social justice, equity among all people, and the creation and maintenance of a "level playing field" for all racial, ethic, religious, cultural, sexual preference, and socioeconomic groups.

In sum, then, a significant difference exists between split conceptions and ideas linked to developmental systems theories about relations among social context (e.g., socioeconomic status or parenting) and a person's development, not only in regard to the character of the scientific activity associated with the study of these relations but, as well, in the degree of confidence parents might have about the efficacy of their agency with their children and in the sorts of policies and programs policymakers and practitioners might support. To illustrate the different policy implications of split (biogenic, psychogenic, or sociogenic) conceptions and of developmental systems theory, Table 4.1 presents one view of the implications for policies and programs of split, biogenic conceptions of parenting (R. M. Lerner, 2002c). The table presents (A) beliefs about whether the hereditarian, split conception is believed to be either (1) true or (2) false, and (B) public policy and social program implications that would be associated with the hereditarian "split" position were it in fact (1) true or (2) false under either of the two belief conditions involved in A (cf. Jensen, 1973).

In contrast, Table 4.2 presents a view of the different implications for policies and programs of split, sociogenic conceptions of parenting (R. M. Lerner, 2002c). Moreover, Tables 4.1 and 4.2—in the "A.2.B2." quadrant—not only present the policy and program implications of believing that the hereditarian or the strict environmentalist conceptions, respectively, are believed to be false and are in fact false. In addition, they illustrate the policy and program implications of believing relational, developmental systems theory to be true when it is in fact the case (as obviously argued in this book) that it is true.

Table 4.1 demonstrates that if the hereditarian conception is believed to be true, then irrespective of whether it is in fact true (and, it must be emphasized that it is incontrovertibly *not* true; for example, see Braun, 2004; Collins et al., 2000; Garcia Coll et al., 2004; Gottlieb, 1997; Hirsch, 1997; Horowitz, 2000; R. M. Lerner, 2002a; Venter et al., 2001), a range of actions constraining the freedom of association, reproductive rights, and even survival of people would be promoted. However, if the hereditarian

Table 4.1   Policy and Program Implications of (A) Beliefs About Hereditarian Conception of Genes and (B) Its Truth or Falsity

		B. Public policy and social program implications if hereditarian "split" position were in fact:	
		1. True	2. False
	1. True	• repair inferior genotypes, making them equal to superior genotypes • miscegenation laws • restrictions of personal liberties of carriers of inferior genotypes (separation, discrimination, distinct social tracts) • sterilization • elimination of inferior genotypes from genetic pool	• same as A. 1, B. 1
A. Hereditarian "split" conception is believed to be:	2. False	• wasteful and futile humanitarian policies • wasteful and futile programs of equal opportunity, affirmative action, equity, and social justice • policies and programs to quell social unrest because of unrequited aspirations of genetically constrained people • deterioration of culture and destruction of civil society	• equity, social justice, equal opportunity, affirmative action • celebration of diversity • universal participation in civic life • democracy • systems assessment and engagement • civil society

SOURCE: Lerner, R. M. (2002c).

Table 4.2   Policy and Program Implications of (A) Beliefs About Strict Environmentalist Conception of Context and (B) Its Truth or Falsity

| | | B. Public policy and social program implications if strict environmentalist "split" position were in fact: | |
		1. True	2. False
	1. True	• provide all children with same educational or experiential regimen to maximize their common potential/aptitude • eliminate all individualized educational or training programs • standardized assessments for all children • penalties for parents, schools, and communities when children manifest individual differences in achievement • educate all parents, caregivers, and teachers to act in a standard way in the treatment of all children	• same as A. 1, B. 1
A. Strict environmental "split" conception is believed to be:	2. False	• wasteful and counterproductive diversity-sensitive policies • wasteful and counterproductive programs based on individual differences	• programs that are sensitive to individual differences and that seek to promote a goodness of fit between

(Continued)

Table 4.2   (Continued)

	B. Public policy and social program implications ifstrict environmentalist "split" position were in fact:	
	1. True	*2. False*
	• policies and programs to quell social unrest because of unrequited aspirations of people promised that the individualized program they received would make them equal to all other people • deterioration of culture and destruction of civil society	individually different people and contexts • affirmative actions to correct ontogenetic or historical inequities in person–context fit • celebration of diversity • universal participation in civic life • democracy • systems assessment and engagement • social justice • civil society

SOURCE: Lerner, R. M. (2002c).

conception were correctly regarded as false (and, conversely, the developmental systems conception were correctly seen as true), then policies and programs aimed at social justice and civil society for the diverse families and children of America would be promoted. Similarly, Table 4.2 shows that if the developmental systems perspective is correctly seen as true, and if the strict environmentalist conception is correctly regarded as false, corresponding results for social justice and civil society are promoted. This result obtains despite, of course, the fact the strict environmentalist perspective would be associated with a set of problematic policy and program implications that differed from those problems linked to the hereditarian perspective.

Conclusions

Ideas are powerful organizers of individual behavior and social action. Theories of human development can be linked to a more democratic and socially just nation for families and children, or they can be linked to ill-founded inequities, discrimination, or even more horrendous constraints on human freedom and opportunity. The path to pursue in our science and in the applications to policy and practice we support is clear: We should unequivocally pursue and promote developmental systems approaches to research and applications that are pertinent to youth development and, just as strongly, speak out against split, reductionist hereditarian approaches (e.g., behavior genetics and sociobiology) and, of course, if it should again gain favor, we should criticize strict environmentalist ideas as well.

This course has been clearly set for some time. In the mid-1960s, T. C. Schneirla wrote about the social policy implications of Konrad Lorenz's hereditarian ideas about the existence of a human instinct for aggression. In a review of Lorenz's (1966) *On Aggression*, Schneirla (1966) wrote:

> It is as heavy a responsibility to inform man about aggressive tendencies assumed to be present on an inborn basis as it is to inform him about "original sin," which Lorenz admits in effect. A corollary risk is advising societies to base their programs of social training on attempts to inhibit hypothetical innate aggressions, instead of continuing positive measures for constructive behavior. (p. 16)

More recently, Horowitz (2000) pointed to the caution about hereditarian ideas made by Elman, Bates, Johnson, Karmiloff-Smith, Parisi, and Plunkett (1998) in the concluding section of their book, *Rethinking Innateness*. "If our careless, under-specified choice of words inadvertently does damage to future generations of children, we cannot turn with innocent outrage to the judge and say 'But your Honor, I didn't realize the word was loaded'" (p. 8).

Similarly, although Braun (2004) emphasizes that developmental systems theory approaches are still not the predominant frame for science and application and that, as such, progress in promoting positive youth development and health remains limited (see too Benson, 2003b), she also calls for an approach to research and application that is framed by the integrative, relational ideas of developmental systems theory. She notes that:

> One way to begin to move beyond the unproductive debate over nature *versus* nurture is to think more critically about how biological systems function. Genes certainly are one important component of organisms. But, as explicitly noted by Gottlieb and others (Fausto-Sterling, 2000; Lewontin, 2000; Oyama, 2000), genes are always expressed in an environmental context. It is, in other words, impossible to understand human development without taking a conceptual and experimental approach that starts from the premise that biological and environmental systems are indivisible. Human and non-human organisms continuously shape and reshape their physical and social environment. Thus, the constructed dualism of genes versus environment has profound consequences for knowledge production and for how knowledge will be used. To understand how culture is embodied, research on human development and disorders of development requires methodologies that allow for the study of genes in the context of the whole organism living in a changing physical and social environment. The genetic paradigm currently holds great appeal for scientists and the public alike. Without doubt, narrow genetic approaches to the study of development, disease, and behavior have generated and will continue to generate detailed molecular knowledge of the genomes of organisms. Unfortunately, because few have taken a systems approach to exploring the dynamic interplay between genes and the environment, understanding human development and disease is destined to remain partial at best. (Braun, 2004, p. 143)

In summary, to avoid the undesirable policy and program outcomes that may be linked to split conceptions of human development, we will need to alter both our theoretical models and the vocabulary we use to present our beliefs about human development to colleagues and to non-scholarly communities (Hirsch, 1997), and perhaps especially to the media and policymakers—the citizens who to a great extent influence and act on public discourse. We will need to advance models that "avoid all splits" (Overton, 1998) and that, instead, conceptually embrace the dynamic, fused relations between genes and context that is involved in the developmental system (Gottlieb, 1997). It is this gene ← → context fusion that gives the developmental system its organismic integrity, its continuity, *and* its plasticity (Thelen & Smith, 1998).

As illustrated in Tables 4.1 and 4.2, the potential costs, in the form of undemocratic and even life-threatening policies and programs to the health and welfare of diverse families and children, are too great for scholars persuaded by the utility of developmental systems theories to fail to rise to what is in effect a dual challenge—of scientific revision and community outreach. We must pay heed to Lewontin's (1992) caution that the "price" society must pay for the continued presence of split conceptions is the need to remain vigilant about their appearance. We must be prepared to discuss the poor science they reflect and the inadequate bases they provide for public policy and applications pertinent to improving human life (see too Schneirla, 1966; Tobach, 1994). We must be ready to suggest alternatives, such as developmental systems ones, to split views of research about and applications for human development.

Given the enormous, and arguably historically unprecedented, challenges facing the families of America and the world, perhaps especially as they strive to rear healthy and successful young people capable of leading civil society productively, responsibly, and morally across the twenty-first century (Benson, 1997, 2003a, 2003b; Damon, 1997; Damon et al., 2003; R. M. Lerner, Fisher, & Weinberg, 2000), there is no time to lose in the development of such a commitment by the scholarly community. Accordingly, in the next chapters I discuss the implications of developmental systems ideas for framing my theory of positive youth development— of youth thriving and civic engagement—and, in turn, of the use of my theory of positive youth development for envisioning a set of policy and program initiatives pertinent to promoting youth thriving ← → civil society relations.

5

On the Nature of Thriving

The ideas of developmental systems theory (R. M. Lerner, 2002a) provide a useful frame for formulating a model of exemplary positive youth development—of thriving—and of the role of thriving young people—through their civic engagement—in enhancing civil society and advancing liberty. For instance, the relation of individual development to history described within developmental systems theory means that change is a necessary feature of human life. However, change in individual ← → context relations is of course not limitless. Interlevel relations within the human developmental system both facilitate and constrain opportunities for change.

For example, change (e.g., learning a new language with native-speaker fluency in adolescence or young adulthood) is constrained both by past developments (knowledge of one's native language) and by contemporary contextual conditions (the absence or presence of opportunities to immerse oneself in a new language and culture). As a consequence, contemporary developmental systems theories stress that only *relative plasticity* exists across life, and that the magnitude of this plasticity may vary across ontogeny (Baltes et al., 1998; R. M. Lerner, 1984, 2002a).

Nevertheless, I have noted that the presence of relative plasticity legitimates an optimistic and proactive search for characteristics of individuals and of their ecologies that together can be arrayed to promote positive developmental change (Birkel et al., 1989; Fisher & Lerner, 1994; R. M. Lerner, 2002a; R. M. Lerner & Hood, 1986). Accordingly, the emphasis in developmental systems theory on relative plasticity provides a foundation for an applied developmental science aimed at enhancing human development by strengthening the linkages between developing individuals and their changing family and community settings, and for advancing the adaptive (mutually beneficial) character of individual ← → context relations. From this applied developmental science perspective, healthy development involves positive changes in the relation between a developing person—who is committed and able to contribute positively to self, family, and community—and a community that supports the development of such citizens.

As I have defined it, a young person involved across time in such healthy, positive relations with his or her community and on the path to idealized personhood may be said to be *thriving*. Thus, the components of the individual-psychological and social relational features of individual ← → context relations that change over time to constitute such development comprise the thriving process.

Developmental science may be applied in several ways to promote thriving. The details of such applications are the focus of subsequent chapters. However, it is important to note here that both public policies and social programs may be used to enhance the orientation of a person to contribute to healthy family life and to democratic community institutions while, at the same time, improving himself or herself in ways that enable such individual actions to be successful. Promotion of a sense of the importance of levels of being beyond the self—what I have defined as one manifestation of a sense of spirituality—and of the importance of undertaking a role to contribute to social well-being (e.g., a moral identity, a sense of civic duty) are exemplars of such an orientation (cf. Erikson, 1959, 1968; R. M. Lerner, 2002b; R. M. Lerner, Bornstein, & Smith, 2003; Youniss et al., 1999; and Youniss & Yates, 1999).

Simultaneously, such applied developmental science may involve furthering the institutions and systems within communities in order to facilitate healthy development (Camino, 2000). As is discussed in greater detail in Chapter 6, examples of such efforts are programs that provide young people with the opportunity to contribute to and take leadership positions in community efforts to improve social life and social justice, and, over time, to develop their commitments to and skills at community building (Benson, 2003a; Damon & Gregory, 2003; Zeldin, Camino, & Wheeler, 2000).

The bases for change in individual ← → context relations, and for both plasticity and constraints in development, lie in the relations that exist among the multiple levels of organization that constitute the substance of human life (Ford & Lerner, 1992; Schneirla, 1957; Thelen & Smith, 1998;

Tobach, 1981). Accordingly, applied developmental science efforts aimed at furthering the thriving process and at fostering in young people a spiritual sense and a moral commitment to make healthy, integrated contributions to self, family, community, and civil society may involve work focused on multiple levels of organization within the developmental system. These levels range from the inner biological to the individual-psychological and the proximal social relational (e.g., involving dyads, peer groups, and nuclear families); to the sociocultural (including both community-based organizations—CBOs—that serve youth, as well as key macro-institutions, such as educational, public policy, governmental, and economic systems); to the natural and designed physical ecologies of human development (Bronfenbrenner, 1979, 2001, in press; Riegel, 1975).

Developmental Regulation and Moral and Civic Identity

Within developmental systems theories, changing relations are the basic unit of analysis (e.g., Bronfenbrenner, 2001; R. M. Lerner, 2002a; Overton, 1998). As such, the regulation across development of these relations must be of central concern in efforts directed to capitalize positively on the relative plasticity of the human development system in order to enhance healthy behavior and development. As emphasized throughout this book, adaptive developmental regulation involves mutually beneficial and sustaining exchanges between individuals and contexts. Moreover, as I have emphasized, consistent with humans' evolutionary heritage, which established mutually supportive individual ← → context relations as integral for human survival, in human development, successful (adaptive, health-promoting) regulations at the level of individual functioning involve changing the self to support the context and altering the context to support the self. Such efforts require the individual to remain committed to contributing to the context and to possess, or to strive to develop, the skills for making such contributions. The importance of skill building in the programs of CBOs that effectively promote youth thriving is noted again later in this book.

Accordingly, policy and program efforts aimed at creating and sustaining effective (healthy) individual ← → context regulations may be directed to, on the one hand, enhancing the person's self-definition or moral sense about embracing the significance of enhancing social justice and democracy. On the other hand, such policies and programs may be directed to improvement across individuals of the systems present within the social context that enable individual freedom and facilitate equity and opportunity for individual program participation in and leadership of community activities. The importance of youth participation in the programs of CBOs that effectively promote youth thriving are noted again later. When these respective contributions are synthesized over time in a manner that involves increases in the thriving of individuals, there is a growth in the institutions of civil society, that is, as noted earlier, in the "space" between people and government (O'Connell, 1999). A system of positive human development is therefore present.

In short, a social system that celebrates individuality and individual initiative will be one that individuals seek to serve and sustain. Such a relation is the essence of the mutual individual $\leftarrow \rightarrow$ context benefits defining adaptive developmental regulation. From the perspective of the integrated levels of organization comprising this developmental system, there are universal, structural, and cultural components, on the one hand, and society-specific components, on the other hand, of the relations across life between person and context that enable effective contributions to self and to society to occur, and therefore for thriving to exist.

The universal components of the developmental process constituting thriving involve the *structure* of the regulatory connection between person and context. From a developmental systems perspective that is informed by the neotenous character of human evolution (see Chapter 2), the key unit of analysis in the study of human development is the integrated relation between the individual level of organization and the multilevel ecology of human development. This ecology is composed of other people (e.g., peer groups, families) and the institutions of society and culture that are constituted by both cultural institutions, such as schools and religious institutions, and conceptual or ideological institutions, such as the values that exist in a society regarding the desired features of human functioning.

A relation that subserves the maintenance and perpetuation of the developmental system is one wherein the individual acts to support the institutions of society and, simultaneously, where these institutions support the healthy and productive functioning and development of the individual (Elder, 1998; Ford & Lerner, 1992). In such a relation, the actions of the individual on the context and the actions of the context on the individual are fused in the production of healthy outcomes for both the individual and the institutions (Elder, 1998).

As such, the key feature of the thriving process is one wherein the regulation of individual ← → context relations eventuates in such outcomes at multiple levels of the developmental system, for example, the person, the family, and the community (Brandtstädter, 1998; Heckhausen, 1999). In fact, a key, structural value of all societies (i.e., a universal structural value of all societies) is that individuals' regulation of their individual ← → context relations should make positive contributions to self, family, community, and society (Elder, 1998). In all societies, then, healthy and valued (or "idealized") personhood is seen as a period, or *stage*, wherein such generative regulation is produced (Csikszentmihalyi & Rathunde, 1998; Erikson, 1959).

Ideally, then, a thriving youth will become an adult generating productive and culturally valued contributions to self, family, community, and civil society. These contributions will have an intergenerational impact. Idealized personhood maintains civil society by contributing to the current components of community, business, and civic life. It also perpetuates civil society by imbuing these components with assets for future adaptation to historical change. *Children are these assets.* Most important, then, a key facet of idealized personhood is socialization—as parents, teachers, or mentors—of the members of the next generation to become active agents of civil society. The importance of healthy adult ← → youth relations in the programs of CBOs that effectively promote youth thriving are noted later in this book. Indeed, along with youth skill building and youth participation, healthy adult ← → youth relations are discussed as constituting the "Big Three" components of effective youth-serving programs, that is, the activities that are key to promoting positive youth development (e.g., Blum, 2003; Rhodes, 2002; Rhodes & Roffman, 2003; Roth & Brooks-Gunn, 2003a, 2003b).

Of course, in different societies there is variation in what a person must do to manifest the structural values of productive and healthy personhood. That is, how a person must function to manifest structurally valued regulation will vary from social-cultural setting to setting and across historical (and ecological) conditions (Elder, et al., 1993; Erikson, 1959). For example, in the United States, regulations that support individual freedom, equity, and democracy are highly valued. In other societies, regulations that support inter-individually invariant belief in or obedience to religious dicta may be of superordinate value.

In all cases, however, each society will show variation within a given historical moment in what behaviors are judged as valuable in (consistent with) supporting the universal structural value of maintaining or perpetuating individual ← → context regulations subserving mutually beneficial individual and institutional relations (Meyer, 1988). As a consequence, then, the indicators of what an individual must manifest as he or she develops from infancy to adult personhood may vary across place and time (Elder, et al., 1993). There may be variation across different societies and points in time within the same society in definitions of individual ← → context relations that comprise exemplary development, or thriving, and thus in the specific behaviors that move a young person along a life path wherein he or she will possess the functional values of society and attain structurally valued personhood. Simply, there may be both historical and cultural variation in the specific, functionally valued components of the thriving process.

Thriving, Liberty, and Moral Duty

Developmentally emergent and contextually mediated successful regulations of positive individual ← → context relations ensure that individuals have the nurturance and support needed for healthy development. Simultaneously, such regulation provides society with people who have the mental capacities and the behavioral skills—the inner and outer lives—requisite to maintain, perpetuate, and enhance socially just, equitable, and democratic social institutions (R. M. Lerner, Freund, DeStefanis, & Habermas, 2001; R. M. Lerner & Spanier, 1980).

This mutual interdependency between person and context can foster, in ideal circumstances, the prospering (healthy, positive, and productive development) of individuals and their social worlds. In such circumstances, individuals will manifest exemplary positive development. They will thrive. Such individuals are committed to contributing to social justice and equity for all individuals in society because society is committed to ensuring justice and equality of opportunity and treatment (equity) for them. Through civic engagement they enter onto a life path marked by the Five Cs, discussed in Chapter 1, and as well, they pursue the noble purpose of becoming productive adult members of their communities, persons contributing positively to self, others, and the institutions of civil society. This type of developmental regulation—between thriving individuals and their civil society—is the essence of a system marked by liberty.

In such a system, it is the moral duty of the people who live within the system and who are affected by the system to sustain and further it (Wilson, 1993). I derive this normative moral principle (this categorical imperative, if you will) from the facts of human evolution (see Chapter 2) and human development (see Chapter 3). However, as I noted, this derivation is an instance of the naturalistic fallacy.

In my view, moral behavior is behavior that supports a system marked by liberty; it is civically engaged behavior predicated on the person's belief that contributions to family, community, and civil society are the "right thing" to do—that one is duty bound to "matter" beyond one's self (cf. Wilson, 1993). In this view, moral development involves the increasing consistency between an individual's behavioral attributes and those characteristics of personal and social functioning requisite for maintaining and enhancing developmental regulations associated with liberty, with the idea of America. It is my contention that the moral valence of behavior—a person's noble purpose (Damon et al., 2003)—can be gauged by the goodness of fit between the individual's behavioral repertoire and what is required to instantiate the thriving young individual ← → civil society relation.

It is this set of arguments that comprises my intentional commission of a version of the supposed naturalistic fallacy (Kohlberg, 1971; Wilson, 1993). A discussion of this philosophical issue is important for situating my theory of youth moral and civic identity development within other discussions of moral development among youth. In addition, this discussion of the supposed naturalistic fallacy will enable me to bring into sharper relief the precise features of the structure and function of the individual ← → context relations that link exemplary positive development (thriving), civic engagement, and liberty.

Committing the Naturalistic Fallacy and (Perhaps) Getting Away with It

There are various forms of the alleged "naturalistic fallacy," that is, of the belief that one can derive universal statements about how one ought to act from observing what is the character of human actions. As did Lawrence Kohlberg (1971) in an essay on moral development and moral philosophy, I believe that one can in fact "commit the naturalistic fallacy and get away with it" (p. 151). However, the route I take in embracing this supposed fallacy is different from the one followed by Kohlberg (1971).

I agree with Kohlberg (1971) that the fallacy is in fact a philosophical problem only if one is confused about the distinctions among cultural relativism, ethical relativism, and scientific neutrality. People vary in how they act and in what they believe. The certain existence of such variation—which may be labeled *cultural relativism* (Kohlberg, 1971)—says nothing, however, about whether there may be ways rationally and empirically to appraise whether some behavior is consistent with universal moral principles. As Kohlberg explained (1971):

> Value relativism is often a confusion between the idea that "everyone has their own values," and the idea that "everyone ought to have their own values." In other words, the value-relativity position often rests on logical confusion between matters of fact (there are no standards accepted by all men), and matters of value (there are no standards which all men ought to accept. (p. 156)

Interestingly, this confusion is also a version of the naturalistic fallacy. That is, one derives from the observation that there is no unanimity about moral values the statement that there are no possible universal moral statements.

Following Brandt (1961), Kohlberg (1971) defined ethical relativism as the observation of cultural relativism coupled with the view that such relativism is logically necessary. However, as does Kohlberg, I argue that the presence of cultural relativism does not mean that relativism is logically necessary. As does Kohlberg, I argue that ethical relativism is an intellectual "legislative mandate," not an empirical or theoretical necessity. Asserting that because one has failed to observe a phenomenon does not foreclose in science the need to search for, or the possibility of, finding empirical support for such a phenomenon. Indeed, if scientists go on to take the view that (1) because of ethical relativism, (2) people ought to be free to adopt and follow their own moral principles; and therefore that (3) science cannot be used to decide, from among the range of such principles that might be generated, one or ones that reflect universal moral statements; then (4) a triple type of logical fallacy is being committed.

First, such scientific neutrality is ill founded because it presupposes—without empirical support—that there are no universal statements. Second, the stance is anti-intellectual in that it contends that the scientific method is useless as a means to assess any fit between observations or theoretical or a priori statements. Third, such neutrality is internally contradictory in that it generates a universal principle—that all personal or subgroup moral stances inherently exist with equal validity or value—to account for the inability to decide among statements that are by definition not universal. Kohlberg (1971) points out the latter problem by noting that there is a:

confusion between (b), the relativistic ethical proposition "no moral beliefs or principles are absolutely valid" and (c), the nonrelativistic liberal's proposition, "It is a valid moral principle to grant liberty and respect to any human being regardless of his moral beliefs or principles." We shall argue that (c) is valid but does not depend for support on (b). Indeed, if the principle of tolerance, (c), is ethically valid, the principle of ethical relativity, (b), cannot be, since the principle of tolerance, if valid, is not itself "relative," "arbitrary," etc. (p. 159)

In short, then, scientific neutrality as it has been enacted in the study of moral development for more than half a century (cf. Kohlberg, 1963, 1968, 1971) is predicated on several interrelated logical errors, that is, conceptual problems that assume rather than empirically test ethical relativity.

Given, then, that I agree with much of Kohlberg's critique of moral relativism and that I share with him an interest in integrating *is* and *ought* statements, where do we differ? Kohlberg (1971) notes that there are at least three instances of the naturalistic fallacy. He contends that his work reflects the commission of only one of these instances. So does mine. However, we differ in regard to the instance we follow.

Neither Kohlberg nor I subscribe to the instance of the naturalistic fallacy that uses either people's judgments of moral behavior or their reports of actions that bring or do not bring gratification as the basis for formulating universal moral statements. However, Kohlberg (1971) intentionally "commits" the naturalistic fallacy by asserting that "any conception of what moral judgment ought to be must rest on an adequate conception of what is" (p. 222), that is, that "every constructive effort at rational morality, at saying what morality ought to be must start with a characterization of what is, and in that sense commits 'the naturalistic fallacy'" (pp. 222–223).

In the commission of this instance of the naturalistic fallacy, Kohlberg presented a theory that described the development of moral reasoning as progressing through three levels of thinking (pre-conventional, conventional, and post-conventional) and indicated (at least in the formulation of his theory that was operational at the time of his 1971 essay) that there were two distinct stages of development associated with each level.

Kohlberg's (1971) specification of the levels and stages in his theory of moral reasoning development involved a sequence that described thought attaining, at its highest level, an orientation to ideas of social justice and human welfare and, at Stage 6, the belief that human life is sacred and requires a universal valuing of respect for the individual. Kohlberg (1971) notes that these "moral categories come from both the Piagetian psychological tradition and from traditional ethical analysis" (p. 167), which he explains drew heavily from the writings of Kant and Dewey.

However, given that Kohlberg's conceptions of levels and stages were formulated a priori, that is, before the collection of data (and I have noted in Chapter 1 that this procedure is generally the case with developmental theories), the fit between these categories and his observations of changes in moral reasoning is irrelevant to the structure of the specified content of these categories. Formulated independent of data and on the basis of consistency with cognitive developmental theory and philosophical analyses of a priori categorical imperatives, the degree to which observed patterns of age changes or age differences in moral reasoning conform to the a priori categories says nothing about the adequacy of the logical process through which Kohlberg developed this theory. Internal coherence and logical consistency are the criteria by which these stages should be evaluated, not whether there are data that converge or diverge with the categories of the theory.

For a variety of reasons, any given set of empirical samples might diverge completely from fit with a priori categories. For example, imagine that samples of moral reasoning were collected in the early 1940s in Germany from among ardent supporters of Hitler and of the Nazi worldview. Such data would diverge from Kohlberg's a priori categories. Such divergence, however, even if replicated with data from several other samples (e.g., contemporary Skin Head or White Supremacist groups or members of the Taliban) would be irrelevant to the validity of Kohlberg's (1971) stage formulation.

Indeed, given the empirical fact of cultural relativism, it could be the case that no set of observations available to a researcher would fit with the theory. Nevertheless, such inconsistency would in no way bear on the adequacy of the theory, given the method used by Kohlberg to generate his ideas, the a priori nature of the categories he formulated, and the theoretical purposes of his theory. In essence, then, Kohlberg merges *ought* and *is* by starting from *ought* statements and seeking to verify them from observing what is. However, given the nature of his theory, no number of *is* observations (whether they converge with his theory or not) can be used to address the adequacy of his *oughts*.

Thus, although Kohlberg willingly commits the naturalistic fallacy, his taking this philosophical step fails to merge science and moral functioning or moral development. Ironically, it is the third instance of the naturalistic fallacy—an instance that Kohlberg (1971) eschews—that does legitimate such a merger. It is the one I adopt. Moreover, although

Kohlberg (1971) claims that "science cannot prove or justify a morality because the rules of scientific discourse are not the rules of moral discourse," he does believe that "science can contribute to a moral discourse as to why one moral theory is better than another" (p. 223). Although I believe that these two statements cannot on close scrutiny be held as logically compatible (i.e., they can be shown to violate Aristotle's law of the excluded middle), I will argue that my commission of the naturalistic fallacy can both decide whether a given set of behaviors is "morally" better than another set and that, by so doing, can in fact use science to justify a definition of moral behavior and development.

Kohlberg (1971) described this instance of the naturalistic fallacy that I adopt as "that of assuming that morality or moral maturity is part of man's biological nature . . ." (p. 222). As may be clear from my arguments in preceding chapters, this is precisely what I am arguing. If human evolution has involved:

1. A particular type of behaviors as requisite for human reproduction and survival, and if

2. These behaviors involve the regulation of mutually supportive relationships between individuals and their social worlds

then it may be the case that:

a. Human psychological and social functioning, when it is optimal, supports this individual ← → content regulation, and
b. Institutions of human society (families, communities, systems of government, and cultural structures) emerge—under conditions of civil society—to support individuals and their abilities to contribute to their social worlds.

If so, it is a reasonable—and empirically testable—hypothesis that human thought about what is moral and reflective of good should embody the idea that adaptive developmental regulations epitomize the essence of moral thinking and behaviors. This hypothesis is consistent with Wilson's (1993) conception of political liberty (see his discussion on page 14 in Chapter 1), with his notion of the evolutionary basis of humans' moral sense (see page 14), and with his notion of the links between duty, selfhood, community, and liberty (see page 16). Indeed, across the history of a civil society involving liberty and of the development of individuals living within it, there should be increasing congruence between the individual reasoning and actions of healthy, thriving people and a subscription to the idea that behaviors and developments that support adaptive developmental regulation, and hence adaptive individual ← → context relations, are moral behaviors.

Accordingly, I merge *ought* and *is* by starting from *is* statements (about the course of human evolution and development) and offer a conception of what "ought to be" based on an analysis of the requirements for humans to enact optimally, and for society to institutionalize ideally, the behaviors that afford healthy, positive functioning, and thriving for individuals and for civil society—and thus for liberty—in their social world. As such, there are and can be further empirical instances of the use of this approach to understanding the integration of moral and civic life in individuals and institutions.

Moreover, and eschewing any hint of relativism or neutrality that may be associated with other empirically oriented approaches to human values, I believe that the instantiation of the naturalistic fallacy that may be reflected in my theory embraces the idea that all human behaviors and all group or national institutional action agendas can be evaluated in regard to whether they reflect consistency with adaptive developmental regulation. When this is the case, then individual liberty and freedom will be embedded in civil society, and "noble purpose" (Damon et al., 2003) will be the avowed aim of people and of institutions living within such a system. Moral functioning exists when individual thriving and civil society are merged through mutually beneficial exchanges—that is, through individual ← → context relations or, in other terms, adaptive developmental regulations.

Is the Naturalistic Fallacy Even a Fallacy?

As explained by Wilson (1993), David Hume (1740/1978), a member of the British School of Empiricism (of which John Locke, David Hartley, Alexander Bain, and George Berkeley were "classmates"; Boring, 1950; Misiak & Sexton, 1966), was arguably the key philosopher articulating the challenge of identifying an empirical basis for morality, that is, of ascertaining a natural basis for morality that was not dependent on revealed religion. That is, Hume observed that moral philosophers would move from noting that some aspect of human life is the case to asserting that this feature of behavior ought to be the case, for example, as in "men make and keep promises" then becoming "men ought to keep promises" (Hume, 1740/1978, pp. 469–470; cited in Wilson, 1993, p. 237). Thus, Wilson (1993) notes that:

I learned from Hume, as did legions of my fellow students, that this transition is impossible; one cannot infer an "ought" statement from an "is" statement; in modern parlance, one cannot infer values from facts. It is logically untenable. (p. 237)

However, and perhaps remarkably to those whose familiarity with the "is to ought" controversy began with the controversy surrounding Kohlberg's (1971) work and not Hume's (1740) ideas from two centuries earlier, Wilson (1993) explains that Hume in fact believed that one could legitimately move from is to ought *if and only if* one did so from the basis of empirical regularities and not from a reliance solely on reasoned argumentation. In other words, "Hume's famous separation of 'is' from 'ought' was meant as a challenge only to those systems of moral thought that attempted to rely on reason to prove a moral obligation, and only to 'vulgar systems' at that" (Wilson, 1993, p. 238).

Accordingly, although Kohlberg (1971) explicitly notes that a legitimate basis for moving from *is* to *ought* cannot be derived from the empirical study of the biological foundations of human development, and urges instead that moving from *is* to *ought* has its basis in an a priori theory of developmental progressions in moral reasoning, such an argument is antithetical to Hume's formulation of the "is to ought" problem. Indeed, if one uses Hume's formulation of what is and is not appropriate in making "is to ought" statements as the baseline from which to judge attempts to adequately address this issue, then Kohlberg has in effect hung himself on his own petard in at least two ways. He has used a pre-empirical set of statements to justify his purported contradiction of the naturalistic fallacy and, as well, he has explicitly eschewed a key domain of science (evolutionary biology) as a means to identify the empirical bases that Hume (1740/1978) believed were requisite to specify in statements deriving an *ought* from an *is*.

Is the Naturalistic Fallacy Even Relevant?

There is another way to understand my solution to the naturalistic fallacy. It may perhaps be seen as a solution that defines away the problem. My theory links (in an inevitable and necessary fusion):

1. Evolutionarily based and structurally invariant (universal) adaptive developmental regulations—defined as individual ← → context relations; and

2. Culturally specific, and hence potentially societally and historically distinct, functions (sets of behaviors, such as academic competence); that

3. Together constitute the means through which individuals may enact adaptive individual ← → context relations.

In short, my theory proposes that moral functioning in any society and at any point in history involves a fusion of structurally invariant ← → functionally variant relations between individuals and their contexts.

Accordingly, and borrowing from a corresponding argument made in regard to structures of general cognitive development formulated by cognitive developmental scholar David Henry Feldman (1994), I am in effect making a non-universal universal statement. My statement is non-universal in the sense that part of the structure ← → function fusion I describe (the function portion) is stipulated to be necessarily culturally and historically relative, and it is universal in that the other part of the fusion I describe, as well as the very presence of such a fusion in human life, are generalizable, invariant, and regarded as requisite across time and place for human life to be sustained. That is, specifically, I am arguing that:

1. The facts of human evolution and human development lead to the statement that behavior that reflects or supports individual ← → context relations, that is, mutually beneficial (i.e., adaptive) developmental regulations, are moral behaviors.

2. However, the facts of human evolution and human development involve an understanding that the structure ← → function relation comprising adaptive developmental regulations derives from plastic phylogenetic and ontogenetic developmental systems.

3. The plasticity of these developmental systems are embedded in history, and this temporality gives the systems the attribute of continuous change.

4. Continual change means that the integrated structure ← → function relations that are present or, more important for the present discussion, that are adaptive at one point in time may not be adaptive at a subsequent time.

5. Therefore, it is possible that a particular structure ← → function relation (e.g., a normative moral "statement," for example, "Children should be seen and not heard") may be universal at one point in time but, as history (evolution) proceeds, this attribute may not be universal at a subsequent time (for example, the statement may change to one of "Children should be participants in family decisions and should play an active role in generating the rules that govern their behavior").

6. Accordingly, the universalism of the structure ← → function relational "unit" is always necessarily relative to the developmental system as it exists at a given point in history. For example, the structure of the human family and the strict sex differences in roles (i.e., in family functions) that were adaptive 7 million years ago on the African savannah, and thus universally needed for human survival (Fisher, 1982a, 1982b), are in contemporary American society not only not universally needed but, in turn, may be antithetical to the stability of the family. For instance, divorce may be more likely if a spouse is restricted to a traditional or sex-stereotyped role (Hetherington & Kelly, 2002).

7. Therefore, since the developmental systems orientation that frames the present view of moral action gives rise to the idea that the universality of the structure ← → function relational unit is always relative to the extant point in history in which it is referenced, one must conceive of the structure ← → function unit as a whole not as being an absolute entity but as a relativistic one.

8. A presupposition that one must maintain, therefore, given the temporality of the developmental system, is that no structure ← → function relational unit, no moral statement, will *necessarily* remain universal across history.

9. One may use, therefore, the concept of non-universal universality (cf. Feldman, 1994, 2000) to depict the temporal embeddedness of normative statements about morality. One may use the concept to depict the generalizability of what *ought to be* in regard to maintaining or furthering structure ← → function relations that reflect adaptive developmental regulations—that portray optimal thriving individual ← → civil society relations—within a given place and time.

Although an admitted academic oxymoron, the concept of non-universal universality may make the present discussion of the naturalistic fallacy moot. Given that no universal *ought* statements about structure ← → function relational units are being derived from the *is* statements of evolution and human development, the issues surrounding the legitimacy of committing the naturalistic fallacy may, after all, be irrelevant to advancing the present argument about the nature and basis of moral action. I am *not* deriving (because of the defining characteristics of developmental systems theory) a universal (or, in the present context, a universal universal) statement about structure ← → function relational units, but rather only culturally and historically relative, or non-universal universal, statements about such units.

As such, even if one were to maintain (in opposition to the argument made by Wilson, 1993) that the naturalistic fallacy remains a philosophical problem even when (as done within my theory) *ought* statements are derived from the facts of evolutions and human development, it is possible to argue that I am not committing the naturalistic fallacy at all. My ideas about the nature of moral action may hold for the world as we find it now, that is, as the modern culmination of human evolution and as the marker of exemplary exchanges between thriving individuals and democratic civil society, that is, of exchanges that reflect liberty and the idea of America.

Thriving as a Marker of Healthy and Successful Developmental Regulations

Consistent with my use of biological and developmental science to derive *ought* statements about moral functioning, my view of thriving can be linked to the Kantian concept of *practical reason*, a form of reasoning superior to *theoretical reason*, that leads people, in careful consideration of the facts of reality, to be aware of what they "ought" to do and then to do it (Kant, 1781/1966; see too Hume, 1740/1978). In this view, those who adhere to practical reason will likely participate in healthy developmental regulation, contributing not only to their own healthy development but also to the perpetuation of a more moral and civil society. By analogy, by wearing the "veil of ignorance" (Rawls, 1971), individuals will want (i.e., they will believe it is just) to act to support a society that does not discriminate among individuals in providing the right to equal opportunity and freedom but, instead, assures liberty and justice for all (R. M. Lerner, Dowling, & Anderson, 2003).

Whatever the specific behaviors (the functional components of the structure ← → function relational units) involved in thriving at a given time or in a particular place, within developmental systems theories thriving invariantly involves the manifestation by a young person of a systematic enhancement across ontogeny of behaviors that function to enhance adaptive developmental regulation (the structural component of the structure ← → function relational unit). My theory is that this structure ← → function relational unit, as it exists at this point in the history of America, means that healthy, positive, and mutually supportive *relations* between free individuals and their freedom-supporting and social justice- and equity-maintaining contexts constitutes thriving. The structure ← → function relations that foster the development of thriving constitutes the essence of a system marked by liberty and exists because of the linkage between (1) growth in individuals' capacities for, commitments to, and enactments of their contributions to such developmental regulations; and (2) the attainment in adulthood of structurally valued behaviors, that is, of the behaviors that, ideally, reflect the optimal manifestation of actions that maintain, perpetuate, and enhance self and context (Csikszentmihalyi & Rathunde, 1998). In other words, thriving is a developmental concept that denotes a healthy change process linking youth with an idealized adulthood status that enables society to be populated by healthy individuals oriented morally to integratively serve self and civil society (Csikszentmihalyi & Rathunde, 1998).

In short, adaptive developmental regulation results in the emergence among young people of an orientation to transcend self-interest and place value on, and commitments to, actions supportive of a social system promoting equity, democracy, social justice, and personal freedoms. This regulatory system is one that enables the individual and individual initiative to prosper. As such, it is this relation—between an individual engaged in support of a democratic system that, in turn, supports the individual— that is the essence of the mutual, individual ← → context benefits defining healthy developmental regulation.

Adaptive Developmental Regulation and Positive Youth Development

Adaptive developmental regulation creates in youth behaviors valuable for positive individual ← → context functioning, behaviors such as the Five Cs of positive youth development noted earlier: competence, confidence, character, social connection, and caring or compassion (Eccles & Gootman, 2002; R. M. Lerner, Fisher, & Weinberg, 2000; Roth et al., 1998). The development of such functionally valued behaviors in young people, as well as the development of an understanding of, and a commitment to, entities that transcend self and self-interest, result in the emergence in youth of an orientation to contribute to their community, which is the "Sixth C" of positive youth development (Little, 1993, 2000; Youniss et al., 1999). The enactment of such contributions constitutes an index of what Damon et al. (2003) describe as "noble purpose."

A commitment to contribution rests on defining behavior in support of mutually beneficial individual ← → context exchanges as morally necessary. Individuals' moral duty to contribute exists because, as citizens receiving benefits from a social system supporting their individual functioning, it is necessary to be actively engaged in, at least, maintaining and, ideally, enhancing that social system (Youniss et al., 1999).

Thriving and Spiritual Development

The sense of transcendence of self and of zero–sum game self-interest that accrues as integrated moral and civic self-definitions (identities) develop may be interpreted as a growing spiritual sense (Benson, 2003a; Dowling et al., in press-a, in press-b; R. M. Lerner, Dowling, & Anderson, 2003). Erik H. Erikson (1959) discussed the emotional "virtues" that were coupled with successful resolution of each of the eight psychosocial crises he included in his theory of ego development. He specified that fidelity, defined as unflagging commitment to abstract ideas (e.g., ideologies) beyond the self, was the virtue associated with adaptive resolution of the identity crisis of adolescence, and thus with the attainment of a socially prescribed, positive role (cf. Youniss et al., 1999). Commitment to a role was regarded by Erikson (1959) as a means for the behaviors of youth to serve the maintenance and perpetuation of society; fidelity to the ideology coupled with the role meant that the young person would gain emotional satisfaction—which, to Erikson (1959) meant enhanced self-esteem—through contributing to society by the enactment of role behaviors (R. M. Lerner, 2002a, 2002b).

One need not focus only on crisis resolution to suggest that behaviors attained during adolescence in the service of identity development may be coupled with an ideological "virtue," that is, with a sensibility about the meaningfulness of abstract ideas that transcend the self (Youniss et al., 1999). From a perspective that focuses on adaptive developmental regulation within the developmental system, it is possible to suggest that spirituality is the transcendent virtue coupled with the behaviors (roles) predicated on the emergence of an integrated moral and civic identity.

Contemporary researchers (e.g., Youniss et al., 1999) increasingly frame questions about the impact of service activity on the healthy identity development of youth in terms of concepts associated with Erikson's (1959) theory of ego development. Erikson (1959) proposed that, when young people identify with ideologies and histories of faith-based institutions, identities can be placed within a social-historical framework that connects youth to traditions and communities that transcend the immediate moment, thereby providing young people with a sense of continuity and coherence with the past, present, and future.

Consistent with Erikson's prescription, youth service programs sponsored by faith-based institutions such as the Catholic Church are embedded in interpretive values and historical meaning. For example, a parish that sponsors a highway cleanup activity for its youth will likely rely upon a moral and value-laden framework to explain its involvement, describing that involvement in religious traditions and stories (Youniss et al., 1999). Youth who take part in service activities are likely to "reflect on these justifications as potential meanings for their (own) actions. These established meanings, with their historical richness and picturing of an ideal future may readily be seen as nourishment for youths' identity development" (Youniss et al., 1999, p. 244).

As such, youth whose exchanges with their contexts (whose developmental regulations) are marked by functionally valued behaviors should develop integrated moral and civic identities and a transcendent, or spiritual, sensibility (Benson, 2003a, 2003b; Youniss et al., 1999). Such development puts them on a path to "idealized adulthood" (Csikszentmihalyi & Rathunde, 1998), to becoming adult citizens who make generative contributions to self, family, community, and civil society. Youth producing these valued behaviors are manifesting what I have specified is the essence of the thriving process.

There is evidence that, among youth, there are marked increases in spirituality, although not in commitments to organized religious institutions (Benson, 2003a). In addition, Dowling et al. (2004) have found that adolescents' sense of spirituality is linked to thriving in two ways. First, there is a pathway from spirituality to thriving that is mediated by adolescent religiosity. However, there is a direct, and stronger, connection directly between spirituality and thriving.

In short, identity development, reflecting a moral and civic engagement in and commitment to society, is related in several ways to spiritual development in adolescence (Youniss et al., 1999). However, as illustrated by the findings of Dowling et al. (2004), thriving is related also to religiosity among adolescents.

Thriving and Religiosity Among Adolescents

There are moderate-to-weak associations between youth religious practices and beliefs, and both lower probabilities of problem behaviors (e.g., delinquency, drug and alcohol use and abuse, and sexual activity) and higher probabilities of positive behaviors (e.g., prosocial behaviors such as altruism, moral values, and mental health; Bridges & Moore, 2002;

Kerestes & Youniss, 2003). There are also weak-to-moderate associations between positive youth behaviors and parental involvement in religion (Bridges & Moore, 2002). For instance, Metz and Youniss (2003) found that high school students who identified themselves as religious were more likely to volunteer, participate in school organizations, and have higher grade point averages. In addition, religious students were more likely to have parents who had volunteered; these religious, volunteering students were also more likely to be female (Metz & Youniss, 2003).

Bridges and Moore (2002) note that these associations between religiosity and positive youth development are weakened due to the low quality of measures of youth religiosity. In addition, they indicate that there is a lack of sufficient longitudinal data to chart the potentially changing role of religiosity in positive youth development (Bridges & Moore, 2002). Moreover, Kerestes and Youniss (2003) note that charting this role is complicated by the fact that "religion is a multidimensional phenomenon that cannot easily be segregated from the social context in which it is practiced" (p. 170).

In this regard, a promising advance in the measurement of religiosity and its link to positive youth development has been reported by King (in press). King indexed religiosity through the use of multiple indicators that had sound measurement characteristics; as well, she assessed the social capital supporting religious development that was present in the social context of youth. She found that, within a cross-sectional sample of several hundred diverse urban youth, religiously active adolescents who had high levels of social capital (measured by indicators of social interaction, trust, and shared vision) had higher levels of moral functioning.

A Model of the Thriving Process

A model of the thriving process that is derived from developmental systems theory emphasizes the presence of relative plasticity in human development and legitimates an optimistic and proactive search for characteristics of individuals and of their ecologies that, together, can be arrayed to promote positive developmental change (R. M. Lerner, Dowling, & Anderson, 2003). The developmental systems' stress on relative plasticity provides also a foundation for an applied developmental science aimed at enhancing human development through strengthening adaptive developmental regulation, that is, interrelations between an individual and his or her context that maintain and perpetuate healthy, positive functioning for all facets of the relationship (the system). From this perspective, healthy development involves positive changes in the relation between a developing person—who is morally committed and able (skilled) to contribute (i.e., to function, to act effectively) positively (in culturally defined ways) to self, family, and community—and a community supporting the development of such citizens.

A young person may be said to be *thriving*, then, if he or she is involved across time in such healthy, positive relations with his or her community and on the path to what Csikszentmihalyi and Rathunde (1998) describe as "idealized personhood" (an adult status marked by making culturally valued contributions to self, others, and institutions). While the structure of individual ← → context relations (of developmental regulations) remain invariant (e.g., involving bidirectionality and relative plasticity), the components of the individual-psychological and social relational features of individual ← → context relations may show intercultural differences as they change over time to comprise the thriving process. Figure 5.1 illustrates the components of the individual ← → context relations that I believe structure the thriving process among youth.

Community assets are both products and producers of the actions of engaged young people. These young people are thriving in that they are changing in directions indicative of enhanced performance of behaviors (functions) valued in their specific society (e.g., behaviors indicative of competence, confidence, connection, and so on) and are, as a consequence, embedded in individual ← → context regulations that reflect the structural value of contributing to civil society. As illustrated in Figure 5.1, at any one point in time, the presence of these relations reflects well-being.

Thriving youth become generative adults (Erikson, 1959). By acting on their "practical reasoning," their sense of "ought," such adults productively build the assets of their communities and manifest the moral orientation, spirituality, and behavioral commitment to ensure for themselves, their families, and their broader social world the quality, scale, and sustainability of the institutions of social justice and civil society.

To sustain the individual and societal benefits of these individual ← → context relations, socialization must promote: (1) a moral orientation among youth that good is created through contributions to positive individual ← → context relations; and, as a derivative of this orientation, (2) a commitment to build the institutions of civil society by constructing the ecological "space" for individual citizens to promote in their communities institutions of social justice, equity, and democracy. Thus, when young people understand themselves as morally committed to and behaviorally engaged in building civil society, and when they as a consequence

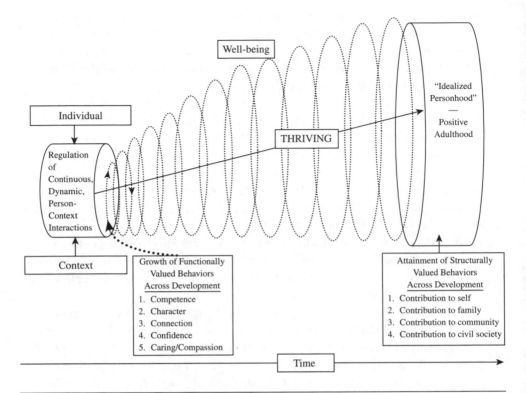

Figure 5.1   The thriving process involves individual ← → context relations that reflect a growth in functionally valued behaviors that, over time, eventuate in the multiple contributions defining idealized personhood.

possess a transcendent sense of the importance in life of a commitment to an enduring nature or being beyond the limits of their own existence, they are able to be agents both in their own, healthy development and in the positive enhancement of other people and of society.

Conclusions

The nature of the links among thriving, civic engagement, and moral development that mark adaptive developmental regulation make it clear that a society interested in the maintenance and enhancement of liberty should develop policies to strengthen, in communities, the capacities of families to provide the individual and ecological assets—the personal and social "developmental nutrients" needed for thriving (Benson, 2003a, 2003b)—that are suggested by Search Institute (Benson, 2003; R. M. Lerner, Theokas, & Jelicic, in press; R. M. Lerner, Fisher, & Weinberg, 2000). These assets are associated with positive youth development—and to an increasing probability of thriving among young people (Scales et al., 2000). Within such a policy context, asset-rich communities would enact activities (e.g., programs) that would provide young people with the resources needed to build and pursue healthy lives that make productive contributions to self, family, and community.

As noted in Chapter 1, one model for designing the individual ← → context system through which such development occurs involves pursuing a vision of family-centered community building (Gore, 2003). The family-centered community-building model suggests that our nation can create a developmental system across generations that builds integrated moral and civic identities in its citizens (Gore, 2003). Such citizens will be able to sustain and to enhance the institutions of civil society.

I discuss in Chapter 7 the family-centered community-building model in greater detail. Here, however, I should note that thriving will more likely emerge when youth develop in such a policy and community action-program context (Benson, 2003b; Benson et al., in press; R. M. Lerner, Fisher & Weinberg, 2000; Pittman et al., 2001; Roth et al., 1998). A competent, confident, connected, caring youth who also possesses character will have the moral orientation and the civic allegiance to use his or her skills to enact in him- or herself and, when a parent, promote in his or her children, behaviors that "level the playing field" for all individuals. Committed—behaviorally, morally, and spiritually—to a better world beyond themselves, they will act to sustain for future generations a society marked by social justice, equity, and democracy and a world wherein all young people may thrive.

To promote a consensus for the creation of a national youth policy predicated on the use of the assets of youth, families, and communities to promote positive development and thriving among America's young people, it is important to understand the interdependency of individuals and contexts that underlie developmental change. This relational emphasis is, as noted throughout this book, a defining feature of developmental systems models of human development. In addition, to build a national youth policy promoting positive youth development, it is important to understand how developmental systems theory enhances understanding and specification of the features of effective youth-serving programs and of policy options that may also be effective in promoting youth thriving and a nation marked by liberty. The next chapter begins this discussion.

6

Programs Promoting
Positive Youth Development
and Civil Society

As noted in Chapter 1, in these early years of the twenty-first century a new, positive, and strength-based vision and vocabulary for discussing America's young people is beginning to emerge. This positive perspective is still not the dominant frame used among scientists or within society more generally for discussing youth (Benson, 2003a; Braun, 2004). The vocabulary of youth deficits is still pervasive (Benson, 2003a; Pittman & Fleming, 1991), and genetic reductionist, split conceptions of human development still influence public discourse to significant degrees (Braun, 2004; R. M. Lerner, 2002c).

Nevertheless, propelled by the increasingly more collaborative contributions of scholars (e.g., Benson, 2003a, 2003b; Benson et al, 2004; Damon & Gregory, 2003; R. M. Lerner, 2002b; Roth et al., 1998; Villarruel, Perkins, Borden, & Keith, 2003), practitioners (e.g., Pittman et al., 2001; Villarruel et al., 2003; Wheeler, 2000, 2003), and policymakers (e.g., Cummings, 2003; Engler & Binsfeld, 1998; Gore, 2003), youth are increasingly seen within numerous sectors of American society as resources to be developed (Catalano et al., 1999). As explained in prior chapters, the new vocabulary of positive youth development emphasizes the strengths that are present within all young people and involves concepts such as developmental assets (Benson, 2003a), moral development (Damon, 1990), noble purpose

(Damon et al., 2003), civic engagement (e.g., Flanagan & Faison, 2001; Flanagan & Sherrod, 1998; Sherrod, Flanagan, & Youniss, 2002a, 2002b; Youniss, McClellan, & Yates, 1999), community youth development (e.g., Villarruel et al., 2003), well-being (Bornstein et al., 2003), and thriving (Dowling et al., 2003, 2004; Furrow et al., 2004; Scales, Benson, Leffert, & Blyth, 2000). All concepts are predicated on the ideas that *every* young person has the potential for successful, healthy development and that *all* youth possess the capacity for positive development.

Across the prior chapters of this book, I have explained that this vision for and vocabulary about positive youth development has evolved over the course of a scientifically arduous path, given the historical precedence of and continued wide subscription to the deficit model of youth. Complicating the acceptance of the new, positive conceptualization of the character of youth as resources for the healthy development of self, families, and communities is the antithetical deficit approach that conceptualizes youth behaviors as deviations from normative development (see Hall, 1904). In this history of the study of youth development, understanding such deviations was not seen as directly relevant to scholarship aimed at discovering the principles of basic developmental processes. Accordingly, the characteristics of youth were regarded as issues of "only" applied concern—and thus of secondary scientific interest. Not only did this model separate basic science from application but, as well, it disembedded the adolescent from the study of normal or healthy development. In short, the deficit view of youth as problems to be managed split the study of young people from the study of health and positive development (R. M. Lerner, 2002c; R. M. Lerner, Brentano et al., 2002; Overton, 1998; Roth & Brooks-Gunn, 2003a).

Other types of "splits" were associated with this deficit model of youth development. As discussed in Chapter 4, the conception of developmental process typically associated with this model often involved causal splits between individual and context, between organism and environment, or—most generally—between nature and nurture (Gottlieb, 1997; R. M. Lerner, 2002a; Overton, 1998). In short, scholars studying human development in general and youth development in particular used a theoretical model that was not useful in understanding the relational nature of development (Overton, 1998), the synthesis between basic and applied science, or how young people developed in normative, healthy, or positive ways. However, the integration of person and context, of basic and applied scholarship, and of young people with the potential for positive development were legitimated by the relational, developmental systems models of development that emerged as cutting-edge scholarship by the end of the twentieth century (Damon, 1998; R. M. Lerner, 1998; 2002a).

Engaging the Developmental System to Promote Positive Development

I have explained that the plasticity of human development emphasized in developmental systems models means that we may always remain optimistic about finding some intervention to reduce problem behaviors. However, plasticity within the developmental system can be directed to the promotion of desired outcomes of change, and not only to the prevention of undesirable behaviors. Pittman (1996; Pittman et al., 2001) has emphasized that prevention is not the same as *provision:* Preventing a problem from occurring does not, in turn, guarantee that we are providing youth with the assets they need for developing in a positive manner.

Simply, problem-free is not prepared (Pittman, 1996). Not having behavioral problems (e.g., not using drugs and alcohol, not engaging in crime or unsafe sex) is not equivalent to possessing the skills requisite to engage productively in a valued job or other role in society. Preventing negative behaviors, then, is not the same as promoting in youth the attributes of positive, healthy development. Accordingly, as noted by several scholars working within a developmental systems framework (e.g., Benson, 1997; Benson et al., 1998; Blyth & Leffert, 1995; Leffert et al., 1998; R. M. Lerner, Brentano, Dowling, & Anderson, 2002b; R. M. Lerner, Ostrom, & Freel, 1997; R. M. Lerner, Rothbaum, Boulos, & Castellino, 2002; R. M. Lerner, Sparks, & McCubbin, 1999; Roth et al., 1997, 1998; Scales et al., 2000; Scales & Leffert, 1999; Villarruel et al., 2003; Wheeler, 2003), to ensure the development of prepared and productive youth, communities need to proactively provide resources to young people so that they develop in positive ways, for example, following the Five Cs of positive youth development discussed earlier.

It is useful to note that each of the Cs represents a cluster of behaviors that community youth development practitioners seek to promote through their youth development programs (e.g., see Villarruel et al., 2003). For instance, as explained by Roth and Brooks-Gunn (2003a):

> The promotion of competence, the first C, includes goals of enhancing participants' social, academic, cognitive, and vocational competencies. Social competence refers to interpersonal skills such as communication,

assertiveness, refusal and resistance, and conflict resolution. Cognitive competence describes cognitive abilities, including logical and analytic thinking, problem solving, decision making, planning, and goal-setting skills. School grades, attendance, test scores, and graduation rates are included under academic competence. Vocational competence pertains to work habits and career choice explorations. Promoting adolescents' confidence, the second C, consists of goals relating to improving adolescents' self-esteem, self-concept, self-efficacy, identity, and belief in the future. Encouraging connections, the third C, involves building and strengthening adolescents' relationships with other people and institutions, such as school. The fourth C, character, is perhaps the most difficult to define. Program goals of increasing self-control, decreasing engagement in health-compromising (problem) behaviors, developing respect for cultural or societal rules and standards and a sense of right and wrong (morality), and spirituality describe character building goals. Developing caring and compassion, the fifth C, implies goals of improving adolescents' empathy and identification with others." (p. 205)

Community-based programs that seek only to prevent problems are not in the main successful in promoting the development of these clusters of behaviors (Roth & Brooks-Gunn, 2003a). As noted later, when I return to a discussion of the "Big Three" components of effective youth development programs, a prevention orientation alone fails to promote positive youth development because such efforts do not provide the program features, or more broadly the developmental assets, that foster the thriving youth ← → civil society relation. What, then, *does* assure, or at least increase the likelihood of, the provision of these assets, of the engagement of youth with their communities, and of these positive youth development outcomes of the Five Cs?

The Contributions of William Damon

What is required to promote thriving young people interacting with the institutions of civil society in mutually beneficial ways? William Damon (1997; Damon & Gregory, 2003) has envisioned the creation of a "youth charter" in each community in our nation and world. The charter consists of a set of rules, guidelines, and plans of action that each community can adopt to provide its youth with a framework for development in a healthy manner. Damon (1997) describes how youth and significant adults in the community (e.g., parents, teachers, clergy, coaches, police, and government and business leaders) can create partnerships to pursue a common ideal of positive moral development and intellectual achievement.

To illustrate, Damon (1997) explains how a youth charter can be developed to maximize the positive experiences and long-term desired developmental outcomes of youth in community sports activities. Damon points out that there many be important benefits of such participation. Young people enhance their physical fitness, learn athletic and physical skills, and, through sports, experience lessons pertinent to the development of character (e.g., they learn the importance of diligence, motivation, teamwork, balancing cooperation versus competition, balancing winning and losing, and the importance of fair play). Moreover, sports can be a context for positive parent–child relations, and such interactions can further the adolescent's successful involvement in sports. For instance, parental support of their male and female adolescents' participation in tennis is associated with the enjoyment of the sport by the youth and with an objective measure of their performance (Hoyle & Leff, 1997).

However, Damon notes as well that organized and even informal opportunities for sports participation for youth, ranging from Little League, soccer, or pickup games in schoolyards, often fall short of providing these benefits for young people. He points out that in modern American society, sports participation is often imbued with a "win at any cost" orientation among coaches and, in turn, their young players. In addition, parents may have this attitude. Together, a value is conveyed that winning is not only the main goal of competition; it is the *only* thing (Damon, 1997, p. 120).

Damon believes that this orientation to youth sports corrupts the purposes of youth participation in sports. Parents and coaches often forget that most of the young people on these teams will not make sports a life career, and, even if they were to do this, they—as well as the majority of young people involved in sports—need moral modeling and guidance about sportsmanship and the significance of representing, through sports, not only physically but psychologically and socially healthy behaviors as well.

In order to enable youth sports to make these contributions to positive adolescent development, Damon envisions the youth charter in regard to youth sports participation as constituting a set of guidelines for the design and conduct of youth sports programs. Adherence to the principles of the charter will enable communities to realize the several assets for young people that can be provided by the participation of youth in sports. Components of the charter include the following commitments:

1. Make youth sports a priority for public funding and other forms of community support (space, facilities, volunteer coaches).

2. Parents and coaches should emphasize standards of conduct as a primary goal of youth sports.

3. Young people should be provided opportunities to participate in individual as well as team sports.

4. Youth sports programs should encourage broad participation by ordinary players as well as stars. And

5. Sports programs for youth must be carefully coordinated with other community events for young people. (Damon, 1997, pp. 123–125)

As illustrated by the youth charter for sports participation, embedding youth in a caring and developmentally facilitative community can promote their ability to develop morally and to contribute to civil society. In a study of about 130 African American parochial high school juniors, the students' working at a soup kitchen for the homeless as part of a school-based community service program was associated with identity development and with the ability to reflect on society's political organization and moral order (Yates & Youniss, 1996).

In a study of more than 3,100 high school seniors (Youniss, Yates, & Su, 1997), the activities engaged in by youth were categorized into (1) school-based, adult-endorsed norms; or (2) engagement in peer fun activities that excluded adults. Youth were then placed into groups that reflected orientations to (1) school-adult norms, but not peer fun (the "School" group); (2) peer fun but not school-adult norms (the "Party" group); or (3) both 1 and 2 (the "All-around" group). The School and the All-around seniors were both high in community service, religious orientation, and political awareness. In turn, the Party group seniors were more likely to use marijuana than were the School group (but not the All-around group) seniors (Youniss et al., 1997).

Furthermore, African American and Latino adolescents who were nominated by community leaders for having shown unusual commitments to caring for others or for contributions to the community were labeled "Care Exemplars" and were compared to a matched group of youth not committed to the community (Hart & Fegley, 1995). The Care Exemplars were more likely than the comparison youth to describe themselves in terms reflective of moral characteristics, to show commitment to both their heritage and to the future of their community, to see themselves as reflecting the ideals of both themselves and their parents, and to stress the importance of personal philosophies and beliefs for their self-definitions (Hart & Fegley, 1995).

In sum, then, Damon (1997) envisions that by embedding youth in a community where service and responsible leadership are possible, the creation of community-specific youth charters can enable adolescents and adults together to systematically promote positive youth development. Youth charters can create opportunities to actualize both individual and community goals that eliminate risk behaviors among adolescents and promote in them the ability to contribute to high-quality individual and community life. Through community youth charters, youth and adults may work together to create a system wherein civil society is maintained and perpetuated (Damon, 1997; Damon & Gregory, 2003).

The Promotion of Developmental Assets: The Contributions of Search Institute

What, precisely, must be brought together by such charters to ensure the promotion of positive youth development? Researchers at Search Institute in Minneapolis, Minnesota believe that what is needed is the application of *assets* (Benson, 1997; Benson, Leffert, Scales, & Blyth, 1998; Leffert, Benson, Scales, Sharma, Drake, & Blyth, 1998; Scales & Leffert, 1999). That is, they stress that positive youth development is furthered when actions are taken to enhance the strengths of a person (e.g., a commitment to learning, a healthy sense of identity), a family (e.g., caring attitudes toward children, rearing styles that both empower youth and set boundaries and provide expectations for positive growth), and a community (e.g., social support, programs that provide access to resources for education, safety, and mentorship available in a community; Benson, 1997).

Accordingly, the researchers at Search Institute, led by its president, Peter L. Benson, believe there are both internal and external attributes that comprise the developmental assets needed by youth. Through their research they have identified 40 such assets—20 internal ones and 20 external ones. These attributes are presented in Table 6.1. Benson and his colleagues have found that the more developmental assets possessed by an adolescent, the greater is his or her likelihood of positive, healthy development.

Table 6.1   The 40 Developmental Assets Proposed by Search Institute

Search Institute has identified the following building blocks of healthy development that help young people grow up healthy, caring, and responsible. Search Institute has surveyed almost 100,000 sixth- to 12th-graders in 213 cities and towns across the country to measure their asset levels.

Asset Type	Asset Name and Definition
Support	1. **Family support**—Family life provides high levels of love and support.
	2. **Positive family communication**—Young person and her or his parent(s) communicate positively, and young person is willing to seek parent(s) advice and counsel.
	3. **Other adult relationships**—Young person receives support from three or more nonparent adults.
	4. **Caring neighborhood**—Young person experiences caring neighbors.
	5. **Caring school climate**—School provides a caring, encouraging environment.
	6. **Parent involvement in schooling**—Parent(s) are actively involved in helping young person succeed in school.
Empowerment	7. **Community values youth**—Young person perceives that adults in the community value youth.
	8. **Youth as resources**—Young people are given useful roles in the community.
	9. **Service to others**—Young person serves in the community one hour or more per week.
	10. **Safety**—Young person feels safe at home, school, and in the neighborhood.
Boundaries and Expectations	11. **Family boundaries**—Family has clear rules and consequences, and monitors the young person's whereabouts.
	12. **School boundaries**—School provides clear rules and consequences.
	13. **Neighborhood boundaries**—Neighbors take responsibility for monitoring young people's behavior.
	14. **Adult role models**—Parent(s) and other adults model positive, responsible behavior.
	15. **Positive peer influence**—Young person's best friends model responsible behavior.
	16. **High expectations**—Both parent(s) and teachers encourage the young person to do well.

Constructive Use of Time	17. **Creative activities**—Young person spends three or more hours per week in lessons or practice in music, theater, or other arts.
	18. **Youth programs**—Young person spends three or more hours per week in sports, clubs, or organizations at school and/or in community organizations.
	19. **Religious community**—Young person spends one or more hours per week in activities in a religious institution.
	20. **Time at home**—Young person is out with friends "with nothing special to do," two or fewer nights per week.
Commitment to Learning	21. **Achievement motivation**—Young person is motivated to do well in school.
	22. **School engagement**—Young person is actively engaged in learning.
	23. **Homework**—Young person reports doing at least one hour of homework every school day.
	24. **Bonding to school**—Young person cares about her or his school.
	25. **Reading for pleasure**—Young person reads for pleasure three or more hours per week.
Positive Values	26. **Caring**—Young person places high value on helping other people.
	27. **Equality and social justice**—Young person places high value on promoting equality and reducing hunger and poverty.
	28. **Integrity**—Young person acts on convictions and stands up for her or his beliefs.
	29. **Honesty**—Young person "tells the truth even when it is not easy."
	30. **Responsibility**—Young person accepts and takes personal responsibility.
	31. **Restraint**—Young person believes it is important not to be sexually active or to use alcohol or other drugs.
Social Competencies	32. **Planning and decision-making**—Young person knows how to plan ahead and make choices.
	33. **Interpersonal competence**—Young person has empathy, sensitivity, and friendship skills.

(Continued)

Table 6.1   (Continued)

Asset Type	Asset Name and Definition
	34. **Cultural competence**—Young person has knowledge of and comfort with people of different cultural/racial/ethnic backgrounds.
	35. **Resistance skills**—Young person can resist negative peer pressure and dangerous situations.
	36. **Peaceful conflict resolution**—Young person seeks to resolve conflict nonviolently.
Positive Identity	37. **Personal power**—Young person feels he or she has control over "things that happen to me."
	38. **Self-esteem**—Young person reports having a high self-esteem.
	39. **Sense of purpose**—Young person reports that "my life has a purpose."
	40. **Positive view of personal future**—Young person is optimistic about her or his personal future.

SOURCE: Benson et al. (1998).

For instance, in a study of 99,462 youth in Grades 6 through 12 in public and/or alternative schools from 213 U.S. cities and town who were assessed during the 1996–97 academic year for their possession of the 40 assets presented in Table 6.1, Leffert et al. (1999) found that the more assets present among youth the lower the likelihood of alcohol use, depression or suicide risk, and violence. Figures 6.1, 6.2, and 6.3, taken from the research of Leffert et al., present these findings.

Figure 6.1 displays the level of alcohol use risk for youth in Grades 6–8 combined and for youth in Grades 9–12 combined; as shown in this figure, in both grade groupings alcohol risk decreases with the possession of more assets. Youth with zero to ten assets have the highest risk, followed by youth with 11 to 20 assets, youth with 21 to 30 assets, and youth with 31 to 40 assets. Thus, consistent with Benson's (1997) view of the salience of developmental assets for promoting healthy behavior among young people, both the trend lines represented in the figure and the fact that the last group has the lowest level of risk show the importance of the asset approach in work aimed at promoting positive development in our

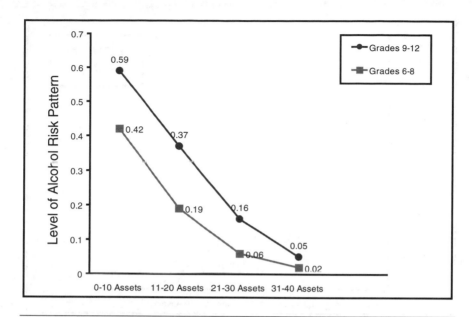

Figure 6.1   Changes in level of alcohol risk in relation to the possession of developmental assets.

SOURCE: Leffert et al. (1999).

nation's children and adolescents. Moreover, the data summarized in both Figures 6.2 and 6.3 replicate the trends seen in Figure 6.1—for males and females in regard to depression/suicide risk in Figure 6.2 and for combinations of males and females in different grade groupings in regard to violence risk in Figure 6.3. This congruence strengthens the argument for the critical significance of a focus on developmental assets in the promotion of positive youth development and, as such, in the enhancement of the capacity and commitment of young people to contribute to civil society.

Other data by Benson and his colleagues provide direct support for this argument. Scales, Benson, Leffert, and Blyth (2000) measured thriving among 6,000 youth in Grades 6 to 12, evenly divided across six ethnic groups (American Indian, African American, Asian American, Latino, European American, and multiracial). *Thriving* was defined as involving seven attributes: school success, leadership, valuing diversity, physical health, helping others, delay of gratification, and overcoming adversity. Most, if not all, of these attributes are linked to the presence of prosocial

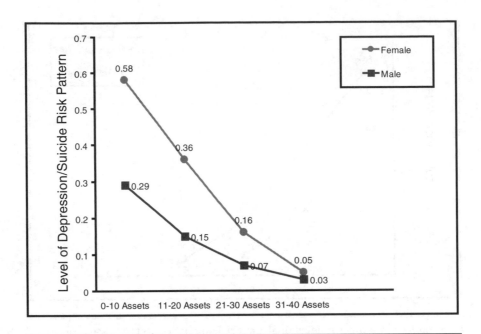

Figure 6.2   Changes in level of depression/suicide risk in relation to the possession of developmental assets.

SOURCE: Leffert et al. (1999).

behavior (e.g., helping others, delay of gratification) and to the behaviors requisite for competently contributing to civil society (e.g., valuing diversity, demonstrating leadership, overcoming adversity). The greater the number of developmental assets possessed by youth, the more likely they were to possess the attributes of thriving. Figures 6.4, 6.5, and 6.6 indicate that as developmental assets increase across the four asset groupings, thriving increases in regard to helping others, valuing diversity, and leadership.

There are other data that support the importance of focusing on developmental assets in both understanding the bases of positive youth development and in using that knowledge to further civil society. Luster and McAdoo (1994) sought to identify the factors that contribute to individual differences in the cognitive competence of African American children in early elementary grades. Consistent with an asset-based approach to promoting the positive development of youth (Benson, 1997; Scales & Leffert, 1998), they found that favorable outcomes in cognitive and socio-emotional development were associated with high scores on an advantage index. This index was formed by scoring children on the basis of the

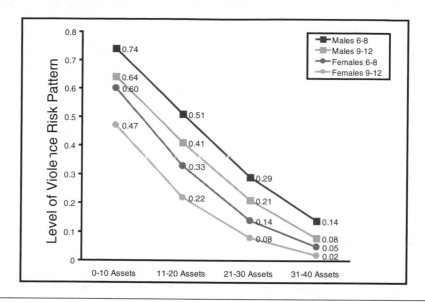

Figure 6.3   Changes in level of violence risk in relation to the possession of
developmental assets.

SOURCE: Leffert et al. (1999).

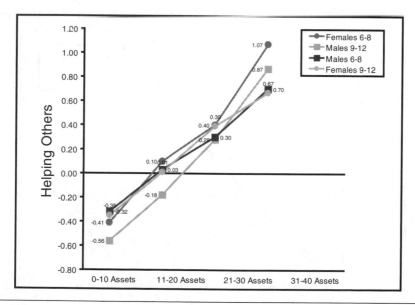

Figure 6.4   Changes in helping others in relation to the possession of
developmental assets.

SOURCE: Scales et al. (2000).

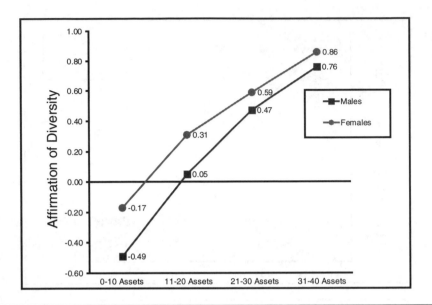

Figure 6.5   Changes in affirmation of diversity in relation to the possession of developmental assets.

SOURCE: Scales et al. (2000).

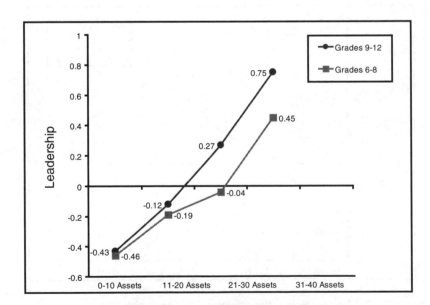

Figure 6.6   Changes in leadership in relation to the possession of developmental assets.

SOURCE: Scales et al. (2000).

absence of risk factors (e.g., pertaining to poverty or problems in the quality of the home environment) and the presence of more favorable circumstances in their lives.

Luster and McAdoo (1994) reported that, whereas only 4 percent of the children in their sample who scored low on the advantage index had high scores on a measure of vocabulary, 44 percent of the children who had high scores on the advantage index had high vocabulary scores. Similar contrasts between low and high scorers on the advantage index were found in regard to measures of math achievement (14 percent versus 37 percent, respectively), word recognition (zero percent versus 35 percent, respectively), and word meaning (7 percent and 46 percent, respectively).

Luster and McAdoo (1996) extended the findings of their 1994 research. Seeking to identify the factors that contribute to individual differences in the educational attainment of African American young adults from low socioeconomic status, Luster and McAdoo (1996) found that assets linked with the individual (cognitive competence, academic motivation, and personal adjustment in kindergarten) and the context (parental involvement in schools) were associated longitudinally with academic achievement and educational attainment.

Conclusions About Developmental Assets and Positive Youth Development

Research reported by Search Institute as well as data provided by other scholars (e.g., Furrow et al., 2004) indicate clearly that individual and contextual assets of youth are linked to their positive development. These data legitimate the idea that the enhancement of such assets—the provision of such developmental *nutrients* (Benson, 2003a, 2003b)—will be associated with the promotion of positive youth development. Importantly, Benson and his colleagues (e.g., Scales et al., 2000) link these assets for positive youth development to effective community-based programs. That is, in their research, Benson and his colleagues find that:

> Time spent in youth programs [was the developmental asset that] appeared to have the most pervasive positive influence in [being a] . . . predictor of . . . thriving outcomes. . . . Good youth programs provide . . . young people with access to caring adults and responsible peers, as well as skill-building activities than can reinforce the values and skills that are associated with doing well in school and maintaining good physical skills. (Scales et al., 2000, p. 43)

Accordingly, policies must be directed to designing, bringing to scale, evaluating, and sustaining programs that are effective in the provision of developmental assets and in using those assets to promote positive development and, ideally, thriving (R. M. Lerner, 2002a, 2002b). As such, it is important to understand the principles behind, and characteristics of, such programs.

Developing Effective Programs for Youth

If programs are to be successful in addressing the combined individual and contextual influences on youth and, in turn, if they are to be associated with positive youth development, it is reasonable to believe that they must engage all levels within the developmental system (Benson, 1997; Benson, 2003a, 2003b; Benson et al., 2004; R. M. Lerner, 1995; Pittman, 1996; Pittman & Irby, 1995; Pittman, Irby, & Cahill, 1995; Trickett, Barone, & Buchanan, 1996). In other words, effective programs engage the system of individual and contextual variables affecting youth development.

By involving multiple characteristics of the young person—for instance, his or her developmental level, knowledge of risk taking, intrapersonal resources (e.g., self-esteem, self-competence, beliefs, and values), interpersonal management skills (e.g., being able to engage useful social support and prosocial behaviors from peers)—successful risk-prevention programs may be developed (Levitt, Selman, & Richmond, 1991). However, as emphasized by the positive youth development perspective I have presented in this book, programs must do more than diminish risk. They must emphasize the strengths and assets of young people, that is, their capacities for positive development, their possession of attributes—*strengths*—that keep them moving forward in a positive developmental path.

Such strengths involve individual attributes, such as self-esteem, spirituality, religiosity, knowledge, skills, and motivation to do well (e.g., Benson, 1997, 2003a). In addition, these strengths are constituted by contextual characteristics such as relations with parents, with other adults, with friends, and with community organizations that are marked by providing models for positive values, providing boundaries and expectations, promoting health and encouraging positive growth, instilling a climate of love and caring and providing youth with a sense of hope for the future, offering positive links to the community, providing opportunities for the constructive use of time, and providing a safe environment that is free from prejudice and discrimination. These individual and contextual strengths are, in essence, the assets for healthy development that are described by Search Institute (e.g., Benson, 1997, 2003a; Scales & Leffert, 1999) and others (e.g., Blum, 2003; Bornstein, 2003; Catalano et al., 1999; Damon, 1997; Damon et al., 2003; Damon & Gregory, 2003; King, in press; R. M. Lerner, Fisher, & Weinberg, 2000; Roth & Brooks-Gunn, 2003a). Focus on these assets provides a means to envision the key features of successful youth programs, ones associated with healthy adolescent development.

As summarized in the report of the Carnegie Council on Adolescent Development, *Great Transitions: Preparing Adolescents for a New Century* (Carnegie Corporation of New York, 1995), programs that build the assets of positive youth development help adolescents meet enduring human needs. That is, if they are to develop into healthy and productive adults, all youth need to:

> (1) Find a valued place in a constructive group; (2) Learn how to form close, durable human relationships; (3) Feel a sense of worth as a person; (4) Achieve a reliable basis for making informed choices; (5) Know how to use the support systems available to them; (6) Express constructive curiosity and exploratory behavior; (7) Find ways of being useful to others; and (8) Believe in a promising future with real opportunities. (Carnegie Corporation of New York, 1995, pp. 10–11)

Moreover, the report goes on to note that:

> Meeting these requirements has been essential for human survival into adulthood for millennia. But in a technologically advanced democratic society—one that places an increasingly high premium on competence in many domains—adolescents themselves face a further set of challenges. They must: (1) Master social skills, including the ability to manage conflict peacefully; (2) Cultivate the inquiring and problem-solving habits of mind for lifelong learning; (3) Acquire the technical and analytic capabilities to participate in a world-class economy; (4) Become ethical persons; (5) Learn the requirements of responsible citizenship; and (6) Respect diversity in our pluralistic society. (p. 11)

What sorts of programs meet these needs? What features should be included in a youth-serving initiative to make it effective?

Key Features of Programs
That Promote Positive Youth Development

Numerous scholars, practitioners, advocates for youth, and policymakers have studied and discussed effective youth programs (e.g., Benson, 1997;

Carnegie Corporation of New York, 1995; Damon, 1997; Dryfoos, 1990, 1998; Hamilton, 1999; R. M. Lerner, 1993, 1995; R. M. Lerner & Galambos, 1998; Little, 1993; Pittman, 1996; Roth et al., 1997, 1998; Schorr, 1988, 1997; Villarruel et al., 2003; Wheeler, 2003). Although all contributors to this discussion have their own ways of phrasing their conclusions, it is possible to provide an overview of the ideal features—the *best practices*—that should be integrated into effective positive youth development programs. These features of best practice involve coordinated attention to the youth's characteristics of individuality and to the specifics of his or her social context.

Catalano et al. (1999) define positive youth development and the programs linked to its occurrence as involving attempts to promote characteristics associated with several of the Five Cs or with some of the ecological developmental assets specified by Search Institute (Benson, 1997, 2003a). Roth and Brooks-Gunn (2003a) also use the Five Cs as a frame for evaluating the effectiveness of programs aimed at promoting positive youth development.

For instance, programs promote positive youth development when they instill in youth attributes of competence such as self-efficacy, resilience, or social, cognitive, behavioral, and moral competence; attributes of confidence such as self-determination and a clear and positive identity; attributes of social connection such as bonding; and attributes of character such as spirituality and a belief in the future (Catalano et al., 1999). In addition, programs promote positive youth development when they promote ecological assets related to empowerment, such as recognition for a young person's positive behaviors, provision of opportunities for prosocial involvement, and support of prosocial norms or standards for healthy behavior (Catalano et al., 1999). In this regard, Roth and Brooks-Gunn (2003a) compare programs that promote the Five Cs—that is, programs that are aimed at youth *development*—with programs that have a youth focus but are not developmental in orientation and, in particular, are not aimed at the promotion of positive development. Roth and Brooks-Gunn (2003a,) note that the youth development programs that promote the Five Cs are "more successful in improving participants' competence, confidence, and connections" (p. 217).

The Big Three Components of Effective Youth Development Programs

What are the specific actions taken by youth development programs that make them effective in promoting the Five Cs? Catalano et al. (1999)

find that the preponderant majority (about 75 percent) of effective positive youth development programs focus on what I termed the "Big Three" design features of effective positive youth development programs (Eccles & Gootman, 2002; Roth & Brooks-Gunn, 2003a, 2003b). That is, the program provides:

1. Opportunities for youth participation in and leadership of activities that

2. Emphasize the development of life skills within the context of a

3. Sustained and caring adult–youth relationship.

For instance, Catalano et al. (1999) note that effective positive youth development programs "targeted healthy bonds between youth and adults, increased opportunities for youth participation in positive social activities, . . . [involved] recognition and reinforcement for that participation" (p. vi) and often used skills training as a youth competency strategy. These characteristics of effective positive youth development programs are similar to those identified by Roth and Brooks-Gunn (2003b), who noted that such programs transcend an exclusive focus on the prevention of health-compromising behaviors to include attempts to inculcate behaviors that stress youth competencies and abilities by "increasing participants' exposure to supportive and empowering environments where activities create multiple opportunities for a range of skill-building and horizon-broadening experiences" (p. 94). In addition, Roth and Brooks-Gunn (2003b) indicate that the activities found in these programs offer both "formal and informal opportunities for youth to nurture their interests and talents, practice new skills, and gain a sense of personal and group recognition. Regardless of the specific activity, the emphasis lies in providing real challenges and active participation" (p. 204).

In this regard, Roth and Brooks-Gunn (2003a) note that when these activities are coupled with an environment that creates an atmosphere of hope for a positive future among youth, when the program "conveys the adults' beliefs in youth as resources to be developed rather than as problems to be managed" (p. 204), then the goals of promoting positive youth development are likely to be reached. In other words, when activities that integrate skill-building opportunities and active participation occur in the presence of positive and supportive adult ← → youth relations, positive development will occur.

Blum (2003) agrees. He notes that effective youth programs offer to young people activities through which to form relationships with caring adults, relations that elicit hope in the young people. When these programs provide the opportunity for youth to participate in community development activities as well, positive youth development occurs (Blum, 2003).

The role of positive adult ← → youth relationships has been underscored as well by Rhodes (2002; Rhodes & Roffman, 2003). Focusing on volunteer mentoring relationships, for instance, Rhodes and Roffman (2003) note that these non-parental relationships "can positively influence a range of outcomes, including improvements in peer and parental relationships, academic achievement, and self-concept; lower recidivism rates among juvenile delinquents; and reductions in substance abuse" (p. 227).

However, Rhodes and Roffman (2003) also note that there is a developmental course to these effects of volunteer mentoring on youth. When young people are in relationships that last a year or longer, they are most likely to experience improvements in academic, psychological, social, and behavioral characteristics. On the other hand, when youth are in relationships that last for between six and 12 months, fewer positive outcomes of mentoring are evident. When young people are in mentoring relationships that end relatively quickly, it appears that mentoring may actually be detrimental. Decrements in positive functioning have been reported in such circumstances (Rhodes, 2002; Rhodes & Roffman, 2003).

Of course, parents may also serve as the adults in positive adult ← → youth relations. Bornstein (2002) notes that the positive influences of parents on their children's health development may be enhanced when parents have several "tools" to facilitate their effective parenting behaviors. These tools include possessing accurate knowledge about child and adolescent development, having good skills at observing their children, possessing strategies for discipline and for problem prevention, and having the ability to provide to their children effective supports for their emotional, social, cognitive, and language development. An additional resource for positive parenting is for adults to have their own sources of social support (Bornstein, 2002).

In addition to the Big Three components of programs that effectively support positive youth development, there are of course other important characteristics of programs that are effective in promoting such development. Among these are the presence of clear goals; attention to the diversity of youth and of their family, community, and culture; assurance that the program represents a safe space for youth and that it is accessible to them; integration of the developmental assets within the community into the program; a collaborative approach to other youth-serving organizations and programs; contributing to the provision of a "seamless" social support across the community; engagement in program evaluation; and advocacy for youth (Dryfoos, 1990, 1998; Eccles & Gootman, 2002; R. M. Lerner, 1995; Little, 1993; Roth & Brooks-Gunn, 2003; Schorr, 1988, 1997). However, youth participation, adult mentorship, and skill building are the bedrocks upon which effective programs must be built. Indeed, as already noted, Scales et al. (2000), in their survey of thriving—of exemplary positive youth development—among 6,000 youth participating in the 1999–2000 Search Institute survey of developmental assets, found that spending time in youth programs was the key developmental asset promoting thriving.

To illustrate the importance for his or her positive development of a young person's involvement in such programs, we focus on the programs of 4-H. This use of 4-H programs is warranted because the programs involved in this youth-serving organization reflect the Big Three design elements that are vital in devising programs effective in promoting exemplary positive youth development, that is, youth participation, adult mentorship, and skill building.

4-H as the Exemplary Programmatic Approach to Promoting Positive Youth Development

The programs of 4-H, the youth-serving programs of the nation's Cooperative Extension Service that are associated with the land-grant colleges and universities of America (R. M. Lerner, DeStefanis, & Ladd, 1998), serve approximately 7 million young people annually. As presented by the National 4-H Council (www.fourhcouncil.edu), the vision of 4-H programs is to create a world in which youth and adults learn, grow, and work together as catalysts for positive change.

Using the Five Cs of positive youth development as the provisional definition of this domain of adolescence functioning, we find that there are several facets of the 4-H approach to programs that reflect the features of effective youth development programs discussed by Catalano et al. (1999). For example, in regard to competence, 4-H programs focus on learning by doing and on the development of practical life skills. In regard to confidence, a goal of 4-H programs is the enhancement of self-determination, independent thinking, and self-esteem. In respect to character, 4-H programs develop in youth a social conscience built on service and volunteerism, and support youth commitment to diversity through embracing and respecting differences. In turn, connection is built as a consequence of the fact that 4-H programs involve youth and adults learning, growing, and working together; caring is enhanced in this context because youth and adults are equal and caring partners in mutually valued work.

Moreover, the emergent development of the Sixth C of positive youth development—contribution—is the ultimate goal of 4-H programs. The actions of 4-H programs promote youth as catalysts in social change, enhance significant youth contributions to their communities, and—by giving youth opportunities to participate in programs built on their own initiative—enable them to be powerful members of society. This focus of 4-H programs on youth participation exemplifies the emphasis in contemporary youth programs away from the focus on prevention of problems that began in the 1970s (Catalano et al., 1999) and toward preparation (skill building) *and* participation and leadership (O'Donoghue, Kirshner, & McLaughlin, 2002). As noted by O'Donoghue et al. (2002):

> Youth participation and power sharing (actively engaging young people as partners in organizational and public decision making) . . . represent a broadening of focus from looking solely at individual-level outcomes to also examining the organizational and community-level impacts of youth participation. (p. 17)

In other words, youth participation represents a key strategy for promoting youth contributions to self and context, to making young people active agents in adaptive developmental regulations that contribute simultaneously to self, family, community, and civil society. Indeed, the theory of positive youth development presented in this book suggests that when youth participation is a part of a set of family and community-based actions that promote the Five Cs, then a young person, motivated by noble purposes (Damon et al., 2003) and fueled by a spirituality that integrates moral and civic actions, will make these several important contributions.

Youth Participation and the Sixth C of Positive Youth Development

The theory of positive youth development that I propose specifies that if young people are engaged in adaptive regulations with their context, if mutually beneficial individual ← → context relations exist, then young people will be on the way to a hopeful future marked by positive contributions to self, family, community, and civil society. Young people will be thriving. As illustrated in Figure 5.1, as a result of such relations youth will manifest several functionally valued behaviors, which in American society can be summarized by the Five Cs (competence, confidence, connection, character, and caring). A thriving youth will be on a developmental trajectory toward an ideal adulthood status, that is, the person will develop behaviors that are valued by society because such behaviors act to structurally maintain it. These behaviors, then, reflect contribution, and, consistent with the mutually beneficial individual ← → context relations that comprise adaptive developmental regulations, such contributions should support the health and positive development of self, others, and the institutions of civil society.

Accordingly, the promotion of positive youth development has at its core the enhancement—through the civic engagement of young people—of the active contribution of the young person to both self and context, of the individual as an active producer of his or her own positive development (R. M. Lerner, 1982; R. M. Lerner & Busch-Rossnagel, 1981; R. M. Lerner, Theokas, & Jelicic, in press; R. M. Lerner & Walls, 1999). As such, among the Big Three characteristics of effective youth programs, youth participation and leadership would seem to be most critical for fostering active contributions. When such participation engages the young person in taking actions that serve both self and context—when the young person behaves to both enhance his or her own life and to be positively civically engaged—positive youth development (thriving) in the direction of an ideal adulthood should be seen. This linkage between youth participation and civic engagement is becoming a prominent part of the youth development field. For instance, as noted by Wheeler (2003):

> The rediscovery of youth leadership development as a core component of positive youth development (PYD) strategies and programs, however, has an even more significant impact: It validates a growing recognition within the philanthropic community and among leadership theorists that personal development and social development are essential conditions for strengthening a community's capacity to respond to its problems and build its future. (p. 491)

She goes on to indicate that:

> A complementary strategy is civic activism, which has reemerged as a viable means for young people to develop and exercise leadership while effecting concrete changes in their communities. In recognizing that young people are capable of addressing societal problems and concerns and in providing a forum for them to do so, civic activism can be a dynamic and powerful strategy. Through civic activism, young people's ideas and energy can

contribute meaningfully as they participate in community building, work toward social change, and apply their leadership skills—all the while gaining access to services, supports, and opportunities that facilitate their own development. (Wheeler, 2003, p. 492)

Consistent with the vision of Wheeler (2003), Kirshner, O'Donoghue, and McLaughlin (2002) define *youth participation* as "a constellation of activities that empower adolescents to take part in and influence decision making that affects their lives and to take action on issues they care about" (p. 5). However, when youth participation occurs in and is enabled by either community-based organizations or by the institutions of civil society, it should involve actions pertinent to both self and context. In other words, when youth participation reflects the adaptive individual ← → context relations indicative of thriving and predicated on the synthesis of moral and civic identity within a young person, it may be characterized as civic engagement.

As such, we may extend the Kirshner et al. (2002) definition of youth participation by linking it to the conception of youth participation presented more than a quarter-century earlier by the National Commission on Resources for Youth (1975), wherein youth participation was seen as:

involving youth in responsible, challenging action, that meets genuine needs, with opportunity for planning and/or decision making affecting others, in an activity whose impact or consequences extend to others, i.e., outside or beyond the youth themselves. (p. 25)

In the context of this conception, youth participation is a core component of civil society (Camino & Zeldin, 2002). As stressed by Wheeler (2003), "Participating as civic activists often becomes the path or gateway to a lifetime of public service" (p. 495).

Skelton, Boyte, and Leonard (2002) agree. They point out that since the mid-1990s there has been a growing awareness "of the need to stress more public and political dimensions of youth civic engagement" (p. 9). Skelton et al. (2002) note that there are four indicators of this emerging stress on the civic contributions made through youth participation. These dimensions of youth civic engagement include

1. The recognition that youth are not future citizens but are citizens in the here and now;

2. The idea that young people do not just engage in individual volunteering but instead are collaborators within a diverse community of engaged citizens;

3. The provision that youth engage in the actual work of contributing to the enhancement of society; and

4. The development within a young person of not only civic values but of skills and capacities pertinent to contributing to civil society as well.

Skelton et al. (2002) indicate that these skills and capacities include "taking responsibility for decisions and choices; learning to speak publicly; the capacity to thoughtfully listen; and working as a team with a diverse group" (p. 9). Skelton et al. (2002) contend that when a young person develops such skills, that person will "discover how he or she fits into and shapes a flourishing democratic society" (p. 9).

Such discovery might be a key contributor to engaging a young person more actively in the individual ← → context relations that are integral to the adaptive developmental regulations that the present theory of positive youth development sees as the basis of youth thriving and of the maintenance and perpetuation of civil society. There is growing evidence that such youth civic engagement activities are associated with lower probabilities of problem behaviors, with higher probabilities of behaviors associated with the Five Cs, and with contributions associated with the Sixth C of contributions to self, others, and institutions that support the adaptive functioning of both levels of the individual ← → context relationship (e g , Sherrod, Flanagan, & Youniss, 2002b; Zaff & Michelsen, 2002).

Nevertheless, this evidence must be regarded as preliminary and in need of enhanced methodological refinement. For example, as noted about other areas of scholarship associated with the study of positive youth development (e.g., the studies linking the assets associated with youth religiosity and positive youth development; Bridges & Moore, 2002; King, in press), there is a need for enhanced, *theory-guided* measures of indicators of such development, and for the use of these indicators within longitudinal research that assesses the links between changes in youth participation and self and context contributions.

Despite the limitations of extant data, the available information about youth participation and contributions to, or civic engagement with, the society within which they are embedded indicates that participation in community-based programs is associated with a higher probability of involvement in school, high school graduation, possession of positive attitudes about civic engagements, and with a lower probability of teenage pregnancy and drug use (Zaff & Michelsen, 2002). In addition, and consistent with my theory about positive youth development, and especially with the idea that thriving youth are on a developmental course toward becoming "ideal adults"—that is, adults involved in individual $\leftarrow \rightarrow$ context contributions—being civically engaged during one's adolescence is associated with undertaking comparable activities in adulthood (Zaff & Michelsen, 2002).

Underscoring the importance of the family in promoting such positive development, Zaff and Michelsen (2002) note that parents influence the civic engagement of their adolescents by serving as role models and by rewarding youth volunteerism. Such influences may be effective. Although youth voting is low, their volunteerism rates are at a historically high level (McLeod, 2000).

Of course, there is variation in the opportunities that youth have for becoming civically engaged. For instance, urban youth have less civic knowledge and lower rates of civic engagement than do suburban youth, due primarily to demographic influences beyond their immediate control (Hart & Atkins, 2002). For instance, Hart and Atkins (2002) note that obstacles to urban youth civic engagement include the presence in the communities within which young urban youth live of adult populations who are less likely to vote than is the case for suburban adolescents; *and,* as a consequence, there is a lessened probability that urban young people will have adult role models for civic participation. In addition, urban schools are less likely to possess the curricular and extracurricular resources needed to imbue youth with the academic and civic skills necessary for civic engagement (Hart & Atkins, 2002).

Accordingly, as both Gore (2003) and Benson (2003b) have emphasized, community-building efforts to engage all young people as leaders of civil society are critically needed both to enhance American democracy across generations and to ensure that future generations of our nation's citizens have the positive personal and civic attributes required to lead healthy individual and social lives. It is vital, then, to ask how might civic engagement of youth be furthered.

Following O'Connell (1999), Camino and Zeldin (2002) note that there are at least five pathways of experience through which young people may become civically engaged:

1. Young people may become involved in public policy discussions and/or consult to organizations or groups involved in such discussions.

2. Youth may participate in community coalitions organized to address some issue of community concern.

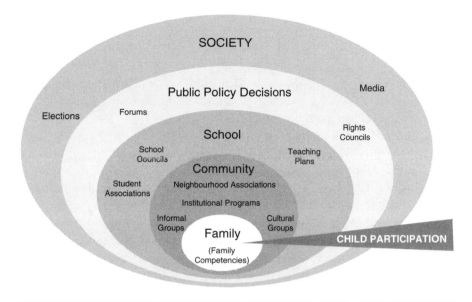

Figure 6.7   As children grow and develop, their opportunities expand from private to public spaces, and from local to global influence.

SOURCE: United Nations Children's Fund (2002). Adapted from R. Nim's PowerPoint presentation at UNICEF's Global Lifestyles Workshop in Salvador (Bahai), Brazil, June 2002.

3. Young people may be part of the decision-making body of an organization (e.g., the National 4-H Council has about one dozen youth members of its Board of Directors; see www.fourhcouncil.edu).

4. Youth may organize and/or become activists in social movements, and

5. Young people may participate in school-based service-learning or community-based learning programs (Kenny, Simon, Brabeck, & Lerner, 2002; Smith et al., in press).

An analogous model of youth participation had been forwarded by the United Nations Children's Fund (UNICEF) in 2002. As shown in Figure 6.7, the opportunities for youth participation are envisioned to expand from private to public arenas, and to change from having local to (potentially) global impacts, as young people develop. The leaders of UNICEF (2002) believe that such growth in youth participation is vital for the expansion of democracy around the world. The UNICEF report, *The*

State of the World's Children 2003 cites Article 12 of the United Nations' Convention on the Rights of the Child in asserting that:

> States parties shall assure to the child who is capable of forming his or her own views the right to express those views freely in all matters affecting the child, the views of the child being given due weight in accordance with the age and maturity of the child. (p. 15)

At this writing, the only two nations in the world who have not ratified this United Nations convention are the United States and Somalia. Somalia does not have a government in place that can provide such ratification. This situation is not the case for the United States of America.

Camino and Zeldin (2002) explain that the effectiveness for positive youth development of the pathways that exist for becoming civically engaged may be enhanced in several ways. These enhancements occur:

1. When youth take "ownership" of their participation—i.e., consistent with the developmental systems theory notion that individuals are producers of their own development (R. M. Lerner, 1982; R. M. Lerner, Theokas, & Jelicic, in press)—the young person shapes his or her role, instead of having it "given" to or imposed on him or her;

2. When civic engagement occurs within the context of healthy and sustained youth–adult partnerships (i.e., when, as in the 4-H model of youth programming, this instance of the Big Three design features of effective youth programs occurs); and

3. When youth civic engagement is facilitated by supportive social and institutional polices (e.g., when, as we have noted with the National 4-H Council, a policy of the organization is to include a critical mass of youth leaders in its leadership, in this case on the Board of Directors; see www.fourhcouncil.edu).

Youthbuild USA as an Exemplar of a Program Promoting Civic Engagement and Community Leadership

YouthBuild USA may be seen as an exemplar of how the combination of these three enhancement strategies not only promotes youth civic engagement but, as well, serves as a means to overcome negative attitudes about young people that may exist in society—for example, attitudes predicated on the deficit model of youth and the notion that young people are problems to be managed (Roth et al., 1998). Stoneman (2002) explains how YouthBuild USA programs—which involve young people in reconstructing dilapidated housing in their communities and participating in professional development, educational, and civic leadership activities—illustrate that youth programs:

> can go far beyond community service without treading down partisan paths. Through involvement in (a) project creation, (b) institution governance, and (c) issue-based advocacy, the energy young people often waste in powerlessness, boredom, and drifting can be unleashed and reinvested in more constructive activities. (p. 221)

Stoneman (2002) has found that all three of these activities are of great interest to young people, especially when presented as leadership development and not civic engagement or civic education. She explains that she has learned that this frame is useful because:

1. It is inherently more interesting to most young people to wonder if they might become leaders than to think of simply being a good citizen.

2. Society needs more ethical and effective leaders at all levels.

3. Every youth program and school would itself be improved if governed with real input from young people; governance is a leadership role.

4. The challenge of leadership roles can engage young people intensely and deeply, liberating their best energies.

5. Real decision-making responsibility can heal two very deep wounds of young people of all backgrounds: (a) low self-esteem due to consistent invalidation of their intelligence; (b) feelings of powerlessness, and its companion anger, due to being raised in a thoroughly adult-dominated world that has not listened to the ideas of young people. (Stoneman, 2002, p. 222)

Stoneman's (2002) vision for addressing the problems inflicted by disenfranchisement by increasing youth empowerment echoes the sentiments of other current and past people working to enhance the lives of America's youth. For instance, Stoneman's (2002) views and those of former Vice President Al Gore (2003) are consonant, in that Gore has observed that:

> Too many young people and families are isolated and feel disconnected. They are disengaged from the civic life of their neighborhoods and communities. They do not have access to the kinds of formal and informal supports they need, not only in times of crisis, but also as a source of strength and nurturance in daily life. One result is that too many young people grow up

without the kinds of opportunities, relationships, and guidance that they need
to become and remain engaged and productive members of our society. (p. vii)

Stoneman's (2002) perspective is also in agreement with the view of
Jane Addams (1910) presented almost a century earlier. Addams, also concerned about the absence of opportunities for youth to contribute to the
social world, noted that "the sense of uselessness (we see today among so
many young people) is the severest shock which the human system can
sustain. If persistently sustained, it results in the atrophy of function"
(Addams, 1910, p. 120). Addams was writing within the early years of the
emergence of the deficit model of youth development (cf. Hall, 1904).
Given that the problems of youth disfranchisement both for young people
and for civil society are comparably identified by both Stoneman (2002)
and Addams (1910), although their statements are separated by almost a
century, we may hope that historians of developmental science will report
that Stoneman's (2002) essay was written during the waning years of the
deficit model.

The development of leaders of our civil society is critical not only
because it will enhance the quality of a young person's individual development but, as Stoneman (2002) suggests, our nation's democracy will
prosper when each person takes an active role in maintaining and extend-
ing the institutions of civil society. Indeed, such leadership is a prime
illustration of the adaptive individual ← → context relation that defines a
thriving young person.

Sherrod, Flanagan, and Youniss (2002b) underscore the importance of
the development of such individual leadership for civil society. They
note that whereas many youth define citizenship as good behavior
(e.g., obeying the law and acting in normatively expected ways), and
while ideological and behavioral commitment to the rule of law is a
necessary component of democratic governance, such commitment is
not sufficient for democracy to flourish (Sherrod et al., 2002b). They
explain that:

A society that is "ruled by people" also depends on citizens who make
informed judgments, who at times object to policies and even (as in many
movements for social justice) disobey unjust laws. Good behavior may be
one aspect of citizenship, but so is activism or taking action to improve the
nation state, which is frequently not considered good behavior. The exercise
of good judgment, as a component of citizenship, involves assessing when
behavior is needed to maintain the status quo and when it is necessary to
take action to change it. (p. 265)

As noted in Chapter 5, such judgment is also an instance of the reciprocal, individual ← → context relations that are requisite for maintaining and enhancing healthy individual development and civil society.

Developing Civically Engaged, Contributing Youth

Sherrod et al. (2002b) note that new developmental research is needed to understand how young people change across the adolescent years regarding the productive and positive emergence of the Sixth C of contribution. For instance, how do youth change from regarding citizenship as obedience and support of the status quo (e.g., as reflecting, for instance, Kohlberg's [1978] "social order and institutional maintenance" stage of moral reasoning) to recognizing that it is incumbent on a citizen to be a reflective evaluator of and active contributor to civil society and community and national governance (Sherrod et al., 2002b)? Such a change involves becoming a leader of society (Stoneman, 2002), a person critically judging the policies and laws of his or her government, and understanding that responsible civic action involves not reflexive agreement with the dictates of any administration but rather acting to extend social justice and equity to all individuals (Sherrod et al., 2002b).

In addition, Sherrod et al. (2002b) indicate that several other questions about the development of civic engagement among youth remain largely unaddressed. For instance, at what periods within development may actions in support of promoting the Sixth C be optimal? Are there particular settings within which the promotion of civic engagement and of contributions to self, family, community, and civil society may be maximized (e.g., school governance, community coalitions, and so on)? Are there particular groups of youth who are most likely to gain from civic engagement programs? In turn, how may the diversity of young people that constitute America be reached?

The research called for by Sherrod et al. (2002b) may be usefully framed by the theoretical model of positive youth development I propose. Such scholarship would be consistent with what appears to be a growing consensus in the field of youth development about the orientation to youth, and to the community-based actions that surround them, needed to promote positive development. That is, my theoretical model emphasizes that youth may act as producers of their own positive development and that, in such circumstances, they will be engaged in mutually beneficial individual ← → context relations with their communities. These ideas are foundations of the currently understood "best practices" in positive youth development programs, in that, as exemplified by both 4-H and YouthBuild USA, effective youth-serving programs foster youth leadership and the enactment of meaningful behaviors (valued skills) by youth within a positive context (involving, centrally, a positive adult–youth relationship).

The connection between youth program best practice and the theoretical ideas that lead to the emphasis on young people as active producers of their own healthy development may be illustrated by the principles of "vital practice for youth and civic development" articulated at a 1996 Wingspread Conference (Skelton et al., 2002). These principles state that:

1. Young people are producers.

2. Young people's intelligence, talents, experience and energy deserve respect.

3. Public work and skill building link together.

4. Young people participate in governance.

5. Young people and adults develop committed, reciprocal relationships.

6. Cooperative action is valued.

7. Young people's public work is visible.

8. Young people's efforts connect with the large civic challenges and questions of meaning in our time.

9. Youth work contributes to community and institutional change. (Wingspread Conference, 1996)

Global Extensions of the Principles of Civic Engagement and Positive Youth Development: Contributions of the International Youth Foundation

The use of the principles of civic engagement and positive youth development forwarded at the Wingspread Conference (1996) is found increasingly in youth-serving programs around the world. Most notably, they are present in the programs offered by the approximately 60 different international partners of the International Youth Foundation (e.g., Kinkade, 2002; Little, 1993; Reese & Thorup, 2003). Reflecting an integrated commitment to these principles underlying the development of civically engaged and positively developing youth, Reese and Thorup (2003, p. 53) note that the mission of the International Youth Foundation

(IYF) is to positively impact the greatest number of young people in as many places as possible, in the shortest amount of time possible, with programs that are effective and in ways that are sustainable; they explain that in order to best pursue this mission, IYF:

> focuses on the ways in which young people can improve their own conditions . . . in which they live. Youth are viewed as protagonists rather than as passive recipients of assistance and as doers rather than as victims of difficult circumstances. IYF and its global network of national, independent nonprofit youth organizations carry out activities in over 60 countries. (pp. 53–54)

Moreover, and reflecting the integrated, developmental systems approach to promoting positive youth development involved in my theory, Reese and Thorup (2003) explain that "IYF emphasizes positive, holistic youth development strategies" (p. 53), including ones that link collaboratively all sectors of society that do—or should—invest in efforts that promote empowered young people to contribute actively and positively to civil society. In explaining the importance of such intersectorial partnering (ISP), Reese and Thorup (2003) extend the set of research issues that were specified by Sherrod et al. (2002b), explaining that:

> ISP is a rapidly changing development strategy, just as youth development is a rapidly changing development field. A key task for social scientists engaged in development work is to deepen their understanding—both qualitatively and quantitatively—of the real benefits and challenges of this approach on global, national, and local levels. (Reese & Thorup, 2003, p. 81)

Conclusions

Despite the clear articulation of the importance of pursuing the research programs called for by Sherrod et al. (2002b) and by Reese and Thorup (2003), youth development scholarship is not yet at a level of productivity to document fully the immediate and long-term outcomes for healthy adolescent and adult development and for civil society of the development of the Sixth C of positive youth development. In addition, despite the growing acceptance of the principles of best practice in programs involving youth participation, leadership, and civic engagement, there have been few translations of these program features into policies that will expand and sustain these actions in support of the positive development, leadership, and contributions of youth.

The research agenda suggested by Sherrod et al. (2002b) and by Reese and Thorup (2003) is complex and assuredly expensive (e.g., the research will require long-term, longitudinal studies of diverse youth and, as such, will involve large groups of young people and the sustained efforts of researchers over the course of several years). Moreover, we have noted that such research will require the development and use of new measures of positive youth development, ones predicated on interest in the presence and growth of the strengths of young people (and not on presence and decrease of problems or deficits). Nevertheless, while such research is challenging, it can be conducted within the context of what is fairly general agreement among developmental scientists about the features that define excellent research design, high quality measurement, and appropriate statistical analyses (e.g., Baltes, Reese, & Nesselroade, 1977; Lerner, in press; McArdle & Nesselroade, 2003; Teti, in press).

However, there is not a comparable degree of consensus in the domain of policy. Of course, perhaps there should not be, since the domains of science and of social values and public policies are qualitatively distinct areas of human life. In addition, whereas researchers would be oriented to move toward agreement about the methods that qualify as good science, citizens may want to maintain a range of viable policy options within society in order to keep democracy vibrant and open for improvement. Nevertheless, just as one might ask a developmental researcher to present the range of theories and methods that might be forwarded to address the study of positive youth development, it is legitimate to ask what are the range of policy ideas that may be useful to put forward to promote positive youth development and contributions by young people to mutually beneficial exchanges between them and their social world. While the list of policy options might not be, and perhaps should not ever be, as complete as the one about scientific methods, it is necessary for such policy options to be detailed if Americans want to promote positive development and civic contributions among all youth and to sustain these efforts across generations. Issues pertinent to developing a national policy for the promotion of positive youth development are discussed in the next chapter.

7

Policies Promoting Positive Youth Development and Civil Society

America is the only Western industrialized nation that does not have a national youth policy (Benson et al., 2004; Hahn, 1994). However, if we value youth as "ends" in themselves, as humans inherently deserving of the best support that can be given them by their society, and if we wish to promote the thriving youth ← → civil society relations upon which liberty rests and the future of American democracy depends, we will create a national policy aimed at promoting positive young development for current and all future generations.

The theory of dynamic, person ← → context relations I have presented in prior chapters provides a model for the general structure of policies that would promote both positive youth development and civil society, that is, the thriving youth ← → civil society relation. The model is predicated on the idea that the plasticity of youth development constitutes a basic strength in all young people; plasticity constitutes a potential for systematic change, and if the strengths of young people are appropriately supported, they may develop in positive directions. The model suggests as well that appropriate support for youth provides the developmental assets needed for furthering their healthy, indeed exemplary, development. Simply, developmental assets are the nutrients for positive development; providing them to young people fosters youth thriving. I have explained how these assets may be developed through three "big" actions associated with programs that are effective in promoting positive youth development: providing youth with positive and supportive relationships

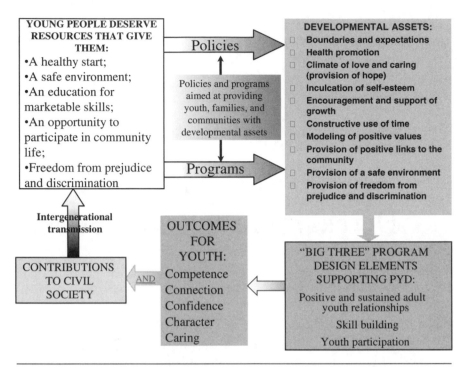

Figure 7.1   When families and communities provide developmental assets to youth in the context of three key components of effective youth programs, positive youth development along a pathway to healthy adulthood results in contributions to self, family and community, and civil society.

with adults; affording youth with opportunities to build the skills needed to make productive contributions to self, family, community, and civil society; and providing youth with opportunities to be civically engaged and to take leadership roles in enacting skills and in making contributions to their communities. I have argued also (and illustrated in Figure 5.1) that when youth develop within families and communities that provide these important assets for positive development, they will thrive during their adolescence. They will be on a developmental path toward an ideal adult status, a status marked by productive contributions to self and others and to the institutions of civil society.

As illustrated in Figure 7.1, youth developing in this manner manifest the Five Cs of positive youth development discussed earlier in the book— competence, connection, character, confidence, and caring (or compassion).

As I noted in Chapter 6, these Cs may be best thought of as clusters of individual attributes; for example, intellectual ability and social and behavioral skills (competence); positive bonds with people and institutions (connection); integrity, moral centeredness, and spirituality (character); positive self-regard, a sense of self-efficacy, and courage (confidence); and humane values, empathy, and a sense of social justice (caring and compassion; Roth & Brooks-Gunn, 2003a). When these five sets of outcomes are developed, civil society is enhanced as a consequence of young people becoming adults who are morally and civically committed to providing the assets they received to succeeding generations. The intergenerational maintenance of this developmental system will assure that America is populated by citizens who are committed to and capable of protecting and advancing liberty.

How does one move from the general model for youth policy illustrated in Figure 7.1 to having actual policies in place? At least four interrelated sets of actions need to be taken:

1. We need to articulate the principles that should guide our specification of the policies that will be derived from our vision of positive youth development and, more concretely, from our theoretical model.

2. We need to develop a set or sets of specific policies that may be derived from our model.

3. We need to devise strategies for translating our vision and policy ideas into effective actions.

4. We need to take action; we need to become active participants in the political process within our democracy.

While this chapter will end with an appeal for the fourth step, the major foci of the chapter will be on the first three types of action.

Principles for Policies Promoting Positive Youth Development

There are three key principles suggested by my theory of positive youth development. Any policy pertinent to young people must be predicated on the first two: (1) that strengths are present among *all* young people; and (2) that there exists the potential to enhance this strength through supporting their healthy development. In other words, policies must be developmental and positive in their orientation to young people. Accordingly, youth deficits and their prevention should be placed on the back burner of the policymaking agenda, and focus should be given to how we can, at each point in the young person's life, find age-appropriate ways to support his or her positive development by building on specific sets of strengths.

Benson et al. (2004) agree with this perspective. They note that public policies for youth need to be sensitive to the development status and pathways of youth, and policies must reflect the tenets of theory and practice that define the positive youth development perspective. For example, policies that are useful for building skills in elementary school-age children (e.g., basic literacy abilities in language, science, civics, mathematics, and health) may not be appropriate for youth in the midst of adolescence (who may need to possess advanced skills in these domains and who may be actively using these skills in interpersonal situations—for instance, dating) in part-time employment positions, and in service in their communities), or for older youth who are contemplating the transition from high school to work or military service (e.g., see Hamilton & Hamilton, 2004).

Accordingly, Benson et al. (2004) indicate that if policies for youth are both to be developmentally appropriate and embrace the cutting edge of science and practice of the field of positive youth development, then:

1. Public policies for youth must move beyond negative outcomes and academic success to encompass both positive and non-academic outcomes.

2. Policies should encompass both children and adolescents, echoing Search Institute's encouragement of thinking about the development of young people across the first two decades of life in a more seamless way.

3. Policies should ensure that a broad range of services, supports, and opportunities are available to young people.

4. The voices and actions of young people as agents of positive change should be prominently featured in social policy.

A third principle of policy design associated with my theory of positive youth development focuses policy on the dynamic relation between the developing youth and his or her context, on the individual ← → context relation, and not on person or context per se. If adaptive human development involves reciprocal links between the engaged and active individual and his or her supportive and changing context, then policies should be focused on strengthening these relations. Simply, to produce and further the thriving youth ← → civil society relations upon which liberty is predicated, policies must be directed to these relations.

Focusing on the young person without attending to his development within a specific family, community, and cultural context will fail to improve his development; such focus will not be sensitive to the specific individual ← → context relations (the specific child effects discussed in Chapter 3) elicited by the person's and the setting's characteristics of individuality. Focusing on the context without attention to the developmental attributes of the growing individual also will fail to improve her development; such focus is not likely to have a better than random chance of attaining a goodness of fit (again see Chapter 3) with her characteristics of individuality and developmental status.

While it is of course the case that a particular policy may seem to be situated logically at the level of either individual or context, this third principle indicates that this focus may be more apparent than real. The education of children and adolescents may serve as an example. Enhancing the knowledge or literacy skills of youth per se is not really the goal of education, especially education financed by public dollars. Rather, the goal of education is to enhance the probability that our young people will become more competent and confident individuals, that they will use their knowledge to become people able to make valued contributions to their lives and to the lives of others. Education serves active citizenship, and, in turn, education for active citizenship should become a core ubiquitous feature of all of American education. In other words, the goal of education is *not* to make a child competent for the sake of possessing a competency, but rather to enable the child to be engaged with society in the exercise of his or her competency. Through education we should seek to increase the probability that individuals will become contributing members of society, productive agents within the thriving youth ← → civil society relation.

To illustrate the problems associated with policies directed not to the individual ← → context relation but rather to one or the other component of this relation, we may consider the nature of family policies in the United States (R. M. Lerner, Sparks, & McCubbin, 1999). The discussion in Chapter 2 of the evolutionary heritage of humans indicated that the healthy rearing of children is the essential function of the family (see too Bowman & Spanier, 1978; R. M. Lerner & Spanier, 1980). However, family policy is not isomorphic with child or youth policy.

For example, family policies may involve aged adults living in retirement and without children or grandchildren. Moreover, many policies and the programs associated with them (e.g., Aid for Dependent Children, AFDC; or the Personal Responsibility and Work Opportunity Reconciliation Act, PRWORA), even when having the avowed interest of impacting children within the family positively, are directed to parents. Such policies Policies do not take a multigenerational approach that provides either (1) independent actions aimed at enhancing directly the lives of both parents and children; or, more preferable in my view, (2) actions directed to enhancing the child ← → parent (family) relation, that is, actions that promote positive development of the family system (e.g., see Corbett, 1995; Huston, 1991; Morelli & Verhoef, 1999; Tout & Zaslow, 2003; Zaslow et al., 1998).

As such, while past or current family policies may influence the financial status of the family, they may not readily impact on, and certainly they fail to emphasize, youth development. That is, these policies do not focus directly on the enhancement of the capacities and the potentials of America's children and adolescents. For instance, a policy or program that provides a job for an unemployed single mother, but results in the placement of her adolescent child in an inadequate after-school care environment for extended periods of time, may enhance the financial resources of the family; however, it may do so at the cost of placing the child in an unstimulating and possibly detrimental environment (R. M. Lerner, Sparks, & McCubbin, 1999).

In sum, there are at least three essential principles for policy design legitimated by my theory of positive development: (1) Policies must take a strength-based approach to youth; (2) policies should be developmental in nature; and (3) policies should focus on (have as their target or unit of analysis) the individual ← → context relation.

When these three principles are translated into ideas for specific policies, they result in the formulation of a set of ideas that engage the breadth of the developmental system involved in promoting positive youth development. They integrate the developing young person, his or her family, the community, and all facets of civil society in the active promotion of positive youth development and, ideally, in producing the thriving youth ← → civil society relation.

The clearest and most complete formulation to date of such a policy agenda is found in Al Gore's (2003; Gore & Gore, 2002) vision of family-centered community building for youth. Accordingly, I focus on Gore's conception of a policy agenda for youth as a means to illustrate the second step required in developing a national policy for youth, that is, proposing a specific set of policy actions that may be derived from theory and that are consistent with the theory-derived principles I have just discussed.

Family-Centered Community Building for Youth

How may a nation pursue the ideas for liberty derived from humans' evolutionary heritage and from the nature of humans' development across life? How can we build communities in our nation that integrate healthy, thriving young people and the institutions of civil society in mutually beneficial ways, ways that link citizenship, civic engagement, and moral commitment together to foster the development of young people into adults who are committed to make positive contributions to self, family, community, and national and global civil society?

In many ways, the discussions across this book have been directed to answering these questions. As such, I have argued that:

1. To sustain the individual and societal benefits of mutually beneficial person-context relations (adaptive developmental regulations), families and communities must promote

2. A moral orientation among youth, that is, an orientation that good is created through a commitment to act to build the institutions of civil society— to construct the ecological "space" for individual citizens to promote in their communities institutions of social justice, equity, and democracy; and therefore that

3. It is critical to align public policies and community actions (e.g., community-based, youth serving programs) in support of the development of such an integrated moral and civic identity.

These ideas are instantiated in an approach to community building envisioned by former Vice President Al Gore. Gore (e.g., 2003; Gore & Gore, 2002) believes that our nation can create a developmental system across generations that builds integrated moral and civic identities in its citizens and that such citizens will be able to sustain and to enhance the institutions of civil society. To create this socially just developmental system, Gore indicates that policies should be developed to enhance in communities the capacities of families to provide the child with the resources needed for his or her positive development, for example, with the developmental assets suggested by Search Institute (Benson, 1997, 2003b).

Gore's (2003; Gore & Gore, 2002) conception of family-centered community building for youth grew out of a conviction about the urgency of "bringing to a renewed level of innovation and energy . . . issues of family and human development—what I call family-centered community building" (Gore, 2003, p. vii). To provide this contribution to policy, Gore proposes a model predicated on the belief that all people should value all young people and, as well, that current social and economic circumstances require community-based efforts in support of this value. In this context, Gore contends that policy should be predicated on the fact that:

> It's neither sufficient nor fair to tell overwhelmed parents that they are solely responsible for building community and doing more for their children. Instead, it is our *shared* task to address more fundamental, systemic questions: Are communities organized in ways that support—rather than thwart—family and human development? Are community policies and institutions accessible to and trusted by families? What kinds of fundamental changes in community life must occur in order to surround families and their children with the relationships, opportunities, and supports they need to thrive? (Gore, 2003, p. vii)

In answer to these questions, Gore formulated the family-centered community building approach to the development of policies and institutions that will be valued and available to families and the young people they are nurturing. He defines this orientation to policy by specifying that:

> To address the primary family and human development issues facing our nation, the family-centered community building approach considers strategies that invest in the human and social capital of a community as well as its productive capacity. These include a range of different strategies that enhance services supporting families, youth development, family education, and parenting and skill-building activities. Family-centered community building also looks at how communities create environmental, social, and educational conditions that enhance individual relationships within families and family relationships within the community. (Gore, 2002, p. viii)

Consistent with the developmental systems idea that the young person plays an active role in his or her own development (see Chapter 3), and with the centrality of the individual ← → context relation in promoting positive youth development (see Chapter 5), Gore underscores the vital role of youth participation and civic leadership in enhancing the healthy development of young people and their communities. He notes that:

Ultimately, building the assets for positive youth development ... will require engaging the human and ecological system in a manner that promotes new leadership in our nation. In particular, for family-centered community building to be sustainable, the key community members among whom leadership must be encouraged are our young people. Empowering youth assures that family-centered community building is done *with* the community and not *for* the community. It also increases the extent to which sustainable change improves the capacities and life chances of all youth and families, and ensures a legacy of contributions to civil society that will enrich all of America for generations to come. (Gore, 2003, p. viii)

In essence, then, Gore (2003) explains that the focus of family-centered community building for youth is on the promotion of positive youth development through enhancing the quality and quantity in communities of the mutually beneficial individual ← → context relations emphasized in my theory of positive youth development. To illustrate this relation, I note that Gore and Gore (2002) indicate that:

The first and most important step our country can take to help families is to change our way of *thinking* about families. . . . Specifically, what's required is a shift from focusing exclusively on the individual to focusing on the family as a complex system, a system whose essential meaning is found in the relationships among the individuals who are connected emotionally and committed to one another as family—those who are, as we have put it here, joined at the heart. (p. 327)

The general policy and program actions illustrated in Figure 7.1 reflect this congruence between my theory and Gore's conception of family-centered community building for youth. This congruence is reflected also in the bottom right-hand quadrants of both Table 4.1 and Table 4.2. Together, the figure and the tables suggest that, to design policies that are consistent with the principles I have derived from my theory of positive youth development, and that Gore (2003) has suggested are involved in the family-centered community building approach to policy, we need to take actions that advance liberty by promoting thriving youth ← → civil society relations. In accordance with my theory, these relations should be marked by:

- Equity, social justice, and equal opportunity
- Sensitivity to individual differences and promotion of a goodness of fit between individually different people and contexts
- Affirmative actions to correct ontogenetic or historical inequities in person–context fit

- Efforts to recognize and celebrate diversity
- Promotion of universal participation in civic life, and hence
- Democracy

The social system that would be created by such community-building policies reflects liberty. It is the operationalization of the idea of America.

A Sample of Policy Proposals

What are the specific policies that reflect these design features and, as well, the principles for policy derived from my theory of positive youth development? It is not feasible to answer this question exhaustively. However, it is possible to illustrate how, pursuant to these principles and design ideas, policies reflecting equity and social justice, which may be instantiated in several key areas of youth development, may promote thriving youth ← → civil society relations.

Going to Scale With Social Programs

A key implication of the policy principles discussed is that, to assure equality of opportunity in life, all programs that are effective in promoting positive youth development need to be supported with resources and systems that enable access to these programs for all youth who need them. Early Intervention programs, Head Start programs, after-school programs, universal health care, and disability services are examples of program domains whose reach (*scale*) needs to be enhanced.

Variations in ways to access such programs, and individuals' treatment by service providers, must not be hidden screening devices that decrease people's ability to use a program. Not only should social services be integrated in all localities, but transportation and child care systems should be coordinated with families to enable people to reach and use programs that are potentially available to them.

Promoting Positive Life Trajectories Through Education

Certainly, the most important opportunity a person has to enhance his or her life chances, to actualize potential, interests, and goals, is to gain knowledge and skills through education. Obviously, and with little disagreement across the political spectrum, high-quality K–12 education must be assured for all children and adolescents in America. As noted by Gore and Gore (2002):

> At the community level, our most important task may be providing meaningful reform of public education for families with children, including changes in local governance and state financing—backed up by a commitment of adequate federal resources to make the improvements real. (p. 332)

To accomplish this goal, greater investment must be made not only in the physical plants of schools and in the technological enhancement of classrooms but in the enhancement of teachers' salaries as well, and by according the teaching profession the respect, status, and gratitude it merits.

However, these necessary educational investments are not sufficient. We must extend universal K–12 education to universal K–16 education. America must assure all young people, and all families, that the opportunities in life available to people trained through a college education will be available to all citizens. In turn, getting children to the threshold of kindergarten ready to learn requires making high-quality child care available to all children and families and, as well, involves affording to child care providers and preschool teachers the same salaries and social regard that should be accorded to K–12 teachers.

Moreover, both as a possible adjunct of or as an alternative to K–16 education, youth should be afforded apprenticeship experiences (Hamilton & Hamilton, 1999, 2004). Here, coordination between classroom instruction and *in vivo* work site or professional experiences can both facilitate the school-to-work transition of young people and assure that business and industry have cohorts of better prepared employees ready to enter and contribute productively to the work force of America.

In addition, out-of-school learning and informal education constitute contexts wherein millions of young people spend many hours each day and week (Villarruel & Lerner, 1994). High-quality community-based programs for out-of-school learning enhance the education of young people—in both traditional academic domains (e.g., through homework programs) and in arenas of citizenship and leadership (e.g., through service learning programs, volunteerism opportunities, or community-based learning) (Bergstrom, 1984, 1995; Smith et al., in press). In addition, by providing young people with high-quality, stimulating, and safe contexts during the non-school hours, these programs support family life, since in many families parents are still at work when their children leave school.

As such, the programs of these community-based organizations (CBOs) are another means for community building for families and for integrating community assets to promote thriving among youth. Moreover, as with K–12 and preschool teachers and child care providers, the youth-serving professionals who work in these CBOs should be given the salaries and social regard they merit. Indeed, creating a new professional specialization—a community youth development professional— should become a priority goal of policymakers who want to recognize the valuable contributions these practitioners make to youth, families, and communities.

Of course, learning is a life-span challenge, and the opportunity to learn should be accorded to people across their lives. Workers and professionals who are retooling, and retired citizens interested in either enriching their lives or in gaining skills to make new contributions to civil society should be given opportunities to make these contributions. In a nation where positive youth development rests in part on positive and healthy adult ← → youth relations, enhancing the productivity and civic engagement of adult and aged citizens may enhance the probability of adults being willing and able to engage young people in positive relations.

One group in particular should be given these learning resources: parents who are making the transition from welfare to work. Welfare-reform initiatives across the states should take seriously the need to invest in real education and job training for parents making this transition. The criterion for these efforts should be that the initiatives maximize education for marketable skills (R. M. Lerner, Fisher, & Weinberg, 2000).

Affording Equity and Social Justice

A pillar of the idea of America is the equality of all people under God and under our laws. While equality of educational opportunity may be a superb means to further this idea, there are other important means as well.

The developmental system is marked by its temporal embeddedness, a link to history that affords humans the ability to change (i.e., that provides a basis for their plasticity). It is antithetical to a system pursuing liberty, therefore, either to deny the inequities of history or to allow to remain invisible contemporary differential opportunities or rights based on race, religion, ethnicity, sexual preferences, disability status, or other characteristics of diversity that are present among America's youth.

Accordingly, equality of opportunity and treatment must be enshrined in policies that ensure level playing fields for all. Affirmative action, the equality of rights and opportunities for gay, lesbian, and bisexual youth, disability laws, and equal treatment of people whether they are married or single are important instances of the means through which social justice can be instantiated (Diamond & Savin-Williams, 2003; Savin-Williams & Diamond, 2004; Helms, 2004; Wheeler, 2003). America's young people are not only able to be represented by their age level. They may also be represented by their other characteristics of diversity. These characteristics are vital parts of their identities (e.g., Diamond & Savin-Williams, 2003; Savin-Williams & Diamond, 2004; Helms, 2003, Wheeler, 2003). Affording social justice to every American youth requires recognition and support of the importance of how any or all of these characteristics of individuality may create a positive sense of self.

The respect for diversity and the accordance of equal opportunities to all has another side to it. Equality before the law does not mean that individual differences should not be taken into account when applying the law to citizens. For instance, America as a nation needs to decide if the punishments given to adults for the violation of criminal laws by adults should apply to children or to disabled (e.g., mentally retarded) individuals. From the point of view of young people as assets to be developed that is inherent in a developmental systems approach to thriving, children should never be tried as adults or given adult punishments (Scott & Woolard, 2004; Steinberg, 2002). Similarly, a person mentally incapable of understanding the nature of his or her acts should not be imprisoned or, especially, executed for them (Scott & Woolard, 2004; Steinberg, 2002).

States within our nation vary in their stances regarding the nature of punishment for the commission of crimes by children or by the mentally disabled (Scott & Woolard, 2004; Steinberg, 2002). A national discussion is needed about how we can treat all American children and mentally disabled citizens in ways that respect the nature of their developmental status and capacities.

Protecting the Social Good

Policies should not only afford individuals rights. They should also structure young people's responsibilities as citizens. Policies should help all institutions of society contribute to the quality of life in communities and across the nation. No one person, interest group, or organization should abrogate unto themselves the right to take actions that infringe on others' freedoms or opportunities to live a positive, healthy life (Wilson, 1993).

From this perspective, then, policy must ensure that the behaviors of interest groups, organizations, or corporations do not impact adversely the personal rights, health, or economic welfare of other individuals or groups. Just as young people's behaviors should be judged in regard to contributions to mutually supportive individual ← → context regulations subserving adaptation and health, so too must lobbying groups, businesses, professions, and political groups be judged in this manner. Accordingly, the protection and preservation of the environment and the ensuring of corporate responsibility and ethics become paramount features of policies that protect liberty.

In addition, policies must not only "protect us from ourselves" but, as emblazoned in our national consciousness as a consequence of September 11, 2001, policies must protect us from others who would attack the United States and act to destroy the idea of America. National security against such aggression, whether in the form of acts of terrorism by a fanatical group of criminals or of acts of war by another nation, must begin within the borders of the nation. There is a twofold challenge here for Americans, however. One is to ensure domestic safety without compromising the civil liberties of any American. Any other stance erodes if not destroys the very liberty enshrined in the idea of America. The other challenge is to ensure domestic peace and tranquility within the context of being an active partner within a global community that seeks to ensure liberty for all people.

Creating Global Citizenship

To ensure liberty through the promotion of thriving youth ← → civil society relations, the goal of America's relations with people of other nations should rest clearly and unequivocally—that is, with no qualifications—on the support of civil society and liberty wherever and whenever possible. To do this we must reorder alliances by sharing resources, expertise, and energy to promote joint defense and strategic planning. We must act as well to promote equitable distribution of resources (e.g., through treaties involving trade, global warming and environmental protection, and energy use), and base our actions on issues of both productivity and use. The goal of such policy revisions is to stabilize democracy now and for future generations.

From a developmental systems theory perspective, the regulations that establish liberty domestically cannot be separated from those that occur in the broader ecology of human development. We cannot advance liberty domestically unless we do so internationally. The promotion of positive youth development and liberty cannot occur in America if democracy, social justice, equity, and freedom are absent in other nations, if there is rampant poverty, unchecked disease, denial of human rights, and environmental degradation across the world. American liberty cannot be sustained within a world system wherein social injustices, seemingly inescapable poverty, and unequal opportunity exist.

Developmental systems theory underscores that in a necessarily integrated global community, liberty will dissipate for all if it is pursued at the cost of allowing social and ecological injustice and inequity to continue in the world. Accordingly, the heritage and duty of America is to keep the light of liberty burning as a beacon for freedom for all of the world. However, to do this, America must use its strength and share its resources to level the playing field for the rest of the world. Simply, America cannot remain a citadel of liberty if poverty, disease, environmental degradation, and injustice reign elsewhere (cf. Reese & Thorup, 2003; Wheeler, 2003).

The developmental system that has resulted in the contingencies between adaptation and mutually beneficial person–context exchanges does not stop at the borders of America. This system embraces all levels of the ecology of human development. In the end, we in America cannot thrive at the expense of the absence or loss of life-sustaining and -rewarding exchanges for individuals in other nations. Ultimately, the only adaptive domestic policy for the United States is one that promotes social justice and equity for all people in the world.

America can, then, be a model for the domestic and international enactment of policies promoting liberty. To serve in this role, America must develop and disseminate instances of its vision for building liberty by supporting the thriving person ← → civil society relationship around the globe. Any action less than this will eventually diminish the opportunity for all people—including all Americans—to live their lives in nations marked by liberty. Our policies and our politicians must commit themselves, then, to enhancing positive youth development globally (cf. Reese & Thorup, 2003).

Making Government a Partner in the Promotion of Youth Thriving ← → Civil Society Relations

As I discuss in greater detail later, in the context of strategies for translating policy ideas into actual policies, there is an important role for government to play in fostering the youth thriving ← → civil society relations that provide the foundation for liberty (cf. Cummings, 2003; Engler & Binsfeld, 1998). As I indicated in Chapter 1, this role is not to create or to orchestrate the operation of the institutions of civil society (O'Connell, 1999). Rather, the proper role of government is to level the playing field for all its young people—to assure equal opportunity within and free access to institutions of civil society. This governmental role is what is meant when we say that America should be a nation "with liberty and justice for all."

Accordingly, a principle that should govern the conduct of government is that, in order to assure adaptive developmental regulations that promote liberty, government must assure that equal opportunities exist for all youth. As a consequence, no governmental impediments should be placed on—and indeed government should facilitate—all young people having the chance to act to maximize their life chances, *as long as these actions do not deny other individuals these same opportunities*. Accordingly, at the same time, youth should be socialized for and given the opportunity to contribute to a civil society that provides these ends and that provides safeguards against the absence or erosion of these opportunities.

Clearly, this view of government stands in contrast to the Social Darwinist-type conception that holds that the proper role of government is to maintain an un-level playing field (cf. Tobach et al., 1974). This position is associated with the contention that differences in location on such a tilted societal plane arise because of differences in proven worth among people or in inherent ability. Such an elitist conception of government, which may be predicated on theories of human development that are antithetical to developmental systems theory (e.g., hereditarian conceptions), would fail to maximize the probability of positive development and thriving among all youth. Such Social Darwinist views are ultimately destructive, both domestically and internationally, of the sustenance of civil society and of creating a global democratic system that is reflective of liberty.

The specific hereditarian ideas discussed and found inadequate in Chapter 4 are reflected in such Social Darwinist thinking, for example, in the flawed ideas involved in human sociobiological theory (e.g., Rushton, 2000; see R. M. Lerner, 2002a, for a critique). In such a view of government, policies—for example, regarding business or corporate responsibility (or, perhaps better, irresponsibility)—accord protection to people's positions not on the basis of their post-birth accomplishments but instead on the basis of a priori differences assigned to people on the basis of racism, classism, sexism, religious intolerance, prejudices about physical ability, or sexual preferences or other lifestyle variations (Tobach et al.,

1974). Such problematic ideas also warrant former Vice President Al Gore's (2002) critique of a government that contends that people have the right to lead by virtue of the station of life into which they were born (e.g., people who were "born on third base and think they hit a triple"; p. 13).

In short, from a developmental systems theoretical perspective, a view of government that ensures liberty involves a key principle through which policy should be formulated. This principle holds that all citizens should have the opportunity to find a life path that supports their abilities and aspirations while, at the same time, contributes to the liberty of all others. As argued earlier, this principle implies that no person or organization should be allowed to inequitably deprive any young person of the opportunity to set his or her own course, to seek to thrive.

This view of policy principles means that civil society and its government should be (1) activist—that is, civil societies should be engaged participants in the work of nations to sustain and enhance political, economic, and environmental justice—and (2) interventionist—that is, civil societies should take leadership in the world community for actions preventing erosions of or attacks on liberty. The price of freedom is eternal vigilance (Lewontin, 1992), and the policies of the United States must act to support democracy throughout the world to ensure that its own youth are free to live and to develop within a democratic and socially just global community, to prevent erosion of democratic systems both nationally and internationally, and to behave as morally conscious world citizens. Policy must be directed to constraining or destroying the capability of individuals, organizations, or foreign governments to deny liberty to its own or to other people.

The events of September 11, 2001, made it abundantly clear that instability within other nations that arises because of inherently undemocratic regimes, or the toleration or support of groups bent on the destruction of liberty and modern civil society, impacts directly the American people. We cannot live in liberty and allow other people to live in anything less.

This principle of universal social justice means that we must create continuity between our nation and others around the globe. We must do more, both domestically and internationally, to accomplish this, and, in part, this means that we need to share more—more of our resources, expertise, energy, and vision.

In sum, across generations, enactment of policies and programs framed by family-centered community building will result in a society where cohorts of young people will be reared by parents who, during their own youth, developed in a civil society and a global community wherein they thrived and where liberty flourished. However, these positive projections about the potential contributions of policies predicated on the promotion of positive youth development through pursuing a family-centered community building approach must be tempered by a recognition that many good ideas—even ones upon which the future likelihood of thriving among our nation's (and the world's) youth may rest—never become actual policies. While ultimately, as noted at the beginning of this chapter, active political participation in the democratic process is required for the translation of ideas into policies, such action should be predicated on sound strategies for enhancing the probability of success. Through what strategies may we advance the present set of ideas about the nature and importance of thriving youth ← → civil society relations for promoting youth thriving, civic engagement, and liberty?

Strategies for Moving Toward a National Youth Policy

I have noted that public policies represent standards or rules (for the conduct of individuals, organizations, and institutions) and reflect values (that structure actions pertinent to particular substantive issues). If we value our youth as ends in themselves, and if we as well wish to foster their positive development and their ability to contribute to mutually beneficial thriving youth ← → civil society relations, we need to ask how we may promote public policies that are legitimated by developmental theory and research pertinent to positive youth development and that reflect the experience and wisdom about best practice derived from the efforts of practitioners and young people themselves.

Building Momentum for Devising a National Youth Policy

Skelton et al. (2002) are concerned with how we might foster a policy context in America that will facilitate engaging youth actively in civil society, and thus promote their positive contributions to self and others—contributions that epitomize the adaptive individual ← → context relations involved in creating liberty. They note that in order to develop such youth-serving policies, structural and functional challenges currently present in our nation must be overcome. For instance, in regard to the structure of the social system within which youth development occurs, they note that:

For the most part, young people's days are spent in a few major systems: schools, juvenile justice systems and United Way funded institutions. . . . In general, these systems are non-responsive to a civic way of being—to democratic practice. Therefore, if we are serious about youth civic engagement, the challenge . . . includes finding ways to address the structural impediments. (Skelton et al., 2002, p. 12)

For instance, Skelton et al. (2002) recommend that schools become more democratic, so that youth have an opportunity to hone decision-making skills and democracy within the institution within which they spend the majority of their waking hours.

Skelton et al. (2002) believe that changes in the functional (behavioral) context of youth are required as well if a policy context supportive of positive youth development is to be created. For instance, they suggest that changed perceptions of young people—from regarding them as individuals having commercial value to people having civic agency—be promoted, and that youth be given opportunities to actively engage in civically important work (Skelton et al., 2002). In addition, and consistent with a key scientific point made repeatedly in this book, Skelton et al. (2002) note that, unless better indicators of positive youth development and of youth civic contributions are developed, structural and functional changes legitimating policy development may go either undetected or poorly documented.

Skelton et al. (2002) are joined by others in identifying structural and functional impediments to developing a national youth policy that promotes positive youth development. One significant contribution to this discussion has been presented by Congressman Elijah E. Cummings (D-Baltimore). Congressman Cummings has specified some of the impediments to youth policy development that arise among both elected officials and the public as a consequence of differences of opinion about what might constitute effective actions to promote positive development among young people. He notes that:

We have yet to achieve a sustained national policy that fully supports the healthy development of young people in this country. . . . Despite our superpower status and our national wealth, America's children are living in a dangerous world. Their development into healthy adults is threatened by appalling rates of infant mortality, health disparities among poor and minority children, unrealized educational goals, unacceptable levels of drug and alcohol abuse, delinquency, and of course, the shocking incidence of gun violence in our nation's schools. In response, we are dedicating billions of dollars in public funding each year to child-oriented programs. No one believes that the results we are achieving by these public investments are sufficient. Both policymakers and the public remain divided, however, as to the substance and scope of the reforms that are required. It is reasonable to ask why a nation with the wealth and intellectual sophistication to send human beings to the moon and map the genetic blueprint of life cannot seem to agree upon how best to be supportive toward its own children and families. (Cummings, 2003, p. ix)

In addition, Cummings believes that:

Part of the answer to that question can be found in American cultural traditions that are ambivalent (at best) about the appropriate role that government should play in influencing childhood development. . . . In the Congress where I serve, as well as in state capitals and across the family dinner tables of America, the debates about how best to empower children to live safer, more productive, and more fulfilled lives are all-too-often driven by ideology or personal experience. Even the traditional language of policy debates about children and their welfare seems inadequate to the challenges that we face. We no longer agree, for example, about which families we are prepared to support. We agree even less often about how best to help those families flourish. (Cummings, 2003, pp. ix–x)

One strategy that Congressman Cummings sees as potentially productive in shrinking the divide within the policymaking community may be a reliance on the role of developmental science as an evenhanded arbiter of differences of opinion about the effectiveness of different approaches to fostering positive development among youth. He suggests that:

The thoughtful, research-based analyses of applied developmental science can inform and help to unify our efforts to protect and uplift the young people of this country. Precisely because we are a diverse nation with widely differing perspectives about how and when children should receive public help, we need hard scientific evidence, presented in a workable, policy-driven context, that can serve to mediate the ideological tensions inherent in our culture. We must begin to distinguish what we know from what we merely believe to be true. Children's lives are at stake. (Cummings, 2003, p. x)

In that developmental scientists are often located within our nation's institutions of higher education, the strategy recommended by Congressman Cummings (2003) is one that relies on colleges and universities to add value to community life by supporting efforts to promote positive development among young citizens (cf. Gore & Gore, 2002).

Senator Edward M. Kennedy (D-Massachusetts) also sees the value of a strategy for policymaking that involves university–community partnerships. He notes that:

> Colleges and universities should not only be accessible to potential students; they should be accessible to their communities as well. For colleges and universities are not just educators; they are also economic engines and essential partners with their communities, and in these roles, they make major contributions to our economy and our society. (Kennedy, 1999, p 197)

Former Michigan Governor John Engler (R-Michigan) and former Lt. Governor of Michigan Connie Binsfeld (R-Michigan) agree with Senator Kennedy about the value of university–community partnerships. Governor Engler and Lt. Governor Binsfel (1998) note that: "Our colleges and universities have an important role to play in gathering and interpreting . . . data. They can give us a good idea of the challenges we face, and where they are" (p. 455).

They believe, as well, that when government works with institutions of civil society, such as the faith community, the power and scope of university–community partnerships are enhanced. Consistent with the Ideas of Reese and Thorup (2003) about intersectorial partnerships (discussed in Chapter 6), Governor Engler and Lt. Governor Binsfeld indicate that "all three sectors—religious, academic, and government—bring tremendous resources to our communities in need. Working together in partnership, these centers of faith, learning, and public authority can achieve much more than any one sector can alone" (p. 452).

The Vision of Peter L. Benson

Peter L. Benson, President of Search Institute, in agreement with Cummings, Kennedy, Engler, and Binsfeld, believes that a developmental science focused on promoting youth-serving community change—in other words, on community building for youth—can be an important strategy in overcoming obstacles to developing a national policy promoting positive youth development. As discussed earlier, the work of Benson and his colleagues at Search Institute (e.g., Benson, 1997, 2003a, 2003b; Leffert et al., 1998; Scales et al., 2000) is aimed at identifying the developmental assets present in youth and their communities that, when integrated, enhance the probability of positive youth development and, under ideal situations, produce exemplary development or thriving.

Accordingly, Benson (2003b) believes that the application of developmental science may help identify for communities and policymakers pathways to community change that would increase the probability of young people possessing the developmental assets, or nutrients for positive development, necessary for becoming active agents of civil society and for their own healthy development. The pathways he describes involve the promotion of:

- Adult engagement in asset-building actions
- Adolescent engagement in becoming proactive in their own development and in activating their asset-building capacity with peers and younger children
- Sector transformation, involving increases in the delivery of developmental nutrients by existing socializing systems such as families, neighborhoods, congregations, schools, youth organizations, and places of work
- Community change, involving multiple actors, settings and ecologies, and
- Social change directed toward creating developmentally attentive and asset-enhancing social norms, media presentations, and local and national policies (Benson, 2003b, p. 217).

Benson (2003b) provides as well a vision for fostering social changes pertinent to all of these pathways. Consistent with other discussions (e.g., Benson et al., 2004; Cummings, 2003; Kennedy, 1999; Pittman, Yohalem, & Irby, 2003; Skelton et al., 2002; Wheeler, 2003), Benson articulates ten strategies for fostering a national climate wherein overcoming impediments to devising a national youth-serving policy can be productively and successfully pursued.

First, and consistent with the repeated call in this book for a new vocabulary for discussing youth—one framed by a strength-based, as compared to a deficit, model—Benson (2003b) notes that the language used to describe young people must be changed. He states, "Recasting youth as resources to be developed rather than 'problems to be fixed' is a reframing necessary for re-engaging and re-energizing citizens and social institutions in creating asset-building relationships with youth" (pp. 217–218).

Benson indicates as well that that university–community collaborations will be important in that, first, research will be needed to develop valid, strength-based indicators of positive youth development; and, second, media will need to be provided with the technical assistance requisite for appropriate use and interpretation of these new measures, so that through their dissemination practices, the public can make this new language part of their everyday vocabulary about youth. Moreover, Benson believes that a related strategy initiative is the use of the approach to developmental theory and research embodied in the present book. He sees such a theoretical frame as maximizing the chances that good science will be usefully embedded within a ecological frame serving programs and policies (Benson, 2003b).

Third, consistent with the ideas of Skelton et al. (2002), Benson (2003b) believes that the first-noted strategy (of using the new, positive youth development vocabulary to discuss young people) will facilitate advances in another domain, that is, there will be a transformation of public perceptions about young people and their capacities and interests. Certainly, a revised vocabulary that is broadly disseminated will facilitate such a transformation. But, in addition, altered perceptions should create different standards or expectations for normative youth behavior. Norms about youth as resources should accrue as this second transformation occurs.

Benson (2003b) believes also that, fourth, local communities should be brought together to identify common ground, areas of agreement pertinent to the goals for and values associated with youth development. Here, William Damon's (1997; Damon & Gregory, 2003) youth charter (discussed in Chapter 6) illustrates what might be done to mobilize such community integration As I have noted, the youth charter is a means by which community members, including youth, join together to specify a common vision for positive youth development and to establish community procedures for nurturing such change.

As exemplified by Damon's (1997; Damon & Gregory, 2003) youth charter, Benson (2003b; see too Benson 1997) believes that community assets must be marshaled to promote the competencies and potentials of youth, and to develop and evaluate initiatives (policies or programs derived from them) designed to promote these positive attributes. Accordingly, policy must go beyond two necessary but not sufficient goals—first, of "meeting basic human needs [through ensuring] economic security, food, shelter, good and useful work, and safety" (Benson, 1997, p. xiii) for youth and the members of their families; and second, targeting and reducing or even eliminating "the risks and deficits that diminish or thwart the healthy development of children and adolescents. Guns, unsafe streets, predatory adults, abuse, family violence, exclusion, alcohol and other drugs, racism, and sexism are among the threats" (Benson, 1997, pp. xiii–xiv). Policy must add the third component—assets—that is crucial for building a strong young person supported through positive relationships with his or her family and community. Indeed, as Benson et al. (1998) note:

> Ultimately, the most critical question is how communities can be supported to integrate and simultaneously pursue strength—building in three community infrastructures—economic, service delivery, and development. The goal of this integration is to develop a combination of policy, resources, and actions, which will meet basic human needs, reduce threats to human development, provide humane and effective access to services, and promote healthy development. (p. 156)

Damon's youth charter underscores also a fifth strategy suggested by Benson (2003b), that of creating means within communities to assure that young people serve as agents in the positive transformation of community life. To accomplish this emphasis on youth leadership, three other strategies—the sixth, seventh, and eighth—are seen by Benson as crucial: sixth, the establishment of positive youth–adult relationships; seventh, the positioning of the family as a central component of youth development; and eighth, making the community the central organizing entity for enhancing youth and families, for furthering the capacity of families to promote their children's positive development.

Thus, in the combined emphasis on the interrelation of youth, families, and communities, Benson (2003b) is here describing key features of the family-centered community building for youth approach (Gore, 2003; Gore & Gore, 2002). Indeed, consistent with this approach, Benson (2003b) believes that attention to the diversity of all of these levels of the ecology of human development must be embraced as a ninth strategic component if we are to create strategies that result in the formulation of a national youth policy.

Finally, as a tenth and culminating strategy, one clearly reflecting his emphasis on empowering youth, families, and communities, Benson (2003b) advises that we must "trust the people" (p. 220). He believes that when young people and the adults who are involved in their lives are empowered and trusted, their actions will provide a potent source for formulating the agenda policymakers might productively pursue. Both because they reflect the behavioral consensus of constituents and because these actions have ecological validity, they represent the steps that empowered youth, families, and communities have actually taken to enhance the positive development and civic contributions and leadership of young people.

In sum, by relying on empowered people—youth and the adults who care for and support them—we may succeed in translating into effective actions our strategies for the creation of a national policy for the promotion of positive youth development; for fostering exemplary exchanges between young people and the institutions of civil society; and for creating the conditions where this generation of American youth and all generations following them will live in a nation and a world where social justice, democracy, and liberty reign.

Conclusions: The Thriving Youth ← → Civil Society Relationship

Clearly, the key to enabling a model for a national youth policy to work is developing one that builds on the existing assets of communities. These assets are the current inventory of building blocks for civil society in America. Accordingly, they must be employed to build the programs that will be associated with the enactment of the model displayed in Figure 7.1. As such, they will be part of a multi-institutional system, changing American society by moving it in the direction of greater equity and access to democratizing resources for all of its diverse citizens.

In this effort, we must all continue to educate ourselves about the best means available to promote enhanced life chances among all of our youth and families, and especially among those whose potential for positive contributions to civil society is most in danger of being wasted (Dryfoos, 1990,1998; Hamburg, 1992; R. M. Lerner, Sparks, & McCubbin, 1999; Schorr, 1988, 1997; Wheeler, 2003). Currently, the collaborative expertise of the research and practitioner communities can provide much of this information, especially if it is obtained in partnership with strong, empowered communities, families, and youth. Policies promoting such coalitions could become an integral component of a national youth and family development policy aimed at creating caring, asset-rich communities with the capacity to further the healthy development of their children and families.

Given the enormous, indeed historically unprecedented, challenges facing the youth of America and the world, and the enormous opportunity we have to capitalize on the strengths of youth not only to meet these challenges but to become thriving agents of democracy, social justice, and civil society as well, there is no time to lose in the development of such asset-rich communities and empowered youth and families working collaboratively to build healthy young people and civil society, to make normative in America the thriving youth ← → civil society relationship.

We must become active producers of the thriving youth ← → civil society relation by engaging in the political process available to us as citizens of America. What we will gain from such actions are new cohorts of healthy, civically engaged youth, individuals on their way to becoming the leaders of a vibrant democracy in which all people have the opportunity to contribute to their own and others' positive development.

In the hands of such young people, there will be a new dawning of the idea of America. There will be liberty and justice for all.

References

Addams, J. (1910). *Twenty years at Hull House*. New York: Macmillan.

Anastasi, A. (1958). Heredity, environment, and the question "how?" *Psychological Review, 65*, 197–208.

Baca Zinn, M., & Eitzen, D. S. (1993). *Diversity in families* (3rd ed.). New York: HarperCollins College Publishers.

Baltes, P. B. (1973). Life-span models of psychological aging: A white elephant? *Gerontologist, 13*, 457–512.

Baltes, P. B. (1987). Theoretical propositions of life-span developmental psychology: On the dynamics between growth and decline. *Developmental Psychology, 23*, 611–626.

Baltes, P. B. (1997). On the incomplete architecture of human ontogeny: Selection, optimization, and compensation as foundations of developmental theory. *American Psychologist, 52*, 366–380.

Baltes, P. B., & Baltes, M. M. (1990). Psychological perspectives on successful aging: The model of selective optimization with compensation. In P. B. Baltes & M. M. Baltes (Eds.), *Successful aging: Perspectives from the behavioral sciences* (pp. 1–34). New York: Cambridge University Press.

Baltes, P. B., Lindenberger, U., & Staudinger, U. M. (1998). Life-span theory in developmental psychology. In W. Damon (Series Ed.) & R. M. Lerner (Volume Ed.), *Handbook of child psychology: Vol. 1 Theoretical models of human development* (5th ed., pp. 1029–1144). New York: Wiley.

Baltes, P. B., Reese, H. W., & Nesselroade, J. R. (1977). *Life-span developmental psychology: Introduction to research methods*. Monterey, CA: Brooks/Cole.

Basler, Roy P. (Ed.). (1969). *Abraham Lincoln: His speeches and writings*. New York: The World Publishing Co.

Behrman, J. R., & Rosenzweig, M. (in press). Does increasing women's schooling raise the schooling in the next generation? *American Economic Review*.

Belsky, J., Lerner, R. M., & Spanier, G. B. (1984). *The child in the family*. Reading, MA: Addison-Wesley.

Bennett, A. J., Lesch, K. P., Heils, A., Long, J., Lorenz, J., Shoaf, S. E., Champoux, M., Suomi, S. J., Linnoila, M., & Higley, J. D. (2002). Serotonin transporter genotype and early experience interact to influence nonhuman primate CNS serotonin turnover. *Molecular Psychiatry, 17*, 118–122.

Benson, P. (1997). *All kids are our kids: What communities must do to raise caring and responsible children and adolescents*. San Francisco: Jossey-Bass.

Benson, P. L. (1990). *The troubled journey: A portrait of 6th–12th grade youth*. Minneapolis, MN: Search Institute.

Benson, P. L. (2003a). Developmental assets and asset-building community: Conceptual and empirical foundations. In R. M. Lerner & P. L. Benson (Eds.), *Developmental assets and asset-building communities: Implications for research, policy, and practice* (pp. 19–43). Norwell, MA: Kluwer Academic Publishers.

Benson, P. L. (2003b). Toward asset building communities: How does change occur? In R. M. Lerner & P. L. Benson. (Eds.), *Developmental assets and asset-building communities: Implications for research, policy, and practice* (pp. 213–221). Norwell, MA: Kluwer Academic Publishers.

Benson, P. L., Leffert, N., Scales, P. C., & Blyth, D. A. (1998). Beyond the "village" rhetoric: Creating healthy communities for children and adolescents. *Applied Developmental Science, 2*(3), 138–159.

Benson, P. L., Mannes, M., Pittman, K., & Ferber, T. (2004). Youth development, developmental assets, and public policy. In R. M. Lerner & L. Steinberg (Eds.), *Handbook of adolescent psychology* (2nd ed., pp. 781–784). New York: Wiley.

Benson, P. L. & Pittman, K. J. (Eds.). (2001). *Trends in youth development: Visions, realities and challenges*. Norwell, MA: Kluwer Academic Publishers.

Bergstrom, J. M. (1984). *School's out*. Berkeley, CA: Ten Speed Press.

Bergstrom, J. M. (1995). *The best summer ever: A parent's guide*. Berkeley, CA: Tricycle Press.

Birkel, R., Lerner, R. M., & Smyer, M. A. (1989). Applied developmental psychology as an implementation of a life-span view of human development. *Journal of Applied Developmental Psychology, 10*, 425–445.

Blum, R. W. (2003). Positive youth development: A strategy for improving health. In. F. Jacobs, D. Wertlieb, & R. M. Lerner (Eds.), *Enhancing the life chances of youth and families: Public service systems and public policy perspectives*. Volume 2 of *Handbook of applied developmental science: Promoting positive child, adolescent, and family development through research, policies, and programs* (pp. 237–252). Editors: R. M. Lerner, F. Jacobs, & D. Wertlieb. Thousand Oaks, CA: Sage Publications.

Blyth, D. A., & Leffert, N. (1995). Communities as contexts for adolescent development: An empirical analysis. *Journal of Adolescent Research, 10*(1), 64–87.

Boring, E. G. (1950). *A history of experimental psychology* (2nd ed.) New York: Appleton-Century-Crofts.

Bornstein, M. H. (1985, November). How infant and mother jointly contribute to developing cognitive competence in the child. *Proceedings of the National Academy of Science USA, 82*, 7470–7473.

Bornstein, M. H. (1989). Between caretakers and their young: Two modes of interaction and their consequences for cognitive growth. In M. H. Bornstein & J. S. Bruner (Eds.), *Interaction in human development* (pp. 197–214). Hillsdale, NJ: Lawrence Erlbaum Associates.

Bornstein, M. H. (Ed.). (1995). *Handbook of parenting*. Mahwah, NJ: Lawrence Erlbaum Associates.

Bornstein, M. H. (Ed.). (2002). *Handbook of parenting* (2nd ed.). Mahwah, NJ: Lawrence Erlbaum Associates.

Bornstein, M. H. (2003). Positive parenting and positive development in children. In R. M. Lerner, F. Jacobs, & D. Wertlieb (Eds.), *Applying developmental science for youth and families: Historical and theoretical foundations*. Volume 1 of *Handbook of applied developmental science: Promoting positive child, adolescent, and family development through research, policies, and programs* (pp. 187–209). Editors: Richard M. Lerner, Francine Jacobs, and Donald Wertlieb. Thousand Oaks, CA: Sage Publications.

Bornstein, M. H., Davidson, L., Keyes, C. M., Moore, K., & The Center for Child Well-Being (Eds.). (2003). *Well-being: Positive development across the life course*. Mahwah, NJ: Lawrence Erlbaum Associates.

Bornstein, M. H., & Tamis-LeMonda, C. S. (1990). Activities and interaction of mothers and their firstborn infants in the first six months of life: Covariation, stability, continuity, correspondence, and prediction. *Child Development, 61*, 1206–1217.

Bornstein, M. H., Tamis-LeMonda, C. S., Tal, J., Ludemann, P., Toda, S., Rahn, C. W., Pêcheux, M.-G., Azuma, H., & Vardi, D. (1992). Maternal responsiveness to infants in three societies: The United States, France, and Japan. *Child Development, 63*, 808–821.

Bowman, H. A., & Spanier, G. B. (1978). *Modern marriage* (8th ed.). New York: McGraw Hill.

Brandt, R. B. (1961). *Value and obligation: Systematic readings in ethics*. New York: Harcourt.

Brandtstädter, J. (1998). Action perspectives on human development. In W. Damon (Series Ed.), & R. M. Lerner (Vol. Ed.), *Handbook of child psychology: Vol. 1 Theoretical models of human development* (5th ed., pp. 807–863). New York: Wiley.

Brandtstädter, J. (1999). The self in action and development: Cultural, biosocial, and ontogenetic bases of intentional self-development. In J. Brandtstädter & R.M. Lerner (Eds.), *Action and self-development: Theory and research through the life-span* (pp. 37–65). Thousand Oaks, CA: Sage.

Braun, L. (2004). Commentary. In C. Garcia Coll, E. Bearer, & R. M. Lerner (Eds.), *Nature and nurture: The complex interplay of genetic and environmental influences on human behavior and development* (pp. 139–143). Mahwah, NJ: Lawrence Erlbaum Associates.

Brazelton, T. B., Koslowski, B., and Main, M. (1974). The origins of reciprocity: The early mother-infant interaction. In M. Lewis and L. A. Rosenblum (Eds.), *The effect of the infant on its caregivers* (pp. 49-76). New York: Wiley.

Bridges, L. J., & Moore, K. A. (2002). Religious involvement and children's well-being: What research tells us (and what it doesn't). *Child Trends Research Brief*. Washington, DC: Child Trends.

Bronfenbrenner, U. (1974). Developmental research, public policy, and the ecology of childhood. *Child Development, 45*, 1–5.

Bronfenbrenner, U. (1977). Toward an experimental ecology of human development. *American Psychologist, 32*, 513–531.

Bronfenbrenner, U. (1979) *The ecology of human development: Experiments by nature and design.* Cambridge: Harvard University Press.

Bronfenbrenner, U. (2001). Human development, bioecological theory of. In N. J. Smelser & P. B. Baltes (Eds.), *International encyclopedia of the social and behavioral sciences* (pp. 6963–6970). Oxford: Elsevier.

Bronfenbrenner, U. (in press). *Making human beings human.* Thousand Oaks, CA: Sage.

Bronfenbrenner, U., & Morris, P. A. (1998). The ecology of developmental process. In W. Damon (Series Ed.) & R. M. Lerner (Vol. Ed.), *Handbook of child psychology: Vol. 1 Theoretical models of human development* (5th ed., pp. 993–1028). New York: Wiley.

Bruer, J. T. (1999). *The myth of the first three years.* New York: The Free Press.

Buss, A. H., & Plomin, R. (1984). *Temperament: Early developing personality traits.* Hillsdale, NJ: Erlbaum.

Camino, L. (2000). Youth–adult partnerships: Entering new territory in community work and research. *Applied Developmental Science, 4, Supplement 1,* 11–20.

Camino, L., & Zeldin, S. (2002). From periphery to center: Pathways for youth civic engagement in the day-to-day life of communities. *Applied Developmental Science, 6,* 213–220.

Campbell, S. (1979). Mother-infant interaction as a function of maternal ratings of temperament. *Child Psychiatry and Human Development, 10,* 67–76.

Carnegie Corporation of New York. (1995). *Great transitions: Preparing adolescents for a new century.* New York: Author.

Catalano, R. F., Berglund, M. L., Ryan, J. A. M., Lonczak, H. S., & Hawkins, J. D. (1999). *Positive youth development in the United States: Research findings on evaluations of youth development programs.* Washington, DC: U. S. Department of Health and Human Services.

Chess, S., & Thomas, A. (1984). *The origins and evolution of behavior disorders: Infancy to early adult life.* New York: Brunner/Mazel.

Chess, S., & Thomas, A. (1999). *Goodness of fit: Clinical applications from infancy through adult life.* Philadelphia, PA: Brunner/Mazel.

Collins, W. A., Maccoby, E. E., Steinberg, L., Hetherington, E. M., & Bornstein, M. H. (2000). Contemporary research on parenting: The case of nature and nurture. *American Psychologist, 55,* 218–232.

Corbett, T. (1995). Changing the culture of welfare. *Focus, 16,* 12–22.

Crockenberg, S. (1986). Are temperamental differences in babies associated with predictable differences in caregiving? In J. V. Lerner & R. M. Lerner (Eds.), *Temperament and social interaction in infants and children: New directions for child development* (pp. 53–73). San Francisco: Jossey-Bass.

Crockenberg, S., & Acredolo, C. (1983). Infant temperament ratings: A function of infants, or mothers, or both? *Infant Behavior and Development, 6,* 61–72.

Csikszentmihalyi, M., & Rathunde, K. (1998). The development of the person: An experiential perspective on the ontogenesis of psychological complexity. In W. Damon (Series Ed.) & R. M. Lerner (Volume Ed.), *Handbook of child psychology: Vol. 1 Theoretical models of human development* (5th ed., pp. 635–684). New York: Wiley.

Cummings, E. (2003) Foreword. In D. Wertlieb, F. Jacobs, & R. M. Lerner (Eds.), *Promoting positive youth and family development: Community systems, citizenship, and civil society.* Volume 3 of *Handbook of applied developmental science: Promoting positive child, adolescent, and family development through research, policies, and programs* (pp. ix–xi). Editors: R. M. Lerner, F. Jacobs, & D. Wertlieb. Thousand Oaks, CA: Sage.

Damon, W. (1997). *The youth charter: How communities can work together to raise standards for all our children.* New York: The Free Press.

Damon, W., & Gregory, A. (2003). Bringing in a new era in the field of youth development. In R. M. Lerner, F. Jacobs, & D. Wertlieb (Eds.). *Applying developmental science for youth and families: Historical and theoretical foundations.* Volume 1 of *Handbook of applied developmental science: Promoting positive child, adolescent, and family development through research, policies, and programs* (pp. 407–420). Editors: R. M. Lerner, F. Jacobs, & D. Wertlieb. Thousand Oaks, CA: Sage.

Damon, W., Menon, J., & Bronk, K. C. (2003). The development of purpose during adolescence. *Applied Developmental Science, 7,* 119–128.

Dannefer, D. (1984). Adult developmental and socialization theory: A paradigmatic reappraisal. *American Sociological Review, 49,* 100–116.

Darwin, C. (1859). *The origin of species by means of natural selection or the preservation of favoured races in the struggle for life.* London: J. Murray.

Dawkins, R. (1976). *The selfish gene.* Oxford, UK: Oxford University Press.

de Beer, G. R. (1959). Paedomorphosis. *Proceedings of the XV International Congress of Zoology, 15,* 927–930.

Diamond, L. M., & Savin-Williams, R. C. (2003). Gender and sexual identity. In. R. M. Lerner, F. Jacobs, & D. Wertlieb (Eds.). *Applying developmental science for youth and families: Historical and theoretical foundations.* Volume 1 of *Handbook of applied developmental science: Promoting positive child, adolescent, and family development through research, policies, and programs* (pp. 101–121). Editors: R. M. Lerner, F. Jacobs, & D. Wertlieb. Thousand Oaks, CA: Sage Publications.

Dowling, E., Gestsdottir, S., Anderson, P., von Eye, A., & Lerner, R. M. (2003). Spirituality, religiosity, and thriving among adolescents: Identification and confirmation of factor structures. *Applied Developmental Science, 7(4),* 253–260.

Dowling, E., Gestsdottir, S., Anderson, P., von Eye, A., Almerigi, J., & Lerner, R. M. (2004). Structural relations among spirituality, religiosity, and thriving in adolescence. *Applied Developmental Science, 8 (1),* 7–16.

Dryfoos, J. G. (1990). *Adolescents at risk: Prevalence and prevention.* New York: Oxford University Press.

Dryfoos, J. G. (1998). *Safe passage: Making it through adolescence in a risky society.* New York: Oxford University Press.

D'Souza, D. (2003). The power of virtue. *Washington Post,* July 4, A 23.

Duncan, G. T., & Magnuson, K. A. (2003). Off with Hollingshead: Socioeconomic resources, parenting, and child development. In H. H. Bornstein & R. H. Bradley (Eds.), *Socioeconomic status, parenting, and child development* (pp. 83–106). Mahwah, NJ: Lawrence Erlbaum Associates.

Dunn, J. & Kendrick, C. (1980). Studying temperament and parent–child interaction: Comparison of interview and direct observation. *Developmental Medicine and Child Neurology, 22,* 484–496.

Eccles, J., & Gootman, J. A. (Eds). (2002). *Community programs to promote youth development.* Washington, DC: National Academy Press.

Eisenberg, L. (1972). The *human* nature of human nature. *Science, 176,* 123–128.

Elder, G. H. (1974). *Children of the Great Depression.* Chicago: University of Chicago Press.

Elder, G. H., Jr. (1998). The life course and human development. In W. Damon (Series Ed.) & R. M. Lerner (Vol. Ed.), *Handbook of child psychology: Vol. 1 Theoretical models of human development* (5th ed., pp. 939–991). New York: Wiley.

Elder, G. H., Modell, J., & Parke, R. D. (1993). Studying children in a changing world. In G. H. Elder, J. Modell, & R. D. Parke (Eds.), *Children in time and place: Developmental and historical insights* (pp. 3–21). New York: Cambridge University Press.

Elman, J. L., Bates, E. A., Johnson, M. H., Karmiloff-Smith, A., Parisi, D., & Plunkett, K. (1998). *Rethinking innateness: A connectionist perspective on development (neural network modeling and connectionism).* Cambridge, MA: MIT Press.

Engler, J., & Binsfeld, C. (1998). Partnership in action. The Governor's clergy summit in the City of Detroit. In R. M. Lerner & L. A. K. Simon (Eds.), *University-community collaborations for the twenty-first century: Outreach scholarship for youth and families* (pp. 451–459). New York: Garland Publishing.

Erikson, E. H. (1959). Identity and the life-cycle. *Psychological Issues 1,* 18–164.

Erikson, E. H. (1968). *Identity, youth and crisis.* New York: Norton.

Fausto-Sterling, A. (2000). *Sexing the body: Gender politics and the construction of sexuality.* New York: Basic Books.

Featherman, D. L., & Lerner, R. M. (1985). Ontogenesis and sociogenesis: Problematics for theory about development across the lifespan. *American Sociological Review, 50,* 659–676.

Feldman, D. H. (1994). *Beyond universals in cognitive development* (2nd ed.). Norwood: Ablex Pub. Corp.

Feldman, D. H. (2000). *Piaget's stages: The unfinished symphony.* Unpublished manuscript. Medford, MA: Eliot-Pearson Department of Child Development, Tufts University.

Feldman, M. W., & Lewontin, R. C. (1975). The heritability hang-up. *Science, 190,* 1163–1168.

Fisher, C. B., and Lerner, R. M. (1994). Foundations of applied developmental psychology. In C. B. Fisher and R. M. Lerner (Eds.), *Applied developmental psychology* (pp. 3–20). New York: McGraw-Hill.

Fisher, H. E. (1982a). Of human bonding. *The Sciences, 22,* 18–23, 31.

Fisher, H. E. (1982b). Is it sex? Helen E. Fisher replies. *The Sciences, 22,* 2–3.

Flanagan, C., & Faison, N. (2001). Youth civic engagement: Implications of research for social policy and programs. *Social Policy Reports, No. 1.*

Flanagan, C., & Sherrod, L. (Eds.). (1998). Political development: Youth growing up in a global community. *Journal of Social Issues, 54*(3).

Ford, D. L., & Lerner, R. M. (1992). *Developmental systems theory: An integrative approach.* Newbury Park, CA: Sage.

Freud, S. (1949). *Outline of psychoanalysis.* New York: Norton.

Freud, S. (1954). *Collected works* (Standard ed.). London: Hogarth.

Furrow, J., Wagner. L.M., Leffert N., & Benson, P.L. (2004). *The measurement of developmental assests in youth and the structure of a self-report survey: Search Institute Profiles of Student Life*: Unpublished Manuscript. Pasadena, CA: Fuller Theological Seminary.

Furrow, J. & Wagener, L. (Eds.). (2003) Special Issue on Beyond the Self: Perspectives on identity and transcendence among youth. *Applied Developmental Science, 7*(3), 116–213.

Furstenberg, F. F., Jr., & Hughes, M. E. (1995). Social capital and successful development among at-risk youth. *Journal of Marriage and the Family, 57,* 580–592.

Garbarino, J. (1992). *Children and families in the social environment* (2nd ed.). New York: Aldine de Gruyter.

Garcia Coll, C., Bearer, E., & Lerner, R. M. (Eds.). (2004). *Nature and nurture: The complex interplay of genetic and environmental influences on human behavior and development.* Mahwah, NJ: Lawrence Erlbaum Associates.

Gore, A. (2002, August 4). Broken promises and political deception. *New York Times* op-ed. p. 13.

Gore, A. (2003). Foreword. In R. M. Lerner & P. L. Benson, P. L. (Eds.). *Developmental assets and asset-building communities: Implications for research, policy, and practice.* Norwell, MA: Kluwer Academic Publishers.

Gore, A., & Gore, T. (2002). *Joined at the heart: The transformation of the American family.* New York: Henry Holt and Company.

Gottlieb, G. (1992). *Individual development and evolution: The genesis of novel behavior.* New York: Oxford University Press.

Gottlieb, G. (1997). *Synthesizing nature-nurture: Prenatal roots of instinctive behavior.* Mahwah, NJ: Lawrence Erlbaum.

Gottlieb, G. (1998). Normally occurring environmental and behavioral influences on gene activity: From central dogma to probabilistic epigenesis. *Psychological Review, 105,* 792–802.

Gottlieb, G. (2004). Normally occurring environmental and behavioral influences on gene activity. In C. Garcia Coll, E. Bearer, & R. M. Lerner (Eds.), *Nature and nurture: The complex interplay of genetic and environmental influences on human behavior and development.* (pp. 85–106). Mahwah, NJ: Lawrence Erlbaum Associates.

Gottlieb, G., Wahlsten, D., & Lickliter, R. (1998). The significance of biology for human development: A developmental psychobiological systems view.

In W. Damon (Series Ed.) & R. M. Lerner (Vol. Ed.), *Handbook of child psychology: Vol. 1 Theoretical models of human development* (5th ed., pp. 233–273). New York: Wiley.

Gould, S. (1977). *Ontogeny and phylogeny.* Cambridge, MA: Harvard University Press.

Gould, S. J. (1981). *The mismeasure of man.* New York: Norton.

Gould, S. J. (1996). *The mismeasure of man* (Rev. ed.). New York: Norton.

Gould, S. J., & Eldridge, N. (1977). Punctuated equilibria: The tempo and mode of evolution reconsidered. *Paleobiology, 3,* 115–151.

Graham, P., Rutter, M., & George, S. (1973). Temperamental characteristics as predictors of behavior disorders of children. *American Journal of Orthopsychiatry, 43,* 328–329.

Griest, D., Forehand, R., Wells, K. C., & McMahon, R. J. (1980). Examination of differences between nonclinic and behavior-problem clinic-referred children and their mothers. *Journal of Abnormal Psychology, 89,* 497–500.

Haeckel, E. (1868). *Naturliche Schopfungsgeschichte.* Berlin: Georg Reimer.

Hahn, A. B. (1994). Toward a national youth development policy for young African-American males: The choices policy makers face. In R. B. Mincy (Ed.), *Nurturing young Black males* (pp. 165–186). Washington: The Urban Institute Press.

Hall, G. (1904). *Adolescence.* New York: Appleton.

Hamburg, D. A. (1992). *Today's children: Creating a future for a generation in crisis.* New York: Time Books.

Hamilton, S. F. (1999). *A three-part definition of positive youth development.* Unpublished manuscript, College of Human Ecology, Cornell University.

Hamilton, S. F., & Hamilton, M. (1999). Creating new pathways to adulthood by adapting German apprenticeship in the United States. In W. R. Heinz (Ed.), *From education to work: Cross-national perspectives* (pp. 194–213). New York, NY: Cambridge University Press.

Hamilton, S. F., & Hamilton, M.A. (2004). Contexts for mentoring: Adolescent–adult relationships in workplaces and communities. In R. M. Lerner & L. Steinberg (Eds.), *Handbook of adolescent psychology* (2nd ed., pp. 395–428). New York: Wiley.

Harley, D. (1982). Models of human evolution. *Science, 217,* 296.

Harris, J. R. (1998). *The nurture assumption: Why children turn out the way they do.* New York: Free Press.

Hart, D., & Atkins, R. (2002). Civic competence in urban youth. In L. Sherrod, C. Flanagan, & J. Youniss, (Eds.). (2002a). *Growing into citizenship: Multiple pathways and diverse influence.* Special Issue of *Applied Developmental Science, 6*(4), 227–236.

Hart, D., & Fegley, S. (1995). Prosocial behavior and caring in adolescence: Relations to self-understanding and social judgement. *Child Development, 66,* 1346–1359.

Hartup, W. W. (1978). Perspectives on child and family interaction: Past, present, and future. In R. M. Lerner & G. B. Spanier (Eds.), *Child influences on marital and family interaction: A life-span perspective* (pp. 23–46). New York: Academic Press.

Hebb, D. O. (1970). A return to Jensen and his social critics. *American Psychologist, 25,* 568.

Heckhausen, J. (1999). *Developmental regulation in adulthood: Age-normative and sociocultural constraints as adaptive challenges.* New York: Cambridge University Press.

Helms, J. E. (2003). Racial identity and racial socialization as aspects of adolescents' identity development. In. R. M. Lerner, F. Jacobs, & D. Wertlieb (Eds.). *Applying developmental science for youth and families: Historical and theoretical foundations.* Volume 1 of *Handbook of applied developmental science: Promoting positive child, adolescent, and family development through research, policies, and programs* (pp. 143–163). Editors: R. M. Lerner, F. Jacobs, & D. Wertlieb. Thousand Oaks, CA: Sage.

Hernandez, D. J. (1993). *America's children: Resources for family, government, and the economy.* New York: Russell Sage Foundation.

Hetherington, E. M., & Kelly, J. (2002). *For better or for worse: Divorce reconsidered.* New York: W. W. Norton & Co.

Hirsch, J. (1970). Behavior-genetic analysis and its biosocial consequences. *Seminars in Psychiatry, 2,* 89–105.

Hirsch, J. (1997). Some history of heredity-vs.-environment, genetic inferiority at Harvard (?), and The (incredible) Bell Curve. *Genetica, 99,* 207–224.

Hirsch, J. (2004). Uniqueness, diversity, similarity, repeatability, and heritability In C. Garcia Coll, E. Bearer, & R. M. Lerner (Eds.), *Nature and nurture: The complex interplay of genetic and environmental influences on human behavior and development* (pp. 127–138). Mahwah, NJ: Lawrence Erlbaum Associates.

Ho, M. W. (1984). Environment and heredity in development and evolution. In M.-W. Ho & P. T. Saunders (Eds.), *Beyond neo-Darwinism: An introduction to the new evolutionary paradigm* (pp. 267–289). London: Academic Press.

Hoffman, R. F. (1978). Developmental changes in human infant visual-evoked potentials to patterned stimuli recorded at different scalp locations. *Child Development, 49(1),* 110–118.

Hogan, R., Johnson, J. A., & Emler, N. P. (1978). A socioanalytical theory of moral development. *New Directions for Child Development, 2,* 1–18.

Homans, G. C. (1961). *Social behavior: Its elementary forms.* New York: Harcourt, Brace & World.

Horowitz, F. D. (2000). Child development and the PITS: Simple questions, complex answers, and developmental theory. *Child Development, 71,* 1–10.

Hoyle, R. H., & Leff, S. S. (1997). The role of parental involvement in youth sport participation and performance. *Adolescence, 32* (125), 233–243.

Hume, D. (1740/1978). *A treatise of human nature* (2nd ed., L. A. Selby-Bigge, Ed., rev. by P. H. Nidditch). Oxford: Clarendon Press.

Huston, A. C. (Ed.). (1991). *Children in poverty: Child development and public policy.* Cambridge: Cambridge University Press.

Inhelder, B., & Piaget, J. (1958). *The growth of logical thinking from childhood to adolescence.* New York: Basic Books

Isaac, G. L. (1982). Models of human evolution. *Science, 17,* 295.

Jensen, A. R. (1969). How much can we boost IQ and scholastic achievement? *Harvard Educational Review, 39,* 1–123.

Jensen, A. R. (1973). *Educability and group differences.* New York: Harper & Row.

Jensen, A. R. (1998). Jensen on "Jensenism." *Intelligence, 26,* 181–208.

Johanson, D. C., & Edey, M. A. (1981). *Lucy: The beginnings of humankind.* New York: Simon & Schuster.

Kant, I. (1781/1966). *Critique of pure reason* (F. Max Muller, Trans.). New York: Anchor Books.

Kennedy, E. M. (1999). University–community partnertships: A mutually beneficial effort to aid community development and improve academic learning opportunities. *Applied Developmental Science, 3,* 197–198.

Kenny, M., Simon, L. A. K., Brabeck, K., & Lerner, R. M. (Eds.). (2002). *Learning to serve: Promoting civil society through service learning.* Norwell, MA: Kluwer Academic Publishers.

Kerestes, M., & Youniss, J. E. (2003). Rediscovering the importance of religion in adolescent development. In. R. M. Lerner, F. Jacobs, & D. Wertlieb (Eds.), *Applying developmental science for youth and families: Historical and theoretical foundations.* Volume 1 of *Handbook of applied developmental science: Promoting positive child, adolescent, and family development through research, policies, and programs* (pp. 165–184). Editors: R. M. Lerner, F. Jacobs, & D. Wertlieb. Thousand Oaks, CA: Sage.

King, P. E. (in press). Religion as a resource for positive youth development: Religion, social capital, and moral outcomes. *Developmental Psychology.*

Kinkade, S. (2002). *Youth in action: Profiles of youth leading change around the world.* Baltimore, MD: International Youth Foundation.

Kohlberg, L. (1963). The development of children's orientations toward a moral order: Sequence in the development of moral thought. *Vita Humana, 6,* 11–33.

Kohlberg, L. (1968). Early education: A cognitive-developmental view. *Child Development, 39,* 1014–62.

Kohlberg, L. (1971). From is to ought: How to commit the naturalistic fallacy and get away with it in the study of moral development. In T. Mischel (Ed.), *Cognitive development and epistemology* (pp. 151–235). New York: Academic Press.

Kohlberg, L. (1978). Revisions in the theory and practice of moral development. *New directions for child development, 2,* 93–120.

Korn, S. J., Chess, S., & Fernandez, P. (1978). The impact of children's physical handicaps on marital quality and family interaction. In R. M. Lerner & G. B. Spanier (Eds.), *Child influences on marital and family interaction: A life-span perspective* (pp. 299–326). New York: Academic Press.

Lee, C., & Bates, J. (1985). Mother–child interaction at age two years and perceived difficult temperament. *Child Development, 56,* 1314–1325.

Leffert, N., Benson, P. L., Scales, P. C., Sharma, A. R., Drake, D. R., and Blyth, D. A. (1998). Developmental assets: Measurement and prediction of risk behaviors among adolescents. *Applied Developmental Science, 2,* 209–230.

Lerner, J. V. (1983). The role of temperament in psychosocial adaptation in early adolescents: A test of a "goodness of fit" model. *Journal of Genetic Psychology, 143,* 149–157.

Lerner, J. V. (1994). *Working women and their families.* Thousand Oaks, CA: Sage.

Lerner, J. V., & Lerner, R. M. (1983). Temperament and adaptation across life: Theoretical and empirical issues. In P. B. Baltes & O. G. Brim, Jr. (Eds.), *Life-span development and behavior* (Vol. 5, pp. 197–231). New York. Academic Press.

Lerner, J. V., & Lerner, R. M. (Eds.). (1989). Longitudinal analyses of biological, psychological, and social interactions across the transitions of early adolescence. Special Issue of the *Journal of Early Adolescence, 9*(No. 3).

Lerner, J. V., Lerner, R. M., & Zabski, S. (1985). Temperament and elementary school children's actual and rated academic performance: A test of a "goodness of fit" model, *Journal of Child Psychology and Psychiatry, 26,* 125–136.

Lerner, R. M. (1982). Children and adolescents as producers of their own development. *Developmental Review, 2,* 342–370.

Lerner, R. M. (1984). *On the nature of human plasticity.* New York: Cambridge University Press.

Lerner, R. M. (1992). *Final solutions: Biology, prejudice, and genocide.* University Park: Penn State Press.

Lerner, R. M. (1993). Investment in youth: The role of home economics in enhancing the life chances of America's children. *AHEA Monograph Series, 1,* 5–34.

Lerner, R. M. (1995). *America's youth in crisis: Challenges and options for programs and policies.* Thousand Oaks, CA: Sage.

Lerner, R. M. (1998). Theories of human development: Contemporary perspectives. In R. M. Lerner (Ed.), *Theoretical models of human development.* Volume 1 of the *Handbook of Child Psychology* (5th ed., pp. 1–24). Editor-in-Chief: William Damon. New York: Wiley.

Lerner, R. M. (2002a). *Concepts and theories of human development* (3rd ed.). Mahwah, NJ: Lawrence Erlbaum Associates.

Lerner, R. M. (2002b). *Adolescence: Development, diversity, context, and application.* Upper Saddle River, NJ: Prentice-Hall.

Lerner, R. M. (2002c). Towards a democratic ethnotheory of parenting for families and policy makers: A developmental systems perspective. *Parenting: Science and Practice, 1(4),* 339–351.

Lerner, R. M. (Ed.). (in press). Special Issue: Innovative methods for studying lives in context. *Research in Human Development, 1(1).*

Lerner, R. M., Anderson, P. M., Balsano, A. B., Dowling, E., & Bobek, D. (2003). Applied developmental science of positive human development. In R. M. Lerner, M. A. Easterbrooks, & J. Mistry (Eds.), *Handbook of psychology: Vol. 6 Developmental psychology* (pp. 535–558). Editor-in-chief: I. B. Weiner. New York: Wiley.

Lerner, R. M., & Benson, P. L. (Eds.). (2003). *Developmental assets and asset-building communities: Implications for research, policy, and practice.* Norwell, MA: Kluwer Academic Publishers.

Lerner, R. M., Bornstein, M. H., & Smith C. (2003). Child well-being: From elements to integrations. In M. H. Bornstein, L. Davidson, C. M. Keyes, K. Moore, & The Center for Child Well-Being. *Well-being: Positive development across the life course* (pp. 501–523). Mahwah, NJ: Lawrence Erlbaum Associates.

Lerner, R. M., Brentano, C., Dowling, E. M., & Anderson, P. M. (2002). Positive youth development: Thriving as a basis of personhood and civil society. In R. M. Lerner, C. S. Taylor, & A. von Eye (Eds.), *New directions for youth development: Theory, practice and research: Pathways to positive development among diverse youth* (pp. 11–34). Vol. 95; G. Noam, Series Ed. San Francisco: Jossey-Bass.

Lerner, R. M., & Busch-Rossnagel, N. A. (Eds.). (1981). *Individuals as producers of their development: A life-span perspective.* New York: Academic Press.

Lerner, R. M., De Stefanis, I., & Ladd, G. T. (1998). Promoting positive youth development: Collaborative opportunities for psychology. *Children's Services: Social Policy, Research, & Practice, 1(2),* 83–109.

Lerner, R. M., Dowling, E. M., & Anderson, P. M. (2003). Positive youth development: Thriving as a basis of personhood and civil society. In L. Wagener & J. Furrow (Eds.), [Special Issue]. *Applied Developmental Science, 7,* 172–180.

Lerner, R. M., Fisher, C. B., & Weinberg, R. A. (2000). Toward a science for and of the people: Promoting civil society through the application of developmental science. *Child Development, 71,* 11–20.

Lerner, R. M., Freund, A. M., De Stefanis, I., & Habermas, T. (2001). Understanding developmental regulation in adolescence: The use of the selection, optimization, and compensation model. *Human Development, 44,* 29–50.

Lerner, R. M., & Galambos, N. L. (1998). Adolescent development: Challenges and opportunities for research, programs, and policies. In J. T. Spence (Ed.), *Annual Review of Psychology* (Vol. 49, pp. 413–446). Palo Alto, CA: Annual Reviews.

Lerner, R. M., & Hood, K. E. (1986). Plasticity in development: Concepts and issues for intervention. *Journal of Applied Developmental Psychology, 7,* 139–152.

Lerner, R. M., Jacobs, F., & Wertlieb, D. (Eds.). (2003). *Applying developmental cience for youth and families: Historical and theoretical foundations.* Volume 1 of *Handbook of applied developmental science: Promoting positive child, adolescent, and family development through research, policies, and programs.* Editors: R. M. Lerner, F. Jacobs, & D. Wertlieb. Thousand Oaks, CA: Sage.

Lerner, R. M., & Lerner, J. V. (1987). Children in their contexts: A goodness of fit model. In J. B. Lancaster, J. Altmann, A. S. Rossi, & L. R. Sherrod (Eds.), *Parenting across the life span: Biosocial dimensions* (pp. 377–404). Chicago: Aldine.

Lerner, R. M., & Lerner, J. V. (1989). Organismic and social contextual bases of development: The sample case of early adolescence. In W. Damon (Ed.), *Child development today and tomorrow* (pp. 69–85). San Francisco: Jossey-Bass.

Lerner, R. M., Ostrom, C. W., & Freel, M. A. (1997). Preventing health compromising behaviors among youth and promoting their positive development: A developmental contextual perspective. In J. Schulenberg, J. L. Maggs, & K. Hurrelmann (Eds.), *Health risks and developmental transitions during adolescence* (pp. 498–521). New York: Cambridge University Press.

Lerner, R. M., Rothbaum, F., Boulos, S., & Castellino, D. R. (2002). A developmental systems perspective on parenting. In M. H. Bornstein (Ed.), *Handbook of parenting* (2nd ed., pp. 315–344). Mahwah, NJ: Erlbaum.

Lerner, R. M., & Spanier, G. B. (1980). *Adolescent development: A life-span perspective.* New York: McGraw-Hill.

Lerner, R. M., Sparks, E., & McCubbin, L. (1999). *Family diversity and family policy: Strengthening families for America's children.* Norwell, MA: Kluwer.

Lerner, R. M., Theokas, C., & Jelicic, H. (in press). Youth as active agents in their own positive development: A developmental systems perspective. In W. Greve, K. Rothermund, & D. Wentura (Eds.). *The adaptive self: Personal continuity and intentional self-development.* Göttingen, Germany: Hogrefe/Huber Publishers.

Lerner, R. M., & Walls, T. (1999). Revisiting individuals as producers of their development: From dynamic interactionism to developmental systems. In J. Brandtstädter & R. M. Lerner (Eds.), *Action and self-development: Theory and research through the life span* (pp. 3–36). Thousand Oaks, CA: Sage, Inc.

Leventhal, T., & Brooks-Gunn, J. (2003). Moving on up: Neighborhood effects on children and families. In M. H. Bornstein, & R. H. Bradley (Eds.), *Socioeconomic status, parenting, and child development* (pp. 209–230). Mahwah, NJ: Lawrence Erlbaum Associates.

Levitt, M. Z., Selman, R. L., & Richmond, J. B. (1991). The psychosocial foundations of early adolescents' high-risk behavior: Implications for research and practice. *Journal of Research on Adolescence, 1*(4), 349–378.

Lewis, M., & Rosenblum, L. A. (Eds.). (1974). *The effect of the infant on its caregivers.* New York: Wiley.

Lewontin, R. (2000). *The triple helix: Gene, organism, and environment.* Cambridge: Harvard University Press.

Lewontin, R. C. (1992). Foreword. In R. M. Lerner (Ed.), *Final solutions: Biology, prejudice, and genocide* (pp. vii–viii). University Park: Penn State Press.

Lewontin, R. C., & Levins, R. (1978). Evolution. *Encyclopedia Einaudi* (Vol. 5). Turin: Einaudi.

Linn, P. & Horowitz, F. (1983). The relationship between infant individual differences and mother–infant interaction during the neonatal period. *Infant Behavior and Development, 6,* 415–427.

182   Liberty

Little, R. R. (1993). *What's working for today's youth: The issues, the programs, and the learnings*. Paper presented at the ICYF Fellows Colloquium, Michigan State University.

Lorenz, K. (1940a). Durch Domestikation verursachte Störungen arteigenen Verhaltens. *Zeitschrift für angewandte Psychologie und Charakterkunde, 59*, 2–81.

Lorenz, K. (1940b). Systematik und Entwicklungsgedanke im Unterricht, *Der Biologe 9*, 24–36.

Lorenz, K. (1943a). Die angeborenen Formen möglicher Erfahrung. *Zeitschrift für Tierpsychologie, 5*, 235–409.

Lorenz, K. (1943b). Psychologie and stammesgeschichte. In G. Heberer (Ed.), *Die evolution der organismen* (pp. 105-127). Jena: G. Fischer.

Lorenz, K. (1965). *Evolution and modification of behavior*. Chicago, IL: University of Chicago Press.

Lorenz, K. (1966). *On aggression*. New York: Harcourt, Brace & World.

Lovejoy, C. O. (1981). The origin of man. *Science, 211*, 341–350.

Luster, T., & McAdoo, H. P. (1994). Factors related to the achievement and adjustment of young African American children. *Child Development, 65*, 1080–1094.

Luster, T., & McAdoo, H. (1996). Family and child influences on educational attainment: A secondary analysis of the High/Scope Perry Preschool data. *Developmental Psychology, 32*(1), 26–39.

Magnusson, D. (1999a). Holistic interactionism: A perspective for research on personality development. In L. A. Pervin & O. P. John (Eds.), *Handbook of personality: Theory and research* (2nd ed., pp. 219–247). New York: The Guilford Press.

Magnusson, D. (1999b). On the individual: A person-oriented approach to developmental research. *European Psychologist, 4*, 205–218.

Mash, E. J. (1984). Families with problem children. *New Directions for Child Development, 24*, 65–84.

Mash, E. J., & Johnston, C. (1983). The prediction of mothers' behavior with their hyperactive children during play and task situations. *Child and Family Behavior Therapy, 5*(2), 1–14.

Masters, R. D. (1978). Jean-Jacques is alive and well: Rousseau and contemporary sociobiology. *Daedalus 107*, 93–105.

McArdle, J., & Nesselroade, J. R. (2003). Growth curve analysis in contemporary psychological research. In J. A. Schinka & W. F. Velicer (Eds.), *Research methods in psychology*. Volume 2 of *Handbook of psychology* (Irving B. Weiner, Editor-in-Chief; pp. 447–480). New York: Wiley.

McEwen, B. S., (1997). Possible mechanisms for atrophy of the human hippocampus. *Molecular Psychiatry, 2*, 255–262.

McEwen, B. S. (1998). Protective and damaging effects of stress mediators. *New England Journal of Medicine, 338*, 171–179.

McEwen, B. S. (1999). Stress and hippocampal plasticity. *Annual Review of Neuroscience, 22*, 105–122.

McLeod, J. (2000). Media and civic socialization of youth. *Journal of Adolescent Health, 27,* 45–51.

Meaney, M., Aitken, D., Berkel, H., Bhatnager, S. and Sapolsky, R. (1988). Effect of neonatal handling of age-related impairments associated with the hippocampus. *Science, 239,* 766–768.

Metz, E., & Youniss, J. (2003). A demonstration that school-based required service does not deter—but heightens—volunteerism. *PS: Political Science and Politics, 36*(2), 281–286.

Meyer, J. W. (1988). The social constructs of the psychology of childhood: Some contemporary processes. In E. M. Hetherington, R. M. Lerner, & M. Perlmutter (Eds.), *Child development in life-span perspective* (pp. 47–65). Hillsdale, NJ: Erlbaum.

Misiak, H., & Sexton, V. S. (1966). *History of psychology in overview.* New York: Grune & Stratton.

Morelli, G. A., & Verhoef, H. (1999). Who should help me raise my child? A cultural approach to understanding nonmaternal child care decisions. In L. Balter & C. S. Tamis-Le Monda (Eds.), *Child psychology: A handbook of contemporary issues* (491–509). Philadelphia: Psychology Press.

Müller-Hill, B. (1988). *Murderous science: Elimination by scientific selection of Jews, Gypsies, and others. Germany 1933-1945* (G. R. Fraser, Trans.). New York: Oxford University Press.

National 4-H Council Programs. (n.d.) Retrieved October 7, 2003, from http://www.fourhcouncil.edu/programs/index.asp.

National Commission on Resources for Youth. (1975). *Youth participation: A concept paper* (RFY Reports). New York: Author.

O'Connell, B. (1999). *Civil society: The underpinnings of American democracy.* Hanover, NH: University Press of New England.

O'Donoghue, J. L., Kirshner, B., & McLaughlin, M. (2002) Introduction: Moving youth participation forward. In B. Kirshner, J. L. O'Donoghue, & M. McLaughlin (Eds.), *Youth participation: Improving institutions and communities.* New Directions for Youth Development (Gil G. Noam, Editor-in-Chief, No. 96, pp. 15–26). San Francisco: Jossey-Bass.

O'Leary, K., & Emery, R. (1983). Marital discord and child behavior problems. In M. Levine & P. Satz (Eds.), *Middle childhood: Development and dysfunction* (pp. 345–364). Baltimore: University Park Press.

Overton, W. F. (1998). Developmental psychology: Philosophy, concepts, and methodology. In W. Damon (Series Ed.) & R. M. Lerner (Ed.), *Handbook of child psychology: Vol. 1 Theoretical models of human development* (5th ed., pp. 107–187). New York: Wiley.

Overton, W. F. (2003). Development across the life span: Philosophy, concepts, theory. In R. M. Lerner, M. A. Easterbrooks, & J. Mistry (Eds.), *Handbook of psychology: Vol. 6 Developmental psychology* (pp. 13–42). Editor-in-chief: I. B. Weiner. New York: Wiley.

Oyama, S. (2000). *Evolution's eye: A systems view of the biology-culture divide.* Durham, NC: Duke University Press.

Partanen, J., Brunn, K., & Markkanen, T. (1966). Inheritance of drinking. *The Finnish Foundation for Alcohol Studies, 14, Pediatrics. New Family Science Review,* 5(1 & 2), 97-110.

Patterson, G. R. (1980). A performance theory for coercive family interactions. In R. B. Cairns (Ed.), *Social interaction: Methods, analysis, and illustrations* (pp. 119–162). Hillsdale, NJ: Lawrence Erlbaum Associates.

Patterson, O. (1991). *Freedom.* New York: Basic Books.

Perkins, D. F., & Borden, L. M. (2003). Positive behaviors, problem behaviors, and resiliency in adolescence. In R. M. Lerner, M. A. Easterbrooks, & J. Mistry (Eds.), *Handbook of psychology: Vol. 6 Developmental psychology* (pp. 373–394). Editor-in-chief: I. B. Weiner. New York: Wiley.

Piaget, J. (1960). *The child's conception of the world.* Paterson, NJ: Littlefield, Adams.

Piaget, J. (1965). *The moral judgement of the child.* New York: Harcourt, Brace Jovanovich.

Piaget, J. (1970). Piaget's theory. In P. H. Mussen (Ed.), *Carmichael's manual of child psychology* (pp. 703–732). New York: Wiley.

Pittman, K. (1996). Community, youth, development: Three goals in search of connection. *New Designs for Youth Development,* Winter, 4–8.

Pittman, K. J., & Fleming, W. E. (1991, September). *A new vision: Promoting youth development.* Written transcript of live testimony by Karen J. Pittman given before the House Select Committee on Children, Youth and Families. Washington DC: Center for Youth Development and Policy Research.

Pittman, K., & Irby, M. (1995). *Promoting investment in life skills for youth: Beyond indicators for survival and problem prevention.* Paper presented at the Monitoring and measuring the state of children: Beyond survival, an interactional workshop, Jerusalem, Israel.

Pittman, K., Irby, M., & Cahill, M. (1995). *Mixing it up: Participatory evaluation as a tool for generating parent and community empowerment.* Cambridge, MA: Harvard Family Research Project.

Pittman, K., Irby, M., & Ferber, T. (2001). Unfinished business: Further reflections on a decade of promoting youth development. In P. L. Benson & K. J. Pittman (Eds.), *Trends in youth development: Visions, realities and challenges* (pp. 4–50). Norwell, MA: Kluwer Academic Publishers.

Plomin, R. (1986). *Development, genetics, and psychology.* Hillsdale, NJ: Erlbaum.

Plomin, R. (2000). Behavioural genetics in the 21st century. *International Journal of Behavioral Development, 24,* 30–34.

Plomin, R., Corley, R., DeFries, J. C., & Faulker, D. W. (1990). Individual differences in television viewing in early childhood: Nature as well as nurture. *Psychological Science, 1,* 371–377.

Plomin, R., & Daniels, D. (1987). Why are children in the same family so different from each other? *Behavioral and Brain Sciences, 10,* 1-16.

Proctor, R. N. (1988). *Racial hygiene: Medicine under the Nazis.* Cambridge, MA: Harvard University Press.

Rawls, J. (1971). *A theory of justice.* Cambridge, MA: Belknap Press of Harvard University Press.

Reese, H. W., & Overton, W. F. (1970). Models of development and theories of development. In L. R. Goulet & P. B. Baltes (Eds.), *Life-span developmental psychology: Research and theory* (pp. 115–145). New York: Academic Press.

Reese, W., & Thorup, C. L. (2003). An alliance for youth development: Second generation models on intersectoral partnering (ISP). In D. Wertlieb, F. Jacobs, & R. M. Lerner (Eds.), *Promoting positive youth and family development: Community systems, citizenship, and civil society.* Volume 3 of *Handbook of applied developmental science: Promoting positive child, adolescent, and family development through research, policies, and programs* (pp. 53–84). Editors: R. M. Lerner, F. Jacobs, & D. Wertlieb. Thousand Oaks, CA: Sage.

Rende, R. (2004). Beyond heritability: Biological process in social context. In C. Garcia Coll, E. Bearer, & R. M. Lerner (Eds.), *Nature and nurture: The complex interplay of genetic and environmental influences on human behavior and development* (pp. 107–126). Mahwah, NJ: Lawrence Erlbaum Associates.

Rhodes, J. E. (2002). *Stand by me: The risks and rewards of mentoring today's youth.* Cambridge, MA: Harvard University Press.

Rhodes, J. E., & Roffman, J. G. (2003). Relationship-based interventions: The impact of mentoring and apprenticeship on youth development. In F. Jacobs, D. Wertlieb, & R. M. Lerner (Eds.), *Enhancing the life chances of youth and families: Public service systems and public policy perspectives.* Volume 2 of *Handbook of applied developmental science: Promoting positive child, adolescent, and family development through research, policies, and programs* (pp. 225–236). Editors: R. M. Lerner, F. Jacobs, & D. Wertlieb. Thousand Oaks, CA: Sage.

Riegel, K. F. (1975). Toward a dialectical theory of development. *Human Development, 18,* 50–64.

Roth, J. L., & Brooks-Gunn, J. (2003a). What is a youth development program? Identification and defining principles. In F. Jacobs, D. Wertlieb, & R. M. Lerner (Eds.), *Enhancing the life chances of youth and families: Public service systems and public policy perspectives.* Volume 2 of *Handbook of applied developmental science: Promoting positive child, adolescent, and family development through research, policies, and programs* (pp. 197–223). Editors: R. M. Lerner, F. Jacobs, & D. Wertlieb. Thousand Oaks, CA: Sage Publications.

Roth, J. L., & Brooks-Gunn, J. (2003b). What exactly is a youth development program? Answers from research and practice. *Applied Developmental Science, 7,* 94–111.

Roth, J., Brooks-Gunn, J., Galen, B., Murray, L., Silverman, P., Liu, H., Man, D., & Foster, W. (1997). *Promoting healthy adolescence: Youth development frameworks and programs.* New York: Teachers College, Columbia University.

Roth, J., Brooks-Gunn, J., Murray, L., & Foster, W. (1998). Promoting healthy adolescents: Synthesis of youth development program evaluations. *Journal of Research on Adolescence, 8,* 423–459.

Rothbart, M. K., & Bates, J. E. (1998). Temperament. In N. Eisenberg (Ed.), *Handbook of child psychology: Social, emotional, and personality development* (Vol. 3, pp. 105–176). Editor-in-Chief: William Damon. New York: Wiley.

Rowe, D. (1994). *The limits of family influence: Genes, experience, and behavior.* New York: Guilford Press.

Rushton, J. P. (1999). *Race, evolution, and behavior* (Special Abridged Edition). New Brunswick, NJ: Transaction Publishers.

Rushton, J. P. (2000). *Race, evolution, and behavior* (2nd Special Abridged Edition). New Brunswick, NJ: Transaction Publishers.

Sahlins, M. D. (1978). The use and abuse of biology. In A. L. Caplan (Ed.), *The sociobiology debate.* New York: Harper & Row.

Sameroff, A. J. (1983). Developmental systems: Contexts and evolution. In W. Kessen (Ed.), *Handbook of child psychology: Vol. 1 History, theory, and methods* (pp. 237–294). New York: Wiley.

Savin-Williams. R. C., & Lisa M. Diamond, L. M. (2004). Sex. In R. M. Lerner & L. Steinberg (Eds.). *Handbook of adolescent psychology* (2nd ed., pp. 189–231). New York: Wiley.

Scales, P., Benson, P., Leffert, N., & Blyth, D. A. (2000). The contribution of developmental assets to the prediction of thriving among adolescents. *Applied Developmental Science, 4,* 27–46.

Scales, P., & Leffert, N. (1999). *Developmental assets: A synthesis of the scientific research on adolescent development.* Minneapolis, MN: Search Institute.

Scarr, S. (1992). Developmental theories for the 1990s: Development and individual differences. *Child Development, 63,* 1-19.

Schneirla, T. C. (1957). The concept of development in comparative psychology. In D. B. Harris (Ed.), *The concept of development: An issue in the study of human behavior* (pp. 78–108). Minneapolis: University of Minnesota Press.

Schneirla, T. C. (1966). Instinct and aggression: Reviews of Konrad Lorenz, *Evolution and modification of behavior* (Chicago: University of Chicago Press, 1965), and *On aggression* (New York: Harcourt, Brace & World, 1966). *Natural History, 75,* 16.

Schorr, L. B. (1988). *Within our reach: Breaking the cycle of disadvantage.* New York: Doubleday.

Schorr, L. B. (1997). *Common purpose: Strengthening families and neighborhoods to rebuild America.* New York: Doubleday.

Scott, E. S., & Woolard, J. L. (2004). The legal regulation of adolescence. In R. M. Lerner & L. Steinberg (Eds.), *Handbook of adolescent psychology* (2nd ed., pp. 523–550). New York: Wiley.

Sherrod, L., Flanagan, C., & Youniss, J. (Guest Eds.). (2002a). *Growing into citizenship: Multiple pathways and diverse influence.* Special Issue of *Applied Developmental Science,* 6(4), 264–272.

Sherrod, L. R., Flanagan, C., & Youniss, J. (2002b). Dimensions of citizenship and opportunities for youth development: The *what, why when, where,* and *who* of citizenship development. In L. Sherrod, C. Flanagan, & J. Youniss, (Guest Eds.). (2002a). *Growing into citizenship: Multiple pathways and diverse influence.* Special Issue of *Applied Developmental Science, 6*(4), 264—272.

Skelton, N., Boyte, H., & Leonard, L. S. (2002). *Youth civic engagement: Reflections on an emerging public idea.* Minneapolis, MN: Center for Democracy and Citizenship, University of Minnesota.

Skinner, B. F. (1971). *Beyond freedom and dignity.* New York: Knopf.

Smith, M., Steinman, J., Chorev, M., Hertzog, S., & Lerner, R. M. (in press). Positive youth development promotion through civic engagement: Service-learning versus community collaborative models. In. C. B. Fisher & R. M. Lerner (Eds.), *Applied developmental science: An encyclopedia of research, policies, and programs.* Thousand Oaks, CA: Sage.

Steinberg, L. (2002, November 10). Judging a juvenile killer. *Washington Post,* p. B07.

Stoneman, D. (2002). The role of youth programming in the development of civic engagement. In L. Sherrod, C. Flanagan, & J. Youniss, (Eds.). (2002a). *Growing into citizenship: Multiple pathways and diverse influence.* Special Issue of *Applied Developmental Science, 6*(4), 221–226.

Suomi, S. J. (1997). Early determinants of behavior: Evidence from primate studies. *British Medical Bulletin, 53,* 170–184.

Suomi, S. J. (2000). A behavioral perspective on developmental psychopathology: Excessive aggression and serotonergic dysfunction in monkeys. In A. J. Sameroff, M. Lewis, and S. Miller (Eds.), *Handbook of developmental psychopathology* (2nd ed., pp. 237–256). New York: Plenum Press.

Swartz, D. (1982). Is it sex? *The Sciences, 22,* 2.

Templeton, J. M. (1995). *The humble approach: Scientists discover God.* Philadelphia: Templeton Foundation Press.

Templeton, J. M. & Herrmann, R. L. (1994). *Is God the only reality?: Science points to a deeper meaning of the universe.* New York: Continuum.

Teti, D. M. (Ed.). (in press). *Handbook of research methods in developmental psychology.* Cambridge, MA: Blackwell.

Thelen, E., & Smith, L. B. (1998). Dynamic systems theories. In W. Damon (Series Editor) & R.M. Lerner (Vol. Ed.), *Handbook of child psychology: Vol. I Theoretical models of human development* (5th ed., pp. 563–633). New York: Wiley.

Thomas, A., & Chess, S. (1977). *Temperament and development.* New York: Brunner/Mazel.

Thomas, A., Chess, S., Birch, H. G., Hertzig, M. E., & Korn, S. (1963). *Behavioral individuality in early childhood.* New York: New York University Press.

Tobach, E. (1981). Evolutionary aspects of the activity of the organism and its development. In R. M. Lerner and N. A. Busch-Rossnagel (Eds.), *Individuals as producers of their development: A life-span perspective* (pp. 37–68). New York: Academic Press.

Tobach, E. (1994). . . . . Personal is political is personal is political . . . *Journal of Social Issues, 50,* 221–224.

Tobach, E., Gianutsos, J., Topoff, H. R., & Gross, C. G. (1974). *The four horses: Racism, sexism, militarism, and social Darwinism.* New York: Behavioral Publications.

Tobach, E. & Greenberg, G., (1984). The significance of T. C. Schneirla's contribution to the concept of levels of integration. In G. Greenberg & E. Tobach (Eds.), *Behavioral evolution and integrative levels* (pp. 1–7). Hillsdale, N. J.: Erlbaum.

Tobach, E., & Schneirla, T. C. (1968). The biopsychology of social behavior of animals. In R. E. Cooke & S. Levin (Eds.), *Biologic basis of pediatric practice* (pp. 68–82). New York: McGraw-Hill.

Tout, K., & Zaslow, M. (2003). Public investments in child care quality: Needs, challenges, and opportunities. In. R. M. Lerner, F. Jacobs, & D. Wertlieb (Eds.). *Applying developmental science for youth and families: Historical and theoretical foundations.* Volume 1 of *Handbook of applied developmental science: Promoting positive child, adolescent, and family development through research, policies, and programs* (pp. 339–366). Editors: R. M. Lerner, F. Jacobs, & D. Wertlieb. Thousand Oaks, CA: Sage Publications.

Trickett, E. J., Barone, C., & Buchanan, R. M. (1996). Elaborating developmental contextualism in adolescent research and intervention: Paradigm contributions from community psychology. *Journal of Research on Adolescence, 6,* 245–269.

United Nation's Children's Fund (UNICEF). (2002). *The state of the world's children 2003.* New York: Author.

Velden, M. (2003). The heritability of mental traits in humans: A proposal for a more coherent discussion. *Swiss Journal of Psychology, 62*(1), 5–10.

Venter, J. C., Adams, M. D., Myers, E. W., Li, P. W., Mural, R. J., [plus 270 others]. (2001). The sequence of the human genome. *Science, 291,* 1304–1351.

Villarruel, F. A. & Lerner, R. M. (Eds.). (1994). *Promoting community-based programs for socialization and learning.* New Directions for Child Development (No. 63). San Francisco: Jossey-Bass.

Villarruel, F. A., Perkins, D. F., Borden, L. M., & Keith, J. G. (Eds.). (2003). *Community youth development: Programs, policies, and practices.* Thousand Oak, CA: Sage.

Wade, N. (2002). Schizophrenia may be tied to 2 genes, research finds. *New York Times,* A11.

Wapner, S., & Demick, J. (1998). Developmental analysis: A holistic, developmental, systems-oriented perspective. In R. M. Lerner (Ed.), *Theoretical models of human development.* Vol. 1 of *Handbook of child psychology* (5th ed., pp. 761–805). New York: Wiley.

Washburn, S. L. (1961). *Social life of early man.* New York: Wenner-Gren Foundation for Anthropological Research.

Wheeler, W. (2000). Emerging organizational theory and the youth development organization. *Applied Developmental Science, 4,* Supplement 1, 47–54.

Wheeler, W. (2003). Youth leadership for development: Civic activism as a component of youth development programming and a strategy for strengthening civil society. In R. M. Lerner, F. Jacobs, & D. Wertlieb (Eds.), *Handbook of applied developmental science: Promoting positive child, adolescent, and family development through research, policies, and programs:* Vol. 2. *Enhancing the life chances of youth and families: Public service systems and public policy perspectives* (pp. 491–505). Editors F. Jacobs, D. Wertlieb, & R. M. Lerner. Thousand Oaks, CA: Sage.

Wilson, E. O. (1975). *Sociobiology: The new synthesis.* Cambridge, MA: Harvard University Press.

Wilson, J. Q. (1993). *The moral sense.* New York: Free Press.

Wingspread Conference. (1996, March 1–3). *Emerging best practices: Weaving the work of youth and child development.* Minneapolis, MN: Author.

Yates, M., & Youniss, J. (1996). Community service and political-moral identity in adolescents. *Journal of Research on Adolescence, 6*(3), 271–284.

Youniss, J., McLellan, J. A., & Yates, M. (1999). Religion, community service, and identity in American youth. *Journal of Adolescence, 22,* 243–253.

Youniss, J., & Yates, M. (1999). Youth service and moral-civic identity. A case for everyday morality. *Educational Psychology Review, 11,* 361–376.

Youniss, J., Yates, M., & Su, Y. (1997). Social integration: Community service and marijuana use in high school seniors. *Journal of Adolescent Research, 12*(2), 245–262.

Zaff, J. F., & Michelsen, E. (2002). Encouraging civic engagement: How teens are (or are not) becoming responsible citizens. *Child Trends Research Briefs.* Washington, DC: Child Trends.

Zaslow, M., Tout, K., Smith, S., & Moore, K. (1998). Implications of the 1996 welfare legislation for children: A research perspective. *SRCD Social Policy Report, 12*(3).

Zeldin, S., Camino, L., & Wheeler, W. (Eds.). (2000). Promoting adolescent development in community context: Challenges to scholars, nonprofit managers, and higher education. *Applied Developmental Science, 4, Supplement 1.*

Name Index

Subject Index

About the Author

Richard M. Lerner is the Bergstrom Chair in Applied Developmental Science and the Director of the Applied Developmental Science Institute in the Eliot-Pearson Department of Child Development at Tufts University. A developmental psychologist, Lerner received a Ph.D. in 1971 from the City University of New York. He has been a fellow at the Center for Advanced Study in the Behavioral Sciences and is a fellow of the American Association for the Advancement of Science, the American Psychological Association, and the American Psychological Society. Prior to joining Tufts University, he was on the faculty and held administrative posts at Michigan State University, Pennsylvania State University, and Boston College, where he was the Anita L. Brennan Professor of Education and the Director of the Center for Child, Family, and Community Partnerships. During the 1994–95 academic year, Lerner held the Tyner Eminent Scholar Chair in the Human Sciences at Florida State University. Lerner is the author or editor of 55 books and more than 360 scholarly articles and chapters. He edited Volume 1, on "Theoretical Models of Human Development," for the fifth edition of the *Handbook of Child Psychology*. He is the founding editor of the *Journal of Research on Adolescence* and of *Applied Developmental Science*. He is known for his theory of, and research about, relations between life-span human development and contextual or ecological change. He has done foundational studies of adolescents' relations with their peer, family, school, and community contexts, and is a leader in the study of public policies and community-based programs aimed at the promotion of positive youth development.